MONKS OF MT. TABOR

DIVISION *and* DETENTE

DIVISION *and* DETENTE

The Germanies and Their Alliances

Eric G. Frey

New York
Westport, Connecticut
London

Library of Congress Cataloging-in-Publication Data

Frey, Eric G.
  Division and detente.

  Bibliography: p.
  Includes index.
    1. Germany (West)—Foreign relations—Germany (East)
2. Germany (East)—Foreign relations—Germany (West)
3. Germany (West)—Foreign relations—Europe.
4. Germany (East)—Foreign relations—Europe. 5. Europe
—Foreign relations—Germany (West) 6. Europe—Foreign
relations—Germany (East) 7. Detente. 8. Alliances.
I. Title.
DD258.85.G35F74 1986   327.4304   86-20516
ISBN 0-275-92222-7 (alk. paper)

Library of Congress Catalog Card Number: 86-20516
ISBN: 0-275-92222-7

First published in 1987

Praeger Publishers, 521 Fifth Avenue, New York, NY 10175
A division of Greenwood Press, Inc.

Printed in the United States of America

∞

The paper used in this book complies with the Permanent
Paper Standard issued by the National Information Standards
Organization (Z39.48-1984).

10 9 8 7 6 5 4 3 2 1

To my parents
and to my brothers, Peter and George

Contents

Acknowledgments

This book developed out of my senior thesis, which I wrote at the Woodrow Wilson School of Public and International Affairs at Princeton University in 1984–85. I am deeply indebted to countless people inside and outside of Princeton. I could have never written this book without their help and support. I wish to express my sincere thanks and admiration to Professor Richard Ullman, my thesis advisor, who has guided me with advice and moral encouragement through the arduous process of academic research and writing. His comments and questions throughout the writing process forced me to reconsider my arguments over and over and vastly improved the quality of my work. I would like to thank John Kornblum, former director of central European affairs in the U.S. Department of State and now U.S. consul in West Berlin, who gave me invaluable help at the beginning of my research, as well as Ambassador Jonathan Dean, Professor James McAdams and Professor Angela Stent, who greatly helped me revise my manuscript with their comments and criticisms of an earlier draft. I would also like to express my appreciation of all those people who granted me interviews in the summer and fall of 1984. Their names are listed in the bibliography at the end of the book. My research in the Federal Republic in the summer of 1984 was supported by grants from the Exxon Foundation and the fund of the Dean of the College of Princeton University. I am especially grateful to Mrs. Kessler and the library staff of the *Deutschlandhaus* in Bonn, whose generous assistance greatly facilitated my research during my stay in Bonn. I would also like to thank all my friends and colleagues who assisted me with typing, editing and proofreading, especially Paul Chamberlain, Laura Feig, Debbie Friedman, Carol Kuntz, Charley McPhedran, Ted Schulman, Joel Sipress, and Kate Sonnenberg. Other people whose help I would like to acknowledge include Michelle Browdy, Laura Halbert, Rebecca Kotkin, Andy Meyers, and Kathy Willey. Finally, I would like to express my deepest gratitude to my parents, who have made it possible for me to study at Princeton and have supported me throughout these years with love and encouragement. I owe everything to them.

ix

Introduction

Insiders had suspected for many months that a crisis loomed over West Germany's counterintelligence service. Its director, Hans Joachim Tiedge, suffered from alcoholism and depression and was said to be heavily in debt. Still, when Tiedge disappeared in mid-August 1985, most people in the West German government were not yet seriously worried. Five days later the news fell like a bombshell: a short article in *Neues Deutschland,* the official newspaper of the East German Communist party, reported that Tiedge had defected to East Berlin. The realization that one of West Germany's highest-ranking intelligence officers had been an East German agent only exacerbated the political crisis that began a week earlier when one of the personal secretaries of the West German president and the minister of economics defected to East Germany. West Germany was shaken by one of the most serious spy scandals of the postwar era.

The scandal reverberated far beyond West German borders. While officials in NATO began to evaluate the damage done to the security of the Western alliance, public attention in Western Europe and the United States turned to the unique relationship between the two German states which had made this scandal possible. The public saw two states that are separated by a deep political division but which share the same language, culture, and history. They saw two societies that are divided by an impervious border but which penetrate each other deeply. A large majority of the East German population turns on West German television every night and watches *Dallas, Dynasty,* and the West German evening news — including news about the German Democratic Republic that the East German media does not reveal. Millions of West Germans visit friends and relatives in East Germany, and each year thousands of East Germans cross the border to West Germany. Almost a third of the current West German population was born in territories that now belong to countries of the Eastern bloc. After two decades of an almost complete lack of bilateral relations and a decade of a slow but cumbersome rapprochement, the Federal Republic of Germany (FRG) and the German Democratic Republic (GDR) had only recently entered a new era in their relationship, an era that held the promise of mitigating the most painful aspects of the German division.

The spy scandal demonstrated, however, that neither 15 years of detente nor cultural and national affinity can negate the harsh political realities that developed in the aftermath of World War II. The two German states not only belong to hostile military blocs, but as the front states of the alliances they are often forced to play the role of the vanguards of the North Atlantic Treaty Organization (NATO) and the Warsaw Treaty Organization (WTO). The highest peace-time concentration of troops and armament in history are found on the territory of the two Germanies, which would almost inevitably turn into a battlefield in the case of a third world war. The two German states are also the major battlefields for the wars of propaganda, political bickering, and espionage between the two alliances. Germany is the place where the East-West division is felt most strongly; due to the absence of a peace treaty, it is the one country where World War II has not yet come to an end.

West Berlin's isolated location in particular serves as a permanent reminder of the fragility of the current solution to the "German question." Whether it is travel, diplomatic exchanges, or soccer games, most aspects of normal interstate relations are fraught with major problems on the German border. East and West Germany are unable to agree on fundamental questions such as the nature of their relationship and whether there exist two separate citizenships. They are even at odds over the names for their countries. While East German officials and publications refer to the two countries only as "BRD" and "DDR" (Bundesrepublik Deutschland and Deutsche Demokratische Republik, the German names for FRG and GDR, respectively), the term "BRD" has been officially banned in West Germany because it does not spell out the name "Germany." Meanwhile, a number of West German newspapers refer to the GDR only in quotation marks, thus expressing their refusal to recognize the other Germany's right to exist.[1]

One of the most surprising aspects of the Tiedge case was the absence of any negative repercussions for inter-German ties. When the personal assistant to former West German chancellor Willy Brandt, Günter Guillaume, was uncovered as an East German agent in 1974, Brandt resigned and inter-German relations suffered a significant setback. In 1985, however, the outcome was different. The political leaders in East and West Germany took hardly any notice of the events. A few days after West German intelligence had discovered that the GDR had placed agents in many of the most important political offices in Bonn and had severely imperiled West German security, Bavarian Prime Minister Franz Josef

Strauß, the most prominent exponent of the West German right, met with East German state and party leader Erich Honecker at the semiannual trade fair in Leipzig in an ostentatiously friendly atmosphere. Despite their ideological differences, the two politicians confirmed their interest in an undisrupted continuation of inter-German relations.

This absence of political upheaval as a result of the spy scandal best demonstrates the extent of changes that inter-German relations have undergone since the Cold War years, when every border incident caused a major political crisis, and even since the "heydays of detente" in the mid-1970s. For residents of West Berlin, for people with family and friends across the border, and even for average citizens in the FRG and the GDR, the rapprochement between the two German states has vastly improved their security and their quality of life. The time without official contacts between the two governments, when travel, postal, and telephone service between the FRG and the GDR were severely hampered, and when West Berlin was in constant danger of being cut off from the rest of West Germany, now belongs to history. As U.S.-Soviet relations deteriorated in the early 1980s, the FRG and the GDR embarked on a new and often courageous course designed to preserve the fruits of detente and to improve inter-German relations apart from and sometimes against the will of the superpowers. In the months before the spy scandal erupted, the two German states had achieved significant progress in bilateral economic and political issues.

This development must not be seen in isolation from changes in the international arena. While the German-German rapprochement was in the 1970s and 1980s undoubtedly in the interest of the German people on both sides of the border, the impetus for its development originally came from outside. It was primarily the beginning of detente between the United States and the Soviet Union during the 1960s that forced the FRG and the GDR to settle their differences and arrive at a *modus vivendi*. Inter-German relations were not only a function of the relations between the Western and the Eastern alliances, but in the following years they also became the cornerstone of a new era of detente. When in the 1960s the Western nations moved toward recognizing the post-war order in Europe in order to guarantee the stability of the continent, the unresolved question of the division of Germany constituted one of the most severe obstacles to an agreement. The formal recognition of the division of Germany through the Basic Treaty — signed in 1972 — became a *conditio sine qua non* for the Helsinki Accords of 1975, which ratified the European post-war order and made detente a permanent fixture in the

European political theater. If one defines the goal of detente as overcoming political divisions and reducing the chances of military confrontations, then it becomes understandable why inter-German ties, which are associated with the most severe division and the highest concentration of military activity on the continent, represent the essence of European detente.

Despite this strong dependence of inter-German relations on the general East-West relationship, in the course of the 1970s inter-German relations developed a dynamic of their own. Possibly the most significant change in the political situation of the two Germanies came after 1979 when the decade of detente between the United States and the Soviet Union came to an abrupt end. A number of unrelated events in 1979 and 1980 made these years a genuine watershed in the history of East-West relations: in November 1979 the NATO "double-track" decision to deploy intermediate-range missiles in Europe while simultaneously pursuing arms control talks with the Soviet Union, the December 1979 Soviet invasion of Afghanistan, and the beginning of the Polish crisis in the summer of 1980. On several occasions in the last five years the two German states dared to disregard the lead of their superpowers and to strive for a certain degree of independence in their foreign policies by advancing their bilateral relations despite the growing chill between the United States and the Soviet Union. These attempts were only partly successful, but they still raised old and new concerns among their allies in the East and the West: How reliable are the German states as allies? Do they desire to follow a "separate German way?" Do they seek reunification, and are they willing to abandon their alliances for that goal? These questions were particularly troubling when seen as touching on the future of the European alliance system and thus of Europe's post-war order.

It is the purpose of this book to illuminate this interplay in East-West relations in general and inter-German relations in particular, especially in the period since 1979. Inter-German ties cannot be understood either as a purely national problem or as only the product of U.S.-Soviet relations. The politics of the two Germanies is shaped by a complex interaction of constraints caused by the alliance system, national interests, domestic pressures, and practical bilateral problems. In order to analyze the international dynamics that characterize inter-German politics, one can divide this issue into four distinct parts:

1. The influence of the internal politics of NATO and WTO on the development of inter-German relations. This point concerns the

position and the degree of autonomy of the two German states *within* their respective alliances.

2. The influence of relations *between* the alliances and the superpowers on inter-German relations. Here, the central question is to what extent the FRG and the GDR can insulate their relations from the global climate between East and West.
3. The influence of inter-German relations on the internal politics of the two alliances. Concerning this point, the most fascinating question is whether there exists an all-German nationalism and a desire for reunification that could affect the viability and unity of the alliances.
4. The influence of inter-German relations on global East-West relations. Here, we want to evaluate what inter-German relations can contribute to the process of detente and arms control in Europe.

While all four points are relevant for the understanding of inter-German relations, in the course of the discussion we will see that the importance of the first two questions outweighs that of the latter two. While inter-German relations are strongly influenced by developments within the alliances and by global East-West relations, they have a far smaller impact on global political developments by themselves than is often assumed. This is mainly true because reunification plays such a limited role in inter-German relations. Contrary to widely held views abroad, a German-German rapprochement does not represent a movement toward reunification, but a movement away from it, toward the recognition of the division of Germany and the establishment of normal relations between two separate states.

This theme of reunification versus rapprochement is the focus of Part I of the book, "The Long Road to Rapprochement," which analyzes inter-German relations as a bilateral process between two sovereign states. Here I concentrate on the questions of mutual recognition, economic and humanitarian relations, and national identity. I conclude that inter-German relations should not be regarded as an explosive phenomenon that can change the political order of Europe by itself, but must be seen as an integral part of the larger political developments that shape the future of the European alliances.

With this premise in mind, in Part II of the book, "The Germanies between East and West," I will focus on the notion of an autonomous European detente, the building of political, economic, and humanitarian bridges between Eastern and Western Europe that proceeds independently of the state of U.S.-Soviet relations. As we will see in the discussion of inter-German relations from 1979 to 1985, the two German states have developed a large set of mutual interests in their relationship, which they are often able to realize regardless of the temporary state of East-West relations in most periods. Although tensions between the United States and the Soviet Union will always constitute a problem for inter-German relations, they no longer automatically interrupt a rapprochement between the FRG and the GDR. It requires sensible policies in Bonn and East Berlin and consideration for the interests of the superpowers and their other allies. Most importantly, both German states have to accept that progress in inter-German relations can only occur within the framework of the established alliances. Whenever either of the German states attempts actions that could call its loyalty to its alliance into question, the relationship is bound to lose some of its autonomy. Challenges to the bloc system are bound to hurt the rapprochement between East and West Germany and European detente in general.

The greatest obstacles to inter-German relations today lie in the unresolved questions concerning the status and sovereignty of the two German states and the internal stability of the GDR. Just as for all of Eastern Europe, the GDR's stability will depend mainly on its ability to balance political and economic liberalization with loyalty to the Soviet Union and the preservation of the Communist party's rule. If such a process succeeds in the coming decades, the wall that divides the two German states would still not come tumbling down, but it might become far less impervious and painful than it is today.

NOTE

1.   This conflict over names creates particular problems to the writer on this issue. Similar to the Middle East conflict, even the use of certain terms can be interpreted as a bias toward the position of one of the two sides. For example, the GDR rejects all references to the *Deutsche Frage* or even to the term *Innerdeutsche Beziehungen* because it regards it as an endorsement of the continuous existence of one Germany. Although they grudgingly accept the term *Deutsch-deutsche Beziehungen*, East Germans usually use the expression *Beziehungen zwischen der BRD und der DDR*. Without planning to take a position in this argument, I will not refrain from using the acronyms "FRG," "GDR," and the terms "German question" and "German nation." As a name for the relationship itself, I will use the term "inter-German relations" without endorsing any position in this debate.

PART ONE
The Long Road To Rapprochement

1

INTER-GERMAN RELATIONS BEFORE THE BASIC TREATY

Regardless of whether or not the allies in World War II had planned the division of Germany — and historical evidence suggests that they had not — the development of two hostile political blocs in Europe made the partition inevitable. Although the agreements reached at the conference of Potsdam in July 1945 called for a joint administration of Germany by all four allies, the growing antagonism between the Soviet Union and the Western powers during 1946 and 1947 made the implementation of these agreements an increasingly unlikely prospect. During 1948 the growing rift through Germany was aggravated by the Soviet withdrawal from the Allied Command Council; the implementation of the Marshall Plan, which the Soviet occupied territories refused; the currency reform in the Western zones that divided Germany into two separate economic regions; and the imposition of the Berlin blockade in July. When the establishment of the Council for Mutual Economic Assistance (CMEA) and of NATO in early 1949 completed the division of Europe into two blocs, the German partition was sealed as well; in the same year, both the FRG and the GDR were established.

It is often argued that the formation of the alliances was the sole cause for the division of Germany, suggesting that the elimination of the blocs would also eliminate the German partition. But the interplay between these two developments was more complex. One of the main reasons for the building of the alliances was the desire of the United States and the Soviet Union to deny the other control over all of Germany. Faced with the prospect of Soviet expansionism, U.S. officials preferred a divided Germany to a united one in the Soviet sphere of power.[1] It is likely that a similar analysis prevailed in the Kremlin. One could therefore say that the two security alliances were instruments to guarantee that Germany remained divided. Given Germany's strategic and economic importance, the risk unification and neutralization carried, as it developed in the case of Austria between 1945 and 1955, was unacceptable to both sides. For both the United States and the Soviet Union, the division of Germany was motivated by offensive and defensive ways of thinking: by the desire to incorporate part of Germany into their spheres of power and to deny the other side control over all of the country.

These two strands of thinking in the allied policies toward Germany were subsequently adopted by the governments of the German states. The policies of both the FRG and the GDR toward each other demonstrated offensive and defensive characteristics. Particularly the *Deutschlandpolitik* of Konrad Adenauer, West German chancellor of the conservative government from 1949 to 1963, was characterized by this dual nature. Adenauer's policy followed two contradictory designs. In his ideology and rhetoric, the reunification of Germany was one of the principal goals of the West German state. The Adenauer government took all legal precautions to leave open the possibility of reunification. Instead of a constitution, the new state adopted a temporary "Basic Law." The preamble of this law prohibited all policies that could preclude a future unification. An all-German citizenship was maintained and also automatically granted to people in the GDR.

Meanwhile, Adenauer adopted a policy that made reunification essentially impossible: Western integration. Adenauer contended that only full political, economic, and military integration into the Western alliance would enable the FRG to regain political and economic power and make it a full actor in the international arena. A strong dependence on the United States and participation in the fledgling system of Western European political and economic integration were the cornerstones of Adenauer's foreign policy. By 1955 the chancellor had reached his goals: the FRG gained full sovereignty and became an equal member of NATO.

Adenauer's policy did not avoid controversy; the leaders of the *Sozialdemokratische Partei Deutschlands* (SPD), the main opposition party, as well as members of the ruling *Christlich-Demokratische Union* (CDU) and the *Christlich-Soziale Union* (CSU), the two conservative parties in the coalition government, deplored Western integration on the grounds that it was an obstacle to reunification. Until its Godesberg Program of 1959, the SPD opposed integration into NATO and called for neutralization of the FRG as a precondition for reunification. Adenauer, however, argued that only Western integration could ever lead to reunification under a democratic system; only the full support of the Western alliance would make West Germany powerful enough to enforce its claim for unity and freedom against the Soviet Union. Thus when in 1952, 1955, and again in 1958 Moscow made offers of reunification on the condition that the FRG discontinue its military integration into the Western alliance, Adenauer contended these offers were part of a Soviet propaganda campaign to undermine West Germany's reliability to its Western allies. By making the demand, which for the Soviets was unacceptable, that only after open and free elections in the GDR would the Federal Republic even consider any reunification proposals, the CDU/CSU government effectively rejected these offers.

Despite this one-sided orientation toward the West, the FRG confirmed its commitment to reunification through an aggressive policy against the GDR. Since it refused to accept the division of Germany, it did not recognize the GDR as a legitimate state and continued to claim the right of sole representation of the German people. No official contacts between the two German states were allowed. Even the reunification plans themselves were presented to the Soviet Union and the Western powers but never to the GDR leadership itself. To isolate the GDR internationally, in 1956 the FRG proclaimed the so-called Hallstein Doctrine, which demanded diplomatic relations be broken with any country that recognized the GDR. This doctrine excluded the Soviet Union with whom Bonn had established diplomatic relations in 1955. Although the Hallstein Doctrine succeeded in preventing most countries from establishing diplomatic relations with the GDR, it also precluded relations between West Germany and the other Eastern European states, which had all established close relations with East Berlin.

The ultimate goal of this policy was the political and economic destabilization of East Germany. In the long run, the West Germans asserted, the Soviet Union would have no alternative to withdrawing from the GDR and allowing the return of its occupied territories to the West. Retrospectively, the logical inconsistency of Adenauer's *Deutschlandpolitik* cannot be denied. Given Soviet military power in Central Europe and Moscow's desire for almost absolute military security, nothing made the prospect of reunification on Western terms more unlikely than the integration of the FRG into a hostile military alliance. Whether national unity could have ever been achieved is already questionable. According to former Austrian Chancellor Bruno Kreisky, who negotiated Austria's State Treaty of 1955 with the Soviets and discussed the German question with Soviet Foreign Minister Molotov and his aide Andrei Gromyko, the Soviets regarded reunification even under neutrality as incompatible with Soviet security.[2] It seems that Adenauer was aware of the logical flaw in his approach. However, defining Western integration as a step toward reunification was an effective way of "selling" this policy to a West German public that was not yet convinced of the value of closer ties with the West.[3]

Still, until the early 1960s the political and economic instability of the GDR gave some credibility to the hope for an ultimate reunification. The biggest threat to stability was the mass migration to the Federal Republic, made possible by the open border between the eastern and western sectors of Berlin. Between 1949 and 1961, 2.7 million people (more than 15 percent of the East German population) moved to the FRG. At the height of the flood in July 1961, 2,000 people per day crossed the zonal border in Berlin. As many of them were skilled workers and professionals, this constituted an enormous economic loss for the young state.

The building of the Berlin Wall in August 1961 changed this threatening situation. In the eyes of the *Sozialistische Einheitspartei Deutschlands* (SED), East Germany's ruling party, the building of the wall was a great success. Enjoying the support of the Soviet leadership, which as one of the four occupying powers controlled East Berlin, it committed Moscow to guarantee the survival of the regime of Walter Ulbricht. By stopping the flow of refugees, the wall permitted the economic consolidation of the state. By denying the East Germans an alternative to staying in the GDR, it encouraged the population to accept the regime and appeared to increase the state's legitimacy among its citizens. "The history of the GDR as a separate, normally functioning entity began only with the construction of the wall in Berlin, despite the detrimental effect that this symbol of illegitimate power had on the international reputation of the East German state."[4] The knowledge that the GDR was permanent also strengthened its position in the Warsaw Treaty Organization and improved its standing in the international arena.

Even in the FRG, an increasing number of people realized the GDR would not collapse under economic troubles and popular dissent. The first to change his policy toward the GDR was Willy Brandt, the mayor of West Berlin when the wall was built. Brandt initiated direct negotiations with East Berlin over passes for West Berlin's residents to visit the eastern part of the city.[5] Two years later, Brandt's press secretary, Egon Bahr, presented the theoretical basis for a new policy toward the GDR. In a famous speech in Tutzing on July 15, 1963, Bahr suggested that rather than making unacceptable demands to the Soviet Union and the GDR, West Germany should pursue a policy of small steps toward better relations with the second German state. Just as the East German leaders built the Berlin Wall because they felt threatened, they might be willing to open up the border and modify their repressive policies if less hostile inter-German relations made them feel more secure. Bahr called this approach "change through rapprochement," which subsequently became the slogan for proponents of a new policy toward the GDR.[6]

Just as the sovereign existence of the GDR became an irreversible reality, the rising interest in detente with the Soviet Union in the United States and in other Western European countries exerted pressure on the FRG to abandon its policy of "nonrecognition" of the GDR. And as a growing number of West Germans criticized their government's rigid position on this issue, Bonn's policy was in danger of losing both its compatibility with the external world and its consensus at home.[7]

The West German political establishment, however, was extremely slow in adapting to the new situation. Gerhard Schröder, foreign minister until 1966, attempted to improve relations to the East European countries by establishing trade missions in their capitals. But the East European governments rejected these overtures and demanded full diplomatic recognition, which was prevented by the Hallstein Doctrine.[8] In 1967 the FRG finally abandoned this doctrine by establishing relations with Romania. However, other Eastern European governments refused to open embassies before the FRG recognized the GDR and accepted the Oder-Neiße line as Poland's western border. When Willy Brandt, who became foreign minister in 1966 under the grand coalition of CDU/CSU and SPD, tried to move in this direction, he was stopped by his conservative coalition partners. An exaggerated concern for conservative votes and their rigid interpretation of the West German Basic Law kept the CDU/CSU from abandoning its policy of nonrecognition.

The election victory of a coalition formed by the SPD and the *Freie Demokratische Partei* (FDP), a small liberal party, under the leadership of Willy Brandt in 1969 then marked the beginning of a new era in West Germany's Deutschlandpolitik. In Brandt's inauguration speech on October 28, 1969, a West German chancellor for the first time recognized the existence of a second German state: "A recognition of the GDR by the Federal Republic according to international law is out of the question. Although *there exists two states in Germany,* they are not foreign territory to each other; their relations must be of special nature" [emphasis added].[9] Brandt's goal was unambitious and defensive. It did not call for a change in the nature of the East German regime but rather for the survival of the German nation as a cultural entity — a survival he saw threatened by the lack of human contact between the two German states.

East Germany's stance on the reunification question and national identity was surprisingly similar to West Germany's throughout the 1950s and 1960s. Also the GDR accused the FRG of being illegitimate in the early post-war period. It repeatedly demanded the withdrawal of all U.S. and British troops, the legalization of the Communist party (outlawed in the FRG in 1956), and reunification under a socialist system. After 1955 the leaders of the SED, East Germany's ruling party, realized that West Germany would not soon become socialist. Thus, they abandoned their outspoken calls for reunification and moved towards a theory of "two states — one nation." But the GDR's official ideology still espoused the goal of a confederation of the two states after the dissolution of the bloc system.[10] Only the growing stability of the East German state after the building of the Berlin Wall fueled the concept of a completely separate East German state in the SED's political thought. The East German leadership put uppermost in its demands West German recognition of the GDR as a fully sovereign and legitimate state — a recognition that would codify the permanent division of Germany. Although the constitution of 1968 still defined the GDR as a "socialist state of German nationality," the notion of reunification had all but disappeared in the East German official rhetoric. Instead, the GDR demanded normal diplomatic relations between the two German states on the basis of "peaceful coexistence."[11]

East German policy makers also accepted the reality of two Germanies. Nevertheless, when the new SPD/FDP government in Bonn began its initiative to open a new era in inter-German relations, Ulbricht was unwilling to cooperate. The SED leader not only feared that increased contact with the West could undermine his political control but that an arrangement with the Federal Republic would reduce his state's importance for the Soviet Union. Ulbricht obstructed the negotiations with Bonn by declaring the West German recognition of the GDR's full sovereignty as the precondition for any kind of talks — a demand that was unacceptable to the FRG. But just as the FRG was under pressure from its allies, Ulbricht found himself in conflict with Soviet demands. The Soviets sought Western — including West German — acceptance of the post-war European borders. While the FRG had for two decades refused to recognize the Soviet-imposed border changes, particularly the transfer of the German territories east of the

Oder-Neiße line to Poland, Brandt's new *Ostpolitik* promised to change this revisionist attitude. The FRG's *Ostverträge* (Eastern Treaties) with the Soviet Union and Poland, signed in 1970, created a *modus vivendi* between West Germany and Eastern Europe. Subsequently, the FRG established diplomatic relations with all Eastern European countries except the GDR.

As a next step toward the codification of the status quo, the victor nations of World War II began negotiations to settle the legal and political status of Berlin, a precondition for an inter-German rapprochement. In those negotiations, the conflict between Ulbricht and the Soviet leadership reached a climax. Ulbricht opposed any treaty that would affirm West Berlin's ties to the Federal Republic. The Soviets wished to reach a quick agreement that could pave the way for a Conference on Security and Cooperation in Europe (CSCE) to legitimize the political division of Europe after World War II. In the spring of 1971, Ulbricht attempted to mobilize his friends in the Kremlin to prevent the Soviet Union from signing the Quadripartite Agreement over Berlin. The veteran communist leader not only challenged the Soviet leadership in foreign policy, but also questioned Moscow's ideological predominance.[12] In the summer of 1971, Ulbricht was forced to resign, and a few months later, the Quadripartite Agreement over Berlin was signed. Ulbricht's successor, Erich Honecker, supported Soviet detente policies and chose a course of rapprochement toward the FRG. In contrast to Ulbricht, he was willing to pay the price of increased Western influence within the GDR in exchange for the international recognition and the increased legitimacy which the agreements with the Federal Republic permitted.[13]

NOTES

1.   See John Lewis Gaddis, *The United States and the Origins of the Cold War 1941-1947* (New York: Columbia University Press, 1972), p. 331.

2.   Telephone interview with Dr. Bruno Kreisky on August 29, 1984.

3.   For a discussion of Adenauer's reunification policy, see Karlheinz Niclauß, *Kontroverse Deutschlandpolitik: Die politische Außeinandersetzung in der Bundesrepublik Deutschland über den Grundlagenvertrag mit der DDR* (Frankfurt/Main: Alfred Metzner, 1977), pp. 31-38.

4.   Christoph Royen, *Change and Immobility in Poland, the CSSR and the DRG Problems and Choices for Western Policy* (unpublished manuscript), p. 42.

5.   Gerhard Wettig, *Entspannungskonzepte in Ost und West,* (Koln: Berichte des Bundesinstitutes für internationale und ostwissenschaftliche Studien 16, 1981), p. 29-31.

6.   See text of the speech in Peter Brandt and Peter Ammon, eds., *Die Linke und die nationale Frage: Texte zur Deutschlandpolitik*, pp. 235-40; for a description of Bahr's motives, see his extensive interview in Egon Bahr, *Was wird aus den Deutschen? Fragen und Antworten* (Hamburg: Rowohlt, 1982), pp. 218-21.

7.   Wilhelm Bruns, *Deutsch-deutsche Beziehungen: Prämissen — Probleme — Perspektiven* (Opladen: Leske & Budrich, 1982), pp. 27-28.

8.   Wettig, *Entspannungskonzepte*, pp. 27-8.

9.   Helmut Kistler, *Die Ostpolitik der Bundesrepublik Deutschland* 1966-1973 (Bonn: Bundeszentrals für politische Bildung, 1982), pp. 50-51.

10.   See Wolfgang Vernohr, "35 Jahre DDR und die nationale Frage," *Deutschland Archiv* 17 (December 1984) pp. 1264-66; Gebhard Schweigler, "Whatever Happened to Germany?" in: Ekkehart Krippendorf, and Volker Rittberger, eds., *The Foreign Policy of West Germany: Formation and Contents* (London: SAGE Publications, 1980), p. 106.

11.   Bruns, *Deutsch-deutsche Beziehungen*, pp. 23-4; and Wolfgang Mleczkowski, "Die Entwicklung der innerdeutschen Beziehungen aus DDR-Sicht," *Deutsche Studien* 18 (1980), pp. 114-18.

12.   Angela Stent, "Soviet Policy toward the German Democratic Republic," in: Sarah M. Terry, ed., *Soviet Policy in Eastern Europe* (New Haven: Yale University Press, 1984), pp. 40-1.

13.   Richard Löwenthal, "The German Question Transformed," *Foreign Affairs* 63 (Winter 1984/85), pp. 307-8.

2 THE BASIC TREATY AND ITS CONSEQUENCES

During 1971 and 1972 the East and West German negotiators Egon Bahr and Michael Kohl worked out a set of agreements solving many of the outstanding issues between the two states. In October 1972 they signed a treaty over the question of inter-German traffic that reduced travel restrictions to and from the GDR. On November 8, 1972 Bahr and Kohl reached agreement on the "Treaty over the Basis of Relations between the Federal Republic of Germany and the German Democratic Republic," the so-called Basic Treaty. The two states arrived at compromises on most of the issues that had long divided the two Germanies, but a number of fundamental problems were left unresolved.

Twelve years after the Basic Treaty, its record is rather ambiguous. On one hand, the treaty has led to vast improvements on a range of issues concerning human contacts between the citizens of the two German states. On the other hand, the ongoing conflicts over the status and sovereignty of the two German states and the restriction of inter-German contacts through repressive GDR policies made the results of the new *Deutschlandpolitik* fall short of the expectations of its West German architects. The following section will detail some of the achievements and the principal problems of the German-German relationship since 1969.

SUCCESSES AND SETBACKS IN
INTER-GERMAN NEGOTIATIONS

Access to West Berlin has been the point of greatest vulnerability for the FRG since the Soviet blockade in 1948-49. The threat of being cut off from West Germany constituted a major political and psychological problem for the encircled city, and the GDR had often exploited that point of leverage by slowing down the border controls on the transit routes or hindering travellers from crossing the border. Thus a guarantee for the transit routes to West Berlin, one of the major features of the 1971 Quadripartite Agreement on Berlin, was probably the most concrete achievement of West Germany's new policy toward the GDR. And it is in this area that the progress in inter-German relations can be seen most clearly.

The transit agreement betwen the FRG and the GDR was negotiated during 1970 and 1971 and was signed jointly with the Quadripartite Agreement on Berlin. For the FRG, it has proven the most important aspect of the Berlin settlement. The transit agreement quaranteed safe access on surface transit routes to West Berlin in exchange for a West German annual lump payment of tolls, visa expenses and other costs accruing to the GDR. This payment rose from DM 235 million annually in 1972 to DM 525 million in 1985. The result was impressive: between 1970 and 1980 the number of individuals using the transit routes grew from 7 million to 19 million per year.

However, the agreement did not end all disputes over the routes. As discussed in a later section, East German officials occasionally still caused delays and harassments on the border to reinforce certain political demands. These measures presented a dual problem to West Germans: they made them feel the vulnerability of West Berlin's exposed position and indicated that the GDR was only marginally interested in rapprochement with the West.

The FRG and the GDR also clashed repeatedly over the smuggling of refugees by West Germans through the transit routes. Between 700 and 750 people escape East Germany this way each year, often after paying large sums to professional smuggling organizations. In 1977 the West German Supreme Court ruled that refugee smuggling was not a criminal act and could in some aspects be regarded as a normal business transaction. The GDR interpreted this decision as legitimizing the abuse of the transit agreements and reacted with stricter controls on the borders.[1]

The main West German interest in the wake of the Basic Treaty, besides facilitations for West Berlin, was an improvement of personal contacts between the two German states. The balance sheet on these issues is generally positive. A series of postal agreements, in which the FRG agreed to pay a user's fee to the GDR, intensified the exchange of letters and telephone conversations between two states. The number of phone calls between West and East Germany rose from 500,000 in 1969 to 13.5 million in 1980. Even more striking was the improvement for West Berlin. Before 1970 one could not phone from the western to the eastern part of the city — there existed no phone lines. Ten years later, 9.5 million lines had been built.[2]

The most important personal contacts between the two neighbors are West German visits to the GDR. The traffic agreement of 1972 facilitated visits by West Germans to East German friends and relatives as well as professional trips and tourism. West Germans are now allowed to visit East Germany for up to 30 days per year. The so-called "small border traffic" permits individuals living in the frontier area to undertake day trips to the towns and villages across the border. For the first time the GDR also granted residents of West Berlin the same visiting rights as other West Germans. The results of these agreements were dramatic: from 1972 to 1979 the number of West German visits to the GDR rose from 2.5 million to 8.2 million visits.[3]

This trend, however, was abruptly reversed when the East German government responded to the Polish crisis in the summer of 1980 by raising the so-called minimum currency exchange rate from DM 12 to DM 25 per day and eliminated exemptions for senior citizens and children. The policy originally had been instituted in 1964 and required every visitor to exchange a certain amount of D-Mark into the East German Mark at the official exchange rate of 1:1 for every day of the visit. Since the unofficial market exchange rate in West German banks is closer to 1:5, this provision effectively constitutes a tax for Western visitors.[4] Although the original requirement was inspired by the insatiable East German desire for foreign currency, the increase of 1980 was a purely political act. Fearing a spillover from the rise of Solidarity and the crisis of the Polish regime, the East German leaders sought to reduce Western influence by raising the entrance fee. The measure achieved its purpose: the number of visits from the FRG dropped from 8.2 million in 1979 to 5.2 million in 1981.[5] The number of visits from West Berlin was halved. Despite strong West German pressure from Bonn, the GDR did not reverse the exchange rate increase, and made only small concessions in

1983 and 1984. Nevertheless, the number of visitors regained its pre-1980 level, growing 18 percent during the inter-German thaw in 1984.[6]

For East Germans, however, the freedom to travel to the West has hardly increased. One and a half million East Germans visit the FRG every year, but the great majority are retired people over 65, the only group of people allowed to leave the country on a regular basis. People below retirement age can obtain a passport only in the case of "urgent family affairs," such as weddings and deaths. Although the number of East Germans travelling to the West under this provision has risen from 37,000 in 1981 to 64,000 in 1983, many requests are still denied on arbitrary grounds.[7] Permission to leave the GDR permanently is even more difficult to obtain. Annually, approximately 10,000 individuals are permitted to move to the FRG under the family reunification program, and approximately 1,000 political prisoners are deported to the FRG in exchange for payments by the West German government. But the large majority of applicants (the number is estimated at 500,000) are denied permission to emigrate. As will be discussed later, the GDR relaxed its tight emigration restrictions only during a few months in early 1984, when more than 30,000 people were allowed to move to the West.

One of the central West German demands in the negotiations following the Basic Treaty was the right of West German media correspondents to work in the GDR. The agreement of 1973 granted extensive rights to West German journalists in the GDR, and in October 1973 the first permanent correspondents went to East Berlin. In practice, however, the GDR proved to be less tolerant than originally expected. Since 1975 a number of West German correspondents have been expelled, largely because of contacts with East German dissidents. In 1978 the GDR closed the office of the West German magazine *Der Spiegel* because it published a purported manifesto of an opposition group within the SED; the office has not yet been reopened. Although reporting by the West German media on East Germany is extensive and rather accurate, the uncertainty caused by expulsions and bureaucratic harassment results in a certain degree of self-censorship among Western correspondents.[8]

An area where negotiations succeeded particularly well was the precise determination of the border between the two states through a joint border commission. By 1978 the commission had redrawn almost the entire inter-German border, had reached an agreement to allow fishermen from the West German town of Lübeck to fish in their traditional fishing areas in East German waters, had gained an agreement that allocated East

German tap water to a West German border town, and had negotiated an accord on flood protection. In 1976 the FRG and the GDR agreed on a joint mining project of soft coal in the area of Helmstedt/Harbke along the border.[9] The only major border issue left unresolved — the determination of the border along the Elbe — will be discussed in a later section.

An issue that has eluded agreement for many years is environmental protection. Throughout the 1970s the GDR rejected any negotiations on environmental issues to protest the presence of the Federal Environmental Protection Office in West Berlin. But as the lack of East German emission standards and antipollution regulations became an increasing threat to West German rivers and regions, West German officials stepped up pressure on that subject. FRG officials were particularly concerned over water pollution in two rivers, the Werra and the Weser, that was caused by potash mining in the GDR. The salt content of the two rivers is ten times above the maximum acceptable European Community norms; it has already destroyed most biological life in the waters and now endangers the water supply of several West German cities.

There has been some progress in this area since 1980. East and West German experts began negotiations on the water and air pollution, and in September 1982 the two sides reached an agreement on water pollution in West Berlin. In July 1984 the GDR participated as the only Eastern European country in a European conference on environmental protection and promised significant improvements in emission controls. Although several plans to prevent the pollution of the Werra and Weser Rivers have been put forward by both sides, no agreement has yet been reached on that issue.[10]

THE CONFLICT OVER THE INTERPRETATION OF THE BASIC TREATY

The Basic Treaty permitted the establishment of quasi-normal relations between the GDR and the FRG, but it did not resolve all problems concerning the legal status of the two states. In the Basic Treaty, the FRG abandoned its claim to sole representation and recognized the GDR's sovereignty. However, the negotiators agreed to disagree over basic questions like citizenship and the existence of a single German nation. The question of whether or not the two German states could be foreign territory for each other was circumvented by the establishment of permanent missions instead of embassies. Thus, the

FRG recognized the sovereignty of the GDR and the inviolability of its borders but did not grant full diplomatic recognition to the GDR. Despite these compromises, the "status problems" have lost none of their explosive force in inter-German relations.

The SPD/FDP coalition in Bonn was apparently willing to make further concessions to the East German leadership, but the interpretation of the Basic Treaty by the West German Supreme Court in Karlsruhe on July 31, 1973 significantly reduced the flexibility of the West German government. When the prime minister of Bavaria and leader of the CSU, Franz Josef Strauß appealed the treaty on the grounds that it violated the national imperative to seek reunification of the Basic Law, the court responded with a ruling that affirmed the constitutionality of the Basic Treaty but insisted on a number of restrictions for its interpretation:

- The Basic Law assumes that the German Reich has not perished. Since no peace treaty was ever signed, it continues to exist; the establishment of the Federal Republic only represented a reorganization of part of the Reich.
- The border between the FRG and the GDR is not a normal international border, but resembles more the borders between the states of the Federal Republic.
- Berlin is a state of the Federal Republic and is thus an integral part of the FRG.
- Even after the Basic Treaty the GDR has not become foreign territory for the Federal Republic. Their bilateral relations are not normal diplomatic relations, but are of a special nature.
- There exists only one German citizenship. It is not limited to the Federal Republic but also includes all residents of the GDR. Every East German is therefore automatically also a citizen of the FRG.[11]

Contrary to this interpretation, the GDR insists that the German Reich has perished and that there now exist two fully independent German states that should coexist like all other independent states. Its main interest in the Basic Treaty was to obtain full diplomatic recognition by the FRG. Although they did not achieve their goal, East German officials like to cite Article 2, which calls for "sovereign equality" between the FRG and the GDR, and Article 4, which states that "no state can represent the other in the international arena."[12]

In contrast, the main goal of the FRG in the treaty was the affirmation of a special legal relationship and the intensification of political and personal relations. Thus, West German officials like to highlight Article 7, which calls for the intensification of relations in trade, science and technology, traffic, arts, legal aid, and other areas. In contrast, this article is hardly ever mentioned in East German publications.[13]

Underlying this debate are two different views of detente itself. In Western opinion, detente serves to break down barriers between nations and societies, encouraging the reduction of hostile competition and the convergence of different systems. Thus, the FRG puts emphasis on the establishment of good neighborly relations, an intensification of personal contacts, and cooperation in a wide range of issues. These goals stand in stark contrast to the East German policy of *demarcation*[14] which was first formulated in the early 1970s. Peaceful coexistence, the most common term for detente in the communist literature, implies a *modus vivendi* between two sovereign states as a protection of peace, but not the end to class struggle and ideological competition between societies with different political systems. As rapprochement with the FRG threatened to loosen the SED's political control over East German society, the leadership began to emphasize the differences between the two societies and to intensify the ideological conflict. The GDR increased the fortification of the inter-German border by installing automatic shrapnel guns, maintained its restrictive travel and emigration policy, banned millions of East Germans from any Western contacts by categorizing them as "carriers of state secrets," stepped up its hostile rhetoric against West Germany's polity, and even developed the doctrine of two separate nations in the GDR and the FRG — a capitalist and a socialist one. These practices soon shattered most West German illusions about the prospects for better inter-German relations. West German officials repeatedly contended that demarcation stood in violation of the Basic Treaty and the final accords of the CSCE conference in Helsinki.

Meanwhile, the GDR contended that the West German insistence on special relations violated the intent of the Basic Treaty. Although the Supreme Court's ruling was only valid within the FRG and did not affect the role of the Basic Treaty in the context of international law, the East German leadership was deeply shocked by the decision, since it seemed to carry on the tradition of nonrecognition.[15] The GDR's ambivalent attitude toward the compromises of the Basic Treaty, such as the establishment of permanent missions instead of embassies, explains why the East Germans put far less emphasis on this agreement than on the UN Charter or the Helsinki Accords, in which there is no notion of a special relationship. In contrast, the FRG regards the treaty as the key document in the inter-German relationship.[16]

Given these differences in ideology, the possibility of achieving agreement over the fundamentals of the inter-German relationship and the status problems has remained rather slim. Instead, West German policymakers have tried to focus in their relationship on practical questions where a common interest exists.[17] The negotiations usually followed the general pattern of West German economic benefits in exchange for humanitarian concessions and increased security for West Berlin. While this approach led to the series of agreements and treaties discussed above, it could be only partly successful. Whenever the GDR pressed for its demands, status problems interfered with inter-German negotiations and often made agreement impossible.

This ongoing conflict culminated on October 13, 1980. Three days after the GDR had announced it would triple the minimum currency exchange, Honecker gave a speech in Gera seemingly putting inter-German relations on a new basis. At the core of his speech stood four demands: (1) the transformation of the permanent representations into embassies; (2) the recognition of a separate GDR citizenship; (3) the dissolution of the *Zentrale Erfassungsstelle Salzgitter* which records and documents human rights violations by East German soldiers on the inter-German border; and (4) the precise determination of the Elbe border.[18] What was surprising about this speech were not the demands themselves, but the fact that Honecker made their fulfillment a prerequisite for any further progress in inter-German relations. His speech therefore stood in contradiction to the Basic Treaty; in particular, Honecker's call for the establishment of embassies, a point that was explicitly settled in the Basic Treaty, made many West Germans believe that the GDR no longer accepted the treaty.[19] Although over the course of the next two years Honecker softened his rhetoric, the issues that he raised continued to represent the core of the bilateral problems.

Embassies

The question of whether the two German states should maintain embassies or only permanent missions touches on the basis of inter-German relations — the issue of diplomatic recognition of the GDR as a completely separate state. The FRG insists that since the GDR cannot be foreign territory, the two states cannot establish regular international relations. Thus the Vienna diplomatic convention only applies on a limited basis to inter-German relations. A separate ministry of inner-German relations, not the West German ministry of foreign affairs, is officially in charge of issues concerning the GDR.

Meanwhile, the GDR goes to great lengths to reaffirm the separation between the two states and to reject *any* special nature in their relations. It refuses, for example, to deal with the ministry of inner-German relations, which it regards as a relic of the old reunification policy. Since the West German foreign ministry is not allowed to work with the GDR, inter-German policy is effectively made in the office of the chancellor. In the GDR, it is the foreign ministry that is in charge of inter-German relations. As East German Foreign Minister Oskar Fischer said, "'FRG' is just a division of the ministry like many others."[20]

Ultimately, the positions of both states appear unrealistic and inconsistent. West Germany's refusal to recognize the GDR as foreign territory ignores the reality of a fully sovereign and separate state; even most West German legal experts regard the "umbrella theory" that the German Reich still exists as unfounded.[21] The GDR, meanwhile, loses touch with reality by refusing to acknowledge that there exists a special relationship between the two states. Ironically, the primary evidence for this special quality is the almost obsessive attention East German citizens and policymakers give to their Western neighbor. Most of East Germany's economic, cultural, and political life centers around an *Auseinandersetzung* (a mixture of conflict and cooperation) with West Germany. And as will be discussed later, the benefits that the GDR derives from the special nature of inter-German trade are essential for the prosperity of the country. The artificial nature of the GDR's position is apparent in statements like the response of Ewald Moldt, the East German representative in Bonn, to a question about the relationship between the East and West German Protestant churches: "The relations between the churches will be as troubleless as the relations between Protestants in the GDR and Tanzania."[22]

Citizenship

The issue where the status conflict gains most significance is the question of citizenship. As demanded by its Basic Law, the FRG only recognizes one German citizenship. Since no German can ever be denied this citizenship, and the GDR is not regarded as foreign territory, all East

Germans are automatically also citizens of the Federal Republic. For East German leaders this policy is one of the most painful aspects of their relationship with the FRG. The citizenship question reminds them daily that many West Germans still regard the GDR as a second-class country and its residents as second-class citizens. Even more damaging to their political self esteem is its practical implication: every East German who sets foot on West German territory or enters a FRG embassy can automatically obtain a West German passport without going through any asylum or naturalization process. For a country that is plagued with an endless history of defections and escapes, this policy is especially unsettling.

This permanent challenge to the legitimacy of the East German state has been one of the major obstacles to any relaxation of travel restrictions for East German nationals, restrictions which remain severe even by communist standards. Many observers contend that a solution to the citizenship question would induce the GDR to adopt a more liberal travel policy. If East Germans were no longer automatically granted citizenship rights in the FRG but had to apply for political asylum just like citizens from any other East European state, so the East Germans argue, they will be less tempted to defect. Even if the West German concession were only symbolic and would not affect actual immigration procedures, the worst fears of the SED officials would be alleviated.[23]

Such a step might even mitigate the original reason for the restrictive travel policy. Many observers believe that the lack of freedom to travel, more than the low standard of living or political repression, is the main source of discontent for East Germans, and is thus the most frequent motive to defect. Also, the Hungarian government found that once it allowed people to travel freely, only a few choose not to return. The West German policy concerning GDR citizenship make such a liberalization less likely, as it represents an implicit attack on the legitimacy of the East German leadership. And whenever its legitimacy is questioned, the SED reacts with more repression.[24]

Another negative consequence of the unsettled citizenship question is the failure to reach an agreement on legal aid between the FRG and the GDR. Since the early 1970s, the GDR has boycotted any negotiations on this issue, arguing that legal procedures concern citizens. Thus, before an agreement is reached, the two states must reach a consensus over the definition of both states' citizenships.[25]

One major obstacle to solving the citizenship problem is the status of West Berlin. Since the GDR insists that the city is not part of the Federal

Republic, the recognition of separate East and West German nationalities would require a third citizenship for West Berlin. Such a step would not only force the release of the city from the control of the four occupying powers — a move that not only the Soviet Union would strongly oppose — but it would be incompatible with the West German policy of reinforcing the ties between the isolated city and the mainland. Further, separate citizenship for West Berlin could cause severe psychological strain for its residents who still fear being abandoned by the West. Many West Germans fear that this change could lead to a mass exodus from the city and undermine its economic viability.[26] Although the legal problem could undoubtedly be solved, the underlying fact is that the ambiguous status of the citizenship question has allowed both sides to maintain the status quo in Berlin without fully resolving the surrounding principal questions. As it has often been the case in inter-German relations, ambiguity can occasionally be an asset.

A further reason why the FRG is unwilling to even consider the citizenship issue is the question of self-determination. Article 116 of the Basic Law prohibits revoking the citizenship of any German — a policy that had been practiced frequently by the Nazis. By recognizing a separate GDR citizenship, it is argued, the Federal Republic would deprive 17 million Germans of their citizenship without having given them a chance to express their free and democratic will. Finally, some West Germans fear that a separate citizenship would add to the already disturbing estrangement between the residents of the two German states. If the FRG recognized a separate GDR nationality, East Germans would have less rights in the Federal Republic than citizens from other member states of the European Community. How can the Federal Republic, they ask, allow French people to work in the FRG while denying the same right to people from Dresden and Leipzig?

Most experts agree that in light of the *de facto* recognition of the GDR, West Germany's refusal to recognize its citizenship is just not realistic. According to international law, a state with a sovereign territory and sovereign authority must also have a sovereign nationality.[27] Political leaders in the SPD and FDP have repeatedly raised the issue of whether the FRG should abandon its anachronistic position in exchange for humanitarian concessions, but they have always encountered severe opposition in all political camps.[28]

Indeed, a compromise would not even require the abandonment of principles. In recent years, Honecker has no longer demanded the recognition, but only respect for the GDR citizenship. He was referring in particular to the termination of provocative acts such as stamping "void" on GDR passports, or sending military draft orders to East German officials working in the Federal Republic. Schmidt promised him such respect at their meeting in Werbellin in December 1981, and West German officials now generally avoid such moves. If the FRG committed itself officially to the respect of the GDR citizenship, this could form the basis for an ultimate agreement. However, the current conservative government has shown little inclination to move into this direction.[29]

Salzgitter

The same motives that make the GDR demand the recognition of its citizenship also propel it to require the dissolution of the *Zentrale Erfassungstelle Salzgitter*. This documentation center, located in Lower Saxony, was founded in 1961 as a response to the building of the Berlin Wall. Salzgitter is an agency of the West German state attorney's offices and records any human rights violations by East German soldiers on the border, in particular the shooting at refugees who try to cross the border illegally. Should the perpetrators ever set foot on West German ground, they could be legally prosecuted.

The GDR regards the existence of this institution as a blatant intervention into their internal affairs, and goes so far as to threaten prosecution of its officials when they visit East Germany. Its case against the center appears to be solid, since Salzgitter seems to be in violation even of West German legal principles. Proponents argue that the FRG has the right and the duty to prosecute human rights violations on the other side of the border because the GDR is not foreign territory and its inhabitants are German citizens. But Salzgitter applies West German law to the territory of the GDR, an act that is explicitly prohibited in Article 6 of the Basic Treaty. Thus most legal experts regard it as a relic of the Cold War period and argue for its abolition, especially since its function could also be fulfilled by regular West German district attorneys.[30]

A severe obstacle to the abolition is the federalist nature of West Germany's judicial system. The center is subordinate to the West German state attorneys and is under the jurisdiction of all West German federal states. Its abolition would require the consent of all 11 states, most of which are ruled by conservative governments. In West Germany's domestic setting, this seems to be an impossible task to achieve.

Further, the current West German government regards Salzgitter as a bargaining chip to affect changes in the East German border policy. Bonn's main demand for a quid pro quo is the lifting of the East German *Schießbefehl,* the firing order on the border. The GDR opposes this demand, contending that just like every state in the world it has a right to control its borders, even if that control requires force. While this argument is theoretically correct, the periodic shooting of East Germans had always stirred up moral outrage in West Germany and strengthened the position of those who defend Salzgitter. The deployment during the 1970s of automatic shrapnel guns that kill or maim anyone who tries to cross the border struck a particularly sensitive nerve in the West German public.

The pressure of world public opinion has already induced the GDR to make some concessions in its border policies. In 1983, it began to dismantle the shrapnel guns and had them all removed by early 1985. Also, the number of shooting incidents on the border has dropped significantly in recent years. These developments, however, have not made the escape from the GDR any easier. East German officials have recognized that virtually impenetrable barriers, such as fences with highly sensitive alarm systems, serve the same purpose as shootings but do far less harm to East Germany's international image.[31]

Elbe Border

The exact location of about 60 miles of the inter-German border along the river Elbe, the most petty of the status problems, remains a point of controversy. While GDR insists that the border lies in the middle of the river, the FRG claims the whole Elbe as West German territory and asserts that the border must therefore lie on the Eastern bank. This controversy grows out of the historical divisions between various German principalities as well as the maps of the allied forces after World War II, in which the demarcation lines were inexactly drawn.

The West German position in this debate illustrates well how domestic constraints often prevent the government from pursuing a rational policy towards the GDR. The London Protocol of September 12, 1944 set the border along the borders of the historical principalities, which lay on the Eastern bank of the Elbe. When Adenauer asked the allies for clarification of the controversial issue in 1953, their zonal border memorandum named the middle of the river as the legitimate border. Still, based on the maps from 1944, the FRG continued to claim the whole river for itself.[32] The issue remained unresolved until 1975, when the joint German-German border commission agreed that the FRG had no legitimate claim to the Eastern bank. However, the Bavarian prime minister Franz Josef Strauß and the prime minister of Lower Saxonia Ernst Albrecht objected to this agreement. Since the disputed area is located in Lower Saxonia, the two conservative politicians prevailed. Although the FRG would have received important concessions concerning border regulations and water pollution, West Germany again missed the chance to reach an agreement.[33]

In February 1977, after a border incident on the Elbe, the West German Supreme Court affirmed the FRG's claim to the whole river. That same year the East German Supreme Court decided that the border actually ran along the shipping lane, that is the deepest point of the river. Although the GDR pressed hard toward a final settlement, it finally agreed to exclude the whole issue from the final report of the border commission. The issue was raised again in the meeting between Schmidt and Honecker in the East German town Werbellin in December 1981. Schmidt regarded the Elbe border as a relatively costless way of gaining concessions from the GDR and pressed Albrecht to change his mind on the issue. But Albrecht refused to yield.[34]

The most absurd aspect of this controversy is that it lacks any practical relevance. Since the East German border installations are on the eastern bank, the whole river can be used by West German shippers and fishermen. Similarly, the FRG lets East German border patrol boats use the eastern half of the river, thus implicitly recognizing the middle of the river as the border. Also, there have been no recorded shooting incidents on the Elbe in recent years.

A solution to the border dispute, however, appears to be of strategic importance for the Soviets who are eager to see the last ambiguous borderline between Eastern and Western Europe clarified. Soviet military planners regard those 60 miles as a troubling gray area in their defense plans and have repeatedly pressed the East Germans to use their relations with the FRG for once to the advantage of their own alliance. Consequently a settlement of the Elbe question would represent a success for the GDR within the WTO and would increase its leeway to pursue inter-German relations.[35]

THE STATUS OF WEST BERLIN

The Quadripartite Agreement of 1971 took West Berlin out of global East-West politics and defused the day-to-day conflict over the transit to West Berlin. But despite the efforts of Western negotiators, the vague language of the agreement effectively thwarted a solution to the disputes over the city's status. The fundamental problem that the document could not address was that the Soviet Union had never accepted the Western presence in the city as fully legitimate. After the failure of their strongest challenge to this presence, the Berlin blockade of 1948-49, the Soviets bestowed de facto recognition to the allied occupation of West Berlin, but continued to argue that the Western allies had no rights concerning Berlin as a whole. Insisting that four-power responsibility extended to the western part but not the eastern part of the city, Moscow demanded input into the political fate of West Berlin while denying comparable rights to the Western allies in the east. Since the Western governments rejected this one-sided interpretation, they never felt obliged to grant the Soviets any political input in West Berlin.

The first controversy represents the basis for the second dispute. Since the late 1940s, the Soviet Union and the GDR have contended that West Berlin had to be a completely independent political unit and that any political ties between West Berlin and the FRG were illegal. The FRG and the Western allies, however, insist that West Berlin belongs to West Germany. Both sides cite parts of the same sentence of the Quadripartite Agreement in support of their position: "The governments of the French Republic, the United Kingdom and the United States of America declare that ties between Berlin's Western sectors and the Federal Republic are maintained and developed, whereby they take into consideration that, as in the past, these sectors are not a part (constituent part) of the Federal Republic and are further on not governed by it."[36] While the FRG emphasizes its right to maintain and develop ties with West Berlin, the GDR and the Soviet Union highlight the latter part of the sentence, usually suppressing the first part. Additionally, they often cite a passage of the appendix which prohibits any ties that concern questions of status and security. According to East German rhetoric, this prohibition includes all political ties between the FRG and the city. Thus, the GDR insists that only loose cultural and economic ties to West Germany are permissible under the Quadripartite Agreement.[37]

The Western powers and the FRG refuse even to negotiate over these claims. They argue that the Soviet Union and the GDR violate the four-power status of the city by treating East Berlin as an integral part of the GDR and declaring it the capital of the GDR. Thus, they have no right to interfere with the political status of the western part of the city. The FRG respects the commitments that the Western allies made to the Soviets in the aftermath of the Berlin blockade restricting certain political ties between the city and the FRG. These limits were confirmed by the Quadripartite Agreement although they conflict with the passages in the West German Basic Law that define West Berlin as a constituent state *(Land)* of the Federal Republic. Still, since Bonn fully exploits the ambiguity of the agreements by insisting on all ties that are not explicitly prohibited, West Berlin is treated in most respects as a full and equal member of the Federal Republic. West Berlin's representatives to the *Bundestag,* the West German parliament, are an exception to this rule; they are not elected by popular vote, but indirectly by the city council, and do not participate in some votes.[38]

The underlying source for these ongoing disputes are the semantical and political compromises of the Quadripartite Agreement, which permitted the most fundamental questions to remain unresolved while establishing a *modus vivendi* on certain practical questions. Only the willingness of the Soviets to neglect and even abandon their previous positions on West Berlin during the negotiations in 1970-71 made this treaty possible. As discussed earlier, the Kremlin leadership pressed for the agreement against the opposition of SED leader Walter Ulbricht since they regarded an agreement as a precondition for the desired CSCE conference. The West gained secure access to the city from this agreement, while the GDR had to accept that its legal role was circumscribed. But soon after the ratification of the treaty, the Soviets and the new East German leadership reverted to their old course by interpreting the agreements as narrowly as possible. This practice has led to a range of petty conflicts over the years and has been in the way of many inter-German issues.[39]

The first controversy erupted after the ruling on the Basic Treaty by the West German Supreme Court that confirmed West Berlin's status as a state of the FRG. The GDR not only sharply condemned this ruling, but in the following years even protested against details like the use of the West German flag in West Berlin or the application of the nuclear nonproliferation treaty to West Berlin. But the conflict reached its climax with the establishment of the headquarters of the Federal Environmental Protection Office in West Berlin on June 19, 1974. The GDR barred agency officials from using the transit routes to West Berlin and disrupted traffic to West Berlin for several days. The presence of this office has also stalled the conclusion of an agreement on environmental protection for more than a decade. The conflict again reached a critical point when U.S. President Jimmy Carter and West German Chancellor Helmut Schmidt visited West Berlin in July 1978. East German officials interrupted all surface transit traffic to protest this alleged violation of the independent status of West Berlin. The GDR also attacked West Berlin's participation in the first direct elections to the European Parliament in June 1979. In response, the GDR announced the direct election of East Berlin's representatives to the East German parliament the same month, thus openly violating the Berlin agreements.

In an ironic change of roles, in the Berlin question it is the GDR and the Soviet Union who act as a revisionist force, while the FRG wants to maintain the status quo of the city — the de facto presence of the West German state and society in West Berlin.[40] Just as the existence of the GDR is a reality with which the FRG had to come to terms, so are West Berlin's ties with the Federal Republic a reality that the East Germans cannot ignore. One might ask why both GDR and Soviet Union take such a strong interest in the status of the city and why they are unwilling to accept that West Berlin is a part of the FRG in practically every respect. The motive behind this attitude is partly understandable. The presence of U.S. and British troops in the middle of the Eastern bloc is a thorn in the flesh of the Soviets, and the existence of a West German "island" on East German territory is a permanent reminder for the GDR that the German partition might not last forever. While other cities have remained divided for many decades, an enclave of two million people surrounded by another country seems intuitively to be an unstable situation. Taking a long-term perspective, Soviets and East Germans have reason to hope that one day the United States and Great Britain will renege on their commitment to defend the city. A complete severing of political ties between West Berlin and the FRG would then allow the eventual absorption of the city into the GDR — a prospect that is rendered increasingly unlikely by West Berlin's political integration with the FRG. Still, one may wonder if the Soviets do not also derive certain benefits from the ambiguous situation concerning Berlin, since their role in the future of the city provides them with leverage over both the GDR and the FRG.

The controversy over West Berlin gains practical importance as a significant number of inter-German agreements, such as the treaties on environmental protection, and science and technology, have not been signed because the GDR opposes the inclusion of the city into the accord. It is not coincidental that the first major agreement between the two states, the trade agreement of 1951, skirted the question of West Berlin's status.

The problem of the agreement on cultural exchange is related to West Berlin in a slightly different way. In 1974, the GDR discontinued all negotiations on this subject, and demanded that the FRG first return the works of art from the *Stiftung Preußischer Kulturbesitz* (Prussian Cultural Heritage Foundation). These works had been located on the current territory of East Berlin before 1945, but were moved to the western part of the city during the bombing raids in World War II. After the war, West Berlin combined them in a huge collection and claimed the property rights to them. For both sides, significant values are at stake here. The collection fills a whole museum complex in West Berlin, and includes one of the world's best Rembrandt collections as well as the famous Egyptian Armana-period bust of Nefertiti.

Due to the lack of a formal agreement, West Germany's cultural relations with East Germany, such as the exchange of art exhibitions, theater and musical performances, still lag behind its cultural relations with most other European states. Given the value that West Germans assign to the continuation of the German *Kulturnation,* this deficiency is one of the most severe problems in inter-German relations. But even here, the last three years have yielded some significant progress. Although in July 1980 the East German assembly passed a law declaring the collection to be East German property, in a 1983 about-face, Honecker suddenly agreed to resume cultural negotiations, leaving out the issue of the collection's ownership. Until mid-1985, the talks were held up by disputes over full inclusion of West Berlin and Bonn's demands to allow more Western books and newspapers to be imported into the GDR. After the resumption of a U.S.-Soviet cultural agreement at the summit meeting between U.S. President Ronald Reagan and the CPSU General Secretary Mikhail Gorbachev in Geneva in November 1985, however, East and West German negotiators quickly settled their remaining disagreements and presented the framework for a cultural exchange treaty between the two German states.

Ironically, the continuous disputes regarding West Berlin have always exerted positive influences as well on inter-German relations. Cooperation over the transit question has provided a framework for West German economic aid to the GDR and thus given both sides a major incentive to seek constructive dialogue. Perhaps two-thirds of all inter-German agreements of the last 15 years dealt to some extent with West Berlin, whether transit to the city or West Berlin's relations to its environment. It is also noteworthy that improvements in inter-German relations in the 1980s have further taken the edge off the Berlin problem. The willingness of both sides to leave status problems out of consideration became apparent during Richard von Weizsäcker's official visit to East Berlin in September 1983. The fact that Weizsäcker, who later became president of the Federal Republic, was the first mayor of West Berlin to visit the other side of the city lent special significance to that occasion. Other examples of the relaxation of tensions surrounding West Berlin were the quick transfer of control over the *Schnellbahn,* an above-ground railroad that had been operated by East German authorities since the post-war years, in January 1984, and a series of agreements on issues like West Berlin's garbage disposal, water supply, and communication links with the Federal Republic.[41]

On the more general level of East-West relations, one can argue the city has repeatedly served as a test of the willingness of both sides to pursue confrontation or cooperation. After having been a dangerous source of tensions during the Cold War, Berlin became a major stimulus for detente between the United States and the Soviet Union through the signing of the Quadripartite Agreement. The continuous division of Berlin has also kept the German question alive and has forced the German allies in East and West to maintain their interest in the development of inter-German relations. Finally, the four-power responsibility over the city guarantees the continuous military and political presence of the United States in Central Europe and thus strengthens the West German position *vis-à-vis* the East.

THE SPECIAL CASE OF INTER-GERMAN TRADE

Whenever general assessments are made about inter-German relations, the issue of trade must almost always be excluded. The case of inter-German trade differs from most other aspects of the German-German relationship. While the victor nations were busy dividing Germany into two separate political and economic units, trade between the western and eastern zones had already begun to flourish. In 1951, inter-German trade was formalized through the so-called Berlin Agreement. All status problems, including the status of West Berlin, were circumvented by the definition of the document as an "agreement on trade between the currency zones of the German Mark (DM-West) and the currency zones of the German Mark of the German National Bank (DM-Ost)." The Berlin Agreement was the first major treaty between the two German states; with one short interruption, it has allowed trade relations to flourish independently of political fluctuations and status conflicts.[42]

This does not mean that the FRG and GDR actually agree on the status of inter-German trade. For West Germans, the trade is unlike foreign trade, but has characteristics of both foreign and domestic trade. Not the ministry of foreign trade, but a special board of trustees for intra-zone trade in Berlin has supervised inter-German trade since 1949. In contrast to other trade with Eastern bloc countries, which is automatically legal if not explicitly prohibited, every individual business transaction with the GDR requires the approval of this board, thus providing the West German government with an extraordinary amount of control over trade relations with East Germany.[43]

East Germans reject all arguments about special status but gladly take advantage of the benefits that result from its unique characteristics. These benefits include a clearing agreement over both states' national banks, a permanent interest-free loan to the GDR, exemption from all duties and tariffs, and consequently, the implicit membership of the GDR in the European Community.

The main West German interest in inter-German trade is political. Since the early days of partition, the trade has fulfilled a "bracket function," providing ties between the two Germanies even during the worst political crises.[44] West German officials repeatedly emphasize the political goals of inter-German trade, thus reminding the GDR of the reasons behind the FRG's generosity. In accord with this political goal, the West German government encourages mainly small and medium-size companies to conduct the major part of inter-German trade, because this necessitates more individual contacts for business transactions. Of the 6,000 West German firms that conduct trade with the GDR, 81 percent have fewer than 1,000 employees.

The actual importance of inter-German trade for the West German economy is rather limited. It represents 30 percent of all the FRG's trade with the East, 3 percent of all its foreign trade, and contributes 1.6 percent of the annual GNP. However, for the companies that export to the GDR, inter-German trade constitutes a large part of their revenues and accounts for almost 100,000 jobs. These middle-size companies are part of a group of firms that, as members of the German Council for Industry and Trade, enjoy a large degree of political clout, especially with the conservative parties. Also West Berlin benefits disproportionally from inter-German trade: businesses located in the city contribute only 3 percent of the annual West German GNP, but 28 percent of inter-German trade. Thus, inter-German trade enjoys the support of powerful special interest groups that press for the enhancement of trade relations and oppose the use of trade as a political instrument.[45]

The political goals of the FRG in inter-German trade are not shared by the GDR. Despite an ideology which perceives economics as a fundamentally political phenomenon, East German leaders have always tried to keep business and politics separate in respect to trade with the West. Their reasons were clear: Western trade, and especially inter-German trade, offers significant economic benefits but can also be a political liability. By divorcing trade relations from any political objectives, the GDR has tried to prevent West German leaders from using trade as a political lever.

Given East Germany's dependence on inter-German trade, the threat of West German economic sanctions is real. Trade with the FRG represents approximately 10 percent of all foreign trade and more than half of its trade with the West. Although the GDR regards this trade as regular foreign trade, the benefits which it obtains through West German trade policies are significant and make these transactions far from normal. For example, the FRG exempts goods from the GDR of all duties normally levied on imports, and reduces the value added tax (VAT) which is imposed on domestic trade. The cost of the VAT shortfalls alone amount to DM 290 million annually. They also help make East German goods more competitive and thus contribute to a more balanced trade account between the two states.[46]

The special status of inter-German trade has made the GDR a de facto member of the European Community. The GDR has the same duty-free access to the West German market as, for example, France. It can sell its agricultural goods for the artifically high prices set by the Common Agricultural Policy (CAP), and can take advantage of a number of other EC privileges. This special status of inter-German trade was laid down in the Treaty of Rome of 1959, which led to the formation of the European Community, and was reconfirmed in 1974. Some EC members have repeatedly voiced criticism of the East German privileges, fearing the re-export of GDR goods from the FRG into their countries. However, this potential problem has never become critical. When East German goods move within the EC, duties can be levied on them, and West German firms lose their advantage of the VAT reduction. Thus the incentive for re-export is rather small: only half a percent of all East German goods leave the FRG again.[47]

Another major advantage for the GDR is the clearing agreement between the two states. All business transactions between the FRG and GDR are conducted by the national banks in Bonn and East Berlin and are calculated in so-called *Verrechnungseinheiten* (clearing units — VEs), which are set at a 1:1 ratio to the West German DM. Companies do not pay or get paid directly, but all payments and debts are credited to the other country's account. Since no money ever changes hands, the two accounts must be in balance in the long run.

A necessary part of any clearing agreement is a so-called swing loan, which compensates for short-term imbalances between imports and exports. Although the swing should, as the name implies, be used by both sides, since the early 1960s only the GDR has taken advantage of it. Thus, the swing has become an interest-free loan to the East German government which grew from DM 35 million in 1969 to DM 850 million in 1978. In addition to representing a lucrative deal for the always currency-starved GDR, the swing's main advantage is its positive influence on the East German credit rating among Western banks. The clearing agreement also permits the GDR to conduct trade without any foreign exchange. This arrangement explains why the volume of inter-German trade rose significantly in the early 1980s: the GDR had amassed huge amounts of foreign debt and could not longer obtain any fresh loans from Western banks. Short of foreign exchange, it had to turn to the FRG to cover the importation of basic commodities, including food and energy.

But inter-German trade also has important political characteristics for the GDR. As will be discussed later, the East German leadership has a more severe legitimacy problem than other Eastern European governments. The most effective way of strengthening its legitimacy in the eyes of its own population is by offering an ever rising standard of living. This task becomes particularly difficult because East German economic performance is measured, not against the Soviet Union and Poland, but against the Federal Republic. Due to the GDR's high dependence on foreign trade, it must rely on its external economic relations to provide its citizens with consumer goods and productive employment opportunities. In this strategy, inter-German trade has always held a central position, and has contributed significantly to the fact that the GDR has the highest standard of living of all countries in the Eastern bloc. Consequently, inter-German relations and East-West detente play an essential function in East German domestic economic policy. As will be discussed later, the GDR's economic interest in a stable relationship with the FRG which is insulated from political crises is a powerful explanation for the conciliatory East German policies during and after the intermediate-range nuclear forces (INF) crisis of 1983-84.[48]

The GDR , however, views the value of inter-German trade relations with uneasiness. It fears that too much trade would make the GDR vulnerable to pressure from West German hard-liners and would open the country to more Western influences, thus undermining its policy of demarcation. Hence, the SED leadership has been very careful to limit inter-German trade to politically acceptable levels. Although 50 percent of all machinery is currently supplied by West German companies, in most other fields the West German share is much smaller. For more than a decade, the percentage of inter-German trade in East Germany's foreign trade has remained at ten percent, suggesting that the SED Politbureau has defined this level as the point at which the GDR can maximize its benefits without becoming vulnerable.[49]

This desire to avoid dependence on the FRG accounts for the GDR's policy of trade diversification during the 1970s. East Germany increased its trade with other West European countries other than the FRG much faster than inter-German trade; the ratio of inter-German trade to the GDR's total trade with the West dropped from 1:1 in 1970 to 1:1.75 at the end of the 1970s. In light of the previously low level of Western trade, this swift increase was not that astonishing. Also, the availability of favorable credit conditions from countries such as France and Austria provided an incentive comparable to the GDR's advantages in inter-German trade. Especially large industrial "flagship" plants were increasingly bought in Western countries other than the FRG.[50] This trend caused major consternation in West Germany, where policymakers saw part of their instruments of inter-German rapprochement rendered ineffective.

An even more important consideration for the East German leadership than trade is West German para-economic payments to the GDR. The West German government annually pays about DM 1.5 billion, while the total currency transfers to the GDR amount to almost DM 2.5 billion annually. In 1984, this included DM 525 million in transit fees to West Berlin, DM 200 million postal fees, DM 50 million road tolls, and DM 120 million payments for special construction projects. In addition, West German visitors annually pay DM 400 million through the minimum currency exchange and send approximately DM 700 million as pecuniary gifts to East German friends and relatives.[51]

Finally, the FRG pays about DM 150 million annually, often through payments in kind, for the release of political prisoners. The payments range between DM 30,000 and DM 100,000 per individual, depending on the level of education and severity of offense of the prisoners. These transactions, which West German officials negotiate on an unofficial level with the East German lawyer Wolfgang Vogel, are often criticized on the grounds that they induce the GDR to arrest political dissidents and "sell" them to the West in order to earn foreign exchange. They also induce peculiar situations, such as the voluntary imprisonment of East Germans who wish to leave the country.[52]

Possibly the most important benefit of all West German economic policies toward the GDR, such as the para-economic payments and the swing and other commercial loans, is their implicit financial umbrella: Western banks assume that the Federal Republic would always save the GDR from bankruptcy. This expectation not only allows the East German leadership to obtain more loans in the West than any other Eastern European country, but the improved credit rating saves the East Germans millions of dollars annually in interest payments. One can even argue that improvements in inter-German relations by themselves also improve the credit worthiness of the GDR, and thus reduce East German interest payments.

Given these conditions, West German policymakers have repeatedly wondered whether they could use trade to obtain more political concessions from the GDR. Especially in the 1970s the conservative opposition parties challenged the SPD/FDP coalition government to use economic leverage more effectively. To the chagrin of many West Germans, the trade weapon has never met such expectations.

Since the beginning of inter-German trade, the FRG had maintained an implicit linkage between trade and free transit to West Berlin. When in early 1960, during the height of the Berlin crisis, the East Germans increased the pressure on the city by interrupting transit traffic and harassing travellers, the FRG announced that it would not extend the Berlin Agreement which was due to expire at the end of the year. West German officials, however, soon realized that this measure would hurt their own objectives as much as the GDR, but would do little to change East German behavior. Before the year was over, the crisis was resolved when the trade agreement was renewed without conditions.

The East Germans learned their lesson from this episode: Under the policy of *Störfreimachung* (freeing from disturbances), the GDR cut back significantly on its trade with the FRG. It was not until 1964, that inter-German trade began to increase again. The West Germans also saw the lesson in this event; since 1960, no explicit attempt to link trade to politics has been made. Although in 1965 the FRG confirmed the linkage between trade and transit to West Berlin, the beginning of negotiations on the transit agreement made this policy irrelevant.[53]

The only time East Germany has been willing to make political concessions was in return for direct West German loans to the GDR government. In 1974 the West German government linked the extension of an increased swing to the reduction of the East German minimum foreign currency exchange — and succeeded. However, when Foreign Minister Hans-Dietrich Genscher applied the same strategy after the three-fold increase in the exchange rate in 1980, the East Germans did not yield; instead, they even threatened to cut back on the volume of bilateral trade. As will be discussed later, the reduction of the flow of West German visitors during the Polish crisis was too important for the East German government to be abandoned for economic benefits. Subsequent negotiations on swing extensions yielded few political results. In 1982 in contrast Bonn managed to gain a general amnesty for East Germans who had left the country illegally between 1972 and 1981 in exchange for a renewal of the swing. And in 1985 the GDR pledged to restrict the influx of Tamil refugees who flew to East Berlin and then switched to the western part of the city.[54]

West Germany's insight that the cost of economic linkage outweighed most positive results was not limited to the inter-German relationship. In the course of the 1970s, the FRG generally abandoned its earlier linkage embargo policy towards the East. Trade was increasingly regarded as an economic asset, not a political weapon. In the 1976 campaign, the SPD for the first time ran on a platform which pointed to the fact that eastern trade had created 300,000 jobs in the FRG. After the Soviet invasion of Afghanistan in December 1979, the Federal Republic followed the boycott of the Olympic games in Moscow, but refused to join the U.S. embargo against the Soviet Union. Nor did it sever economic ties with Poland after the declaration of martial law in 1981. Along with other West European countries, the FRG attempted to halt the U.S. embargo against the Siberian pipeline deal with the Soviet Union — and succeeded in the end. Although the issues in the inter-German relationship are more susceptible to economic linkage than in global East-West relations, the use of economic leverage for political ends seems to have become increasingly a policy of the past.[55]

The main problem of linkage is that on a political and economic level, interests in inter-German relations are far more balanced than some West Germans want to believe. West German political goals are at least as salient as East German economic needs. Further impediments to linking trade to politics is the domestic power of West German companies that conduct inter-German trade, the restrictions imposed by the bilateral agreements which the FRG has signed, and the knowledge that other Western countries would willingly take the FRG's place if it reduced German-German trade relations. Most of inter-German economic relations are determined by binding treaties and cannot be broken easily. Also, despite its strong dependence on economic benefits of the inter-German relationship, the East German leaders — like most communist governments — have shown themselves to be extremely reluctant to make major political concessions in direct exchange for financial favors.[56] Even when such trade appeared to take place, as it did in 1984 after the second unrestricted bank loan guaranteed by the West German government, the GDR always denied such a linkage.

The small degree of interdependence of politics and economics also explains why the fluctuations in inter-German trade cannot be linked to the political climate between the two states. Overall, inter-German trade received a significant boost during the 1970s, growing from DM 4.5 billion in 1970 to DM 12 billion in 1980 and to more than DM 15 billion in 1983. But the growth rates have varied widely and often ran counter to political developments. Thus, inter-German trade experienced a slump shortly after the signing of the Basic Treaty in 1972, when the GDR took advantage of its growing international recognition to increase trade with other OECD countries, and grew vigorously during the inter-German chill in 1980-81. Also, the growth rates of the 1970s were only slightly above the growth rates during the 1960s, when political relations were far less developed. Frequently, the cause for trade fluctuations seems to be the economic situation within the GDR. Whenever the GDR suffered from a shortage of foreign exchange, it cut back its imports and tried to boost its exports in the following year.[57]

These observations are striking because they contradict the widely held view that the GDR pursues political relations with the FRG only for the sake of West German loans and inter-German trade. Undoubtedly, economic benefits play an important role in East German decision making, but as these figures show, they do not tell the whole story. Other motives at work in East Germany's policies toward the FRG will be discussed in Chapter 3.

NOTES

1. For a discussion of the transit agreements and their implementation, see Margit Roth, *Zwei Staaten in Deutschland: Die Sozialliberale Deutschlandpolitik und ihre Auswirkungen 1969-1978* (Opladen: Westdeutscher Verlag, 1981), p. 110-18.

2. *Zahlenspiegel: Bundesrepublik Deutschland/Deutsche Demokratische Republik — Ein Vergleich* (Bonn: Bundesministerium für innerdeutsche Beziehungen, 1983), p. 97.

3. Angela Stent, "Soviet Policy toward the German Democratic Republic," in Sarah M. Terry, ed., *Soviet Policy in Eastern Europe* (New Haven: Yale University Press, 1984), p. 51.

4. Margit Roth, *Zwei Staaten in Deutschland: Die Sozialliberale Deutschlandpolitik und ihre Auswirkungen 1969-1978* (Opladen: Westdeutscher Verlag, 1981), pp. 123-24.

5. *Zahlenspiegel*, p. 93.

6. Walter Leisler Kiep, "The New Deutschlandpolitik," *Foreign Affairs* 63 (Winter 1984-85): 317.

7. Figures from *Jahresbericht 1983*, Bundesministerium für innerdeutsche Beziehungen.

8. See Jürgen Döschner, "Zehn Jahre bundesdeutsche Korrespondenten in der DDR," *Deutschland Archiv* 17 (August 1984): 859-69.

9. See Roth, *Zwei Staaten in Deutschland*, pp. 69-70; and Wilhelm Bruns, *Deutsch-deutsche Beziehungen: Prämissen — Probleme — Perspektiven* (Opladen: Leske & Bundrich, 1982), p. 54.

10. See Peter Jochen Winters, "Vereinbarungen und Verhandlunger mit der DDR im Gefolge des Grundlagenvertrages," *Deutschland Archiv* 15 (December 1982); *Der Spiegel* 6/1980 (February 4, 1980) and 22/1982 (May 31, 1982), and FAZ, July 26, 1985.

11. See Roth, *Zwei Staaten in Deutschland*, pp. 42-5, and Bruns, *Deutsch-deutsche Beziehungen*, p. 30-4.

12. Quoted in Bruns, *Deutsch-deutsche Beziehungen*, p. 147.

13. Ibid., p. 34; and Wolfgang Mleczkowski, "Die Enwicklung der innerdeutschen Beziehungen aus DDR-Sicht," *Deutsche Studien* 18 (1980): 111-12.

14. *Abgrenzung*, the German term for this policy, can also be translated as delimitation or delineation. Since the translation most frequently used in English literature is demarcation, I will use it throughout.

15. See "Anmerkungen zu Träumereien einiger Karlsruher Richter," *Neues Deutschland*, August 16, 1973.

16. Bruns, *Deutsch-deutsche Beziehungen*, p. 123.

17. Ibid., pp. 12-13. Helmut Schmidt expressed this view in his meeting with Honecker in December 1981: "The differences in principal questions which we cannot overcome must be mitigated through a net of what is practicable for both sides." Bruns, "Zehn Jahre Grundlagenvertrag," *Deutschland Archiv* 16 (January 1983): 66.

18. *Neues Deutschland,* October 14, 1980.

19. Bruns, *Deutsch-deutsche Beziehungen,* pp. 111-13.

20. Klaus Bölling, *Die fernen Nachbarn: Erfahrungen in der DDR* (Hamburg: Gruner & Jahr, 1983), p. 182.

21. One of the FRG's leading legal experts called the ruling "an unpalatable mush." See Gebhard Schweigler, "Whatever Happened to Germany?" in Krippendorf, Ekkehart, and Volker Rittberger, *The Foreign Policy of West Germany: Formation and Contents* (London: SAGE Publications, 1980), p. 102; and Michael-Kay Wilke, *Bundesrepublik Deutschland und Deutsche Demokratische Republik: Grundlage und ausgewählte Probleme des Gegenseitigen Verhältnisses der beiden deutschen Staaten* (Berlin: Duncker & Humblot, 1976), p. 156.

22. Bölling, *Die fernen Nachbarn,* p. 182.

23. The importance of the citizenship question in the GDR travel policy is hotly debated. For support for the argument above, see for example, Bölling, *Die fernen Nachbarn,* pp. 45-6. For opposing views see Wolfgang Seiffert, "Was bedeutet die Respektierung der Staatsangehörigkeit," *Deutschland Archiv* 17 (November 1984): 1121-25; and Wolfgang Seiffert, "Polen bedroht das Machtmonopol der SED," *Der Spiegel* 43 (1980): 35-9. See also Jonathan Dean, *Inter-German Relations – Will They Change the Political Map of Europe?* (unpublished manuscript, October 4, 1985).

24. Bölling, *Die fernen Nachbarn,* pp. 57-9.

25. Roth, *Zwei Staaten in Deutschland,* pp. 87-8.

26. Interviews with Gebhard Schweigler, Washington D.C., October 29, 1984, and Hans-Peter Schwarze, West Berlin, July 18, 1984.

27. Bruns, *Deutsch-deutsche Beziehungen,* pp. 38-9.

28. These dissident thinkers include the first two West German envoys in East Berlin, Günter Gaus and Klaus Bölling, former FDP General Secretary Günter Verheugen, and former SPD Minister of Justice Jürgen Schmude. See Bruns, *Deutsch-deutsche Beziehungen,* pp. 38-9; Bölling, *Die fernen Nachbarn,* pp. 45-6 and Bölling, "Die offene deutsche Frage," *Der Spiegel,* April 26, 1985. See also *Der Spiegel,* January 12, 1981 and May 27, 1985.

29. Dettmar Cramer, "Ein deutsches Signal?" *Deutschland Archiv* 14 (May 1981): 561-3; and Theo Sommer, "Wie offen ist die deutsche Frage?" *Die ZEIT,* August 17, 1984.

30. Bölling, *Die fernen Nachbarn,* pp. 55-6.

31. See Kiep, "The New Deutschlandpolitik," pp. 317-18, and *Der Spiegel,* March 26, 1984.

32. Roth, *Zwei Staaten in Deutschland,* pp. 71-2.

33. Bölling, *Die fernen Nachbarn,* pp. 50-2.

34. See Roth, *Zwei Staaten in Deutschland,* p. 73, and *Der Spiegel,* March 26, 1984.

35. Bölling, *Die fernen Nachbarn,* p. 52.

36. Quoted after Dieter Mahncke, *Berlin im geteilten Deutschland* (München: R. Oldenbourg, 1973), Appendix A, pp. 267-8.

37. Gerhard Wettig, "Das Problem der Bindungen West-Berlins bei der Anwendung des Viermächteabkommens," *Deutschland Archiv* 12 (September 1979): 935.

38. The dispute over East Germany's capital has had some intriguing and even amusing aspects. The FRG officially refuses to recognize East Berlin as the capital. For many years, West German officials referred to Pankow, an outer district of East Berlin, as the real capital. Meanwhile, the East Germans emphasized the status of East Berlin as their capital with surprising force. The city's official name is "Berlin, Capital of the GDR," often referred to only as "the Capital." This dispute is also the reason why official visits between the FRG and the GDR hardly ever take place in either state's capital, but in remote towns like Kassel, Erfurt and Werbellin. During the preparations for Honecker's planned trip to the Federal Republic in September 1984, the West German efforts to avoid a visit to Bonn was one of the many disputes that ultimately caused Honecker to cancel his trip.

39. See Angela Stent, "Soviet Policy toward the German Democratic Republic," in Terry, *Soviet Policy in Eastern Europe,* p. 54; and Wettig, "Das Problem der Bindungen West-Berlins," pp. 920-22, p. 937.

40. Reimund Seidelmann, "German Defense Policy," in Edwin H. Fedder, ed., *Defense Politics of the Atlantic Alliance* (New York: Praeger, 1980), pp. 71-2.

41. See Wilhelm Kewig, "Entwicklungslinien des völker-und staatsrechtlichen Status von Berlin," *Europa-Archiv* 9/1984: 271-78.

42. Jochen Bethkenhagen, Siegfried Kupper, Horst Lambrecht, "Über den Zusammenhang von außenwirtschaftlichen Interessen der DDR und Entspannung," in *13. Tagung zum Stand der DDR-Forschung in der Bundesrepublik Deutschland* (Koln: Edition Deutschland Archiv, 1980), pp. 10-14.

43. In all areas, except sensitive high technology, the licenses are automatically granted, according to an interview with Anne-Marie Schlemper-Kubista, Bonn, July 11, 1984.

44. Bruns, *Deutsch-deutsche Beziehungen,* pp. 71-5.

45. See Franz Rösch and Fritz Homann, "Thirty Years of the Berlin Agreement — Thirty Years of Inner-German Trade: Economic and Political Dimensions," *Zeitschrift für die gesamte Staatswissenschaft* 137 (1981), pp. 539-47; and Bruns, *Deutsch-deutsche Beziehungen,* pp. 69-71.

46. See Roth, *Zwei Staaten in Deutschland,* pp. 103-4, and Christian Hacke, "Soll und Haben des Grundlagenvertrages," *Deutschland Archiv* 15 (December 1982).

47. See Rösch and Homann, "Thirty Years," pp. 548-52, and Bruns, *Deutsch-deutsche Beziehungen,* p. 71.

48. For a discussion on the GDR's political interests in inter-German trade, see Ilse Spittmann, "Der Milliardenkredit," *Deutschland Archiv* 16 (August 1983): 787; and Jochen Bethkenhagen, "Über den Zusammenhang von außenwirtschaftlichen Interessen der DDR und Entspannung," p. 16.

49. Bethkenhagen, "Über den Zusammenhang," pp. 7-8.

50. Ibid., pp. 14-15; and Rösch and Homann, "Thirty Years," pp. 539-45.

51.   See Rudolf Herlt, "Das Geschäft mit dem Westen," *Die ZEIT 29* (July 13, 1984); and Bethkenhagen, "Über den Zusammenhang," pp. 10-14.

52.   Stent, "Soviet Policy toward the German Democratic Republic," in Terry, *Soviet Policy in Eastern Europe,* p. 50; and Roth, *Zwei Staaten in Deutschland,* pp. 173-6.

53.   See Bethkenhagen, "Über den Zusammenhang," pp. 7-8, and Roth, *Zwei Staaten in Deutschland,* p. 92.

54.   For the amnesty, see Jan Hoesch, "Ein Erfolg im Schatten," *Deutschland Archiv* 15 (October 1982): 1917-19. For the 1985 swing agreements, see FAZ, July 6, 1985.

55.   Angela Stent, *From Embargo to Ostpolitik: The Political Economy of West German-Soviet Relations 1955-1980* (Cambridge, Mass.: Cambridge University Press, 1981), pp. 236-8.

56.   Bruns, *Deutsch-deutsche Beziehungen,* pp. 71-5, 100.

57.   See Jochen Bethkenhagen and Horst Lambrecht, *D i e Außenhandelsbeziehungen der DDR vor dem Hintergrund von Produktion und Verbrauch* (Köln: Berichte des Bundesinstitutes für internationale und ostwissenschaftliche Studien, 1982).

3 THE PARADOX OF RAPPROCHEMENT

The puzzling juxtaposition of constructive cooperation and fierce conflict that characterizes inter-German relations makes it difficult to define a consistent trend in this relationship or to develop a general theory about it. Commentators in newspapers and in politics often vacillate between extremes. Whenever inter-German relations seem to improve, they raise the specter of German reunification, either as a false illusion that Germans are unable to abandon or as a wishful scenario for a better future. And whenever inter-German relations deteriorate, observers deplore the detrimental influence of the East-West conflict and the ideological gap between communist and capitalist — or, depending on the point of view, totalitarian and democratic — societies as the explanation why East and West Germans cannot come together.

The problem with these modes of analysis is their over-emphasis on reunification. As stated previously, the process of inter-German rapprochement, as it has developed since the early 1970s, neither leads toward reunification nor has this as its ultimate goal. Going beyond the standard arguments that suggest that reunification is effectively prevented by the military dominance of the Soviet Union, the fear of an overpowering united Germany, or the lack of national identity in both German states, I argue that reunification through rapprochement is by definition impossible.

A closer look at the development of inter-German relations supports this assertion. It was West Germany's refusal before 1969 to recognize the division of Germany and consequently the existence of the GDR that precluded any improvements in the relations between the two German states. Only after Brandt accepted the sovereignty of the GDR and, though never abandoning it as a long-term ideal, separated the goal of reunification from the realm of practical policy could inter-German relations begin to prosper.

This observation suggests a general rule about the dynamics of inter-German relations, which I call "the paradox of rapprochement:" the striving for reunification and the striving for rapprochement are mutually exclusive. There are two main implications associated with this concept. First, one of the keys for the future improvement of inter-German relations lies in West German compromises on the status questions — the issues concerning the sovereignty and the legitimacy of the East German government. Second, signs of a German-German rapprochement do not constitute a step toward reunification; on the contrary, they always suggest a move away.

This result should not be surprising, once one understands the aggressive nature of any active reunification policy. Except under very rare circumstances, unification means conquest of one country by another. A united Germany under a Western democratic system is equivalent to the extinction of the East German regime; the same would be true for the West German government in the opposite case. Given the differences in the social systems of the two countries, and even the existence of two different elites, it is almost impossible to imagine a scenario under which unification could occur peacefully. The same is true for other attempts at reunification throughout German history. In the Thirty Years War from 1618 to 1648, the Hapsburgs managed to unite the fractionalized German Reich with the help of Wallenstein's army, but ultimately failed due to foreign intervention. Two hundred fifty years later, in 1871, Bismark achieved unification after the defeat of Austria and France; Germany was united by the military hegemony of Prussia. Never have peaceful attempts at German reunification, such as the revolution of 1848, even come close to success. The same is true for the attempted unification of Korea in the Korean War and the reunification of Vietnam in 1975. One is hard pressed to find an example in history when two sovereign, politically and economically viable states decided voluntarily to merge. Since both governments cannot stay in power and the weaker state would ultimately disappear, any self-respecting government would resist such a measure.

It is not surprising that the GDR regarded West Germany's reunification policy as an aggressive act and opposed any improvement in political and human relations as long as the FRG imperiled the sheer existence of the East German state. The fact that the policy consisted mainly of political rhetoric did not make a difference. A genuine rapprochement requires a level of equality and trust which is impossible to achieve in the presence of calls for the extinction of the other state through reunification. Thus, the policy of nonrecognition prevented most contacts between the two states and contributed to their mutual alienation in the political, economic, cultural, and human spheres. This was the problem that Willy Brandt tried to address in his new policy toward the GDR. In addition to his interest in advancing detente in Europe, his main goal was to save the unity of the German nation by establishing closer relations to the GDR. Since this policy required the bestowing of de facto recognition of the East German state and government, it also precluded a reunification for the forseeable future.

The Basic Treaty, however, did not resolve all status problems in the inter-German relationship. The FRG still refuses to regard East Germany as foreign territory, opposes full diplomatic relations, and does not recognize a separate East German citizenship. As we have seen in the previous chapter, these status problems lie at the core of the inter-German conflict. Whenever any movement came into German-German relations, whether for the worse or for the better, the change always became most visible in the way the status problems were handled. This was true for the Polish crisis of 1980 and the INF crisis of 1983-84. As will be discussed in a later chapter, the breakdown of the inter-German thaw in September 1984 was caused as much by the revival of reunification rhetoric among West German conservatives as by Soviet interference. The moment the SED saw its sovereignty and legitimacy questioned, it retreated again to a more hostile policy toward the FRG.

These facts suggests that the solution of the status problems through the full diplomatic recognition of the GDR as a foreign country could bring the inter-German relationship much closer to the kind of relations that exist between other countries with different political and social systems. The ideal example for such intersystemic relations in Europe are Austria and Hungary. Hungarians can travel to the West several times a year and there is an intense level of economic, cultural, and personal exchange between the two countries. If inter-German relations were ever able to reach such a stage, the most painful aspects of the division of Germany would fade away. Under such ideal conditions even the Berlin Wall, the symbol of this division, would become superfluous.[1]

Why can inter-German relations not reach such a level? The reason cannot be the membership of both German states in hostile political alliances alone, for current West German-Hungarian relations are almost as well developed as Austro-Hungarian relations. The existence of the status problems that prevent a normal bilateral relationship seems to be a principal reason. Most experts would reject the hypothesis that the border could be opened simply by recognizing East German citizenship and by transforming the missions into embassies. They would cite the brutal nature of the East German regime and its need to prevent people from escaping this system as the main obstacle to an inter-German rapprochement. Further, they can point to the excessive loyalty of the GDR to the Soviet Union and the East German policy of demarcation, which attempts to isolate the GDR from its Western neighbor and hinder contacts between East and West Germans. Although this position is factually correct, one must ask *why* the GDR is more loyal to Moscow and more repressive towards its own citizens than countries like Poland and Hungary. There is not one single reason why some East European countries are more repressive and intolerant of pluralism than others. In the CSSR, it is mainly a consequence of the 1969 invasion; in Romania, a reflection of Nicolae Ceausecu's style of leadership. In the GDR, however, the cause seems to be structurally determined: the existence of a "legitimacy deficit" of the East German state.

Throughout most of its early history, the GDR was perceived by the West as well as by its own population as an instrument of Soviet military power and repression, but not as a legitimate state. This situation led to a major crisis in June 1953, when the Ulbricht regime was saved from revolting workers by Soviet tanks. The economic troubles of the state, the attraction of the wealthy and democratic Federal Republic, and the international isolation caused by the Hallstein Doctrine aggravated this problem. The GDR appeared to be unable to acquire legitimacy in its own right.

The SED under Ulbricht responded to this challenge by establishing a highly repressive regime, by severing ties to the West, and by creating an almost total dependence on the Soviet Union. The building of the Berlin Wall in August 1961, which made escape from the GDR effectively impossible, was the most important step in this policy; for reasons discussed earlier, it contributed more than any other event to the growing viability and legitimacy of the GDR. Similarly, the GDR's dependence on the Soviet Union served as a substitute for its lack of international recognition. Because the GDR required the Soviet presence in Eastern Europe to legitimize its existence, its membership in the Eastern bloc and its friendship with the Soviets became the *raison d'être* of the second

German state. It provided it with the political and military backing it needed to face the permanent challenge from West Germany.

Although Ulbricht's strategy was an expression of deep-rooted insecurities, it proved to be a success in most respects. By the late 1960s, the GDR had become a political and economic reality which even the Federal Republic could no longer ignore. The signing of the Basic Treaty represented the codification of this new situation and ended East Germany's international isolation. However, the question of legitimacy was not yet completely solved. First, the GDR still could not offer its citizens the same quality of living as the FRG. The viewing of West German television by three-quarters of the East German population heightened the attraction of the other German state. This phenomenon was reinforced by the unresolved questions of diplomatic recognition and citizenship that constantly reminded the East German leadership of the fragile nature of its legitimacy. The response of the SED to these challenges was the intensification of its policy of demarcation. As the flood of West German visitors grew,[2] the leadership increasingly emphasized the differences between the two German states and hindered contacts with West Germans whenever they could. Instead of genuine rapprochement, inter-German relations brought more hostility and barriers.

The East German policy towards the West is characterized by two related dilemmas. The first dilemma is the inability of the GDR to decide if the stability of state and regime are increased or hurt by inter-German relations. On one hand, West German visitors and consumer goods reduce the dissatisfaction with the oppressive nature of the GDR and offer a safety valve for popular discontent. On the other hand, the influx of Western ideas also generates desires for more freedom and encourages protests against the current system. Since 1972, East German policies have been characterized by a vacillation between these two interpretations.

The second dilemma is a vicious circle concerning status problems. Perhaps more than ideology, the oppressive nature of the SED regime has been one of the main reasons for the unwillingness of West Germans to make concessions in status questions. However, these challenges, particularly the citizenship question, have always made the East German leadership feel less secure and have driven them toward more repression and demarcation. This, in turn, exerts a negative influence on West German public opinion, thus reducing the chances for compromises on status questions. And it also keeps the SED from acquiring increased legitimacy by popular support — the key to stability in any Eastern European state.

However, the same dynamics could also work in favor of an inter-German rapprochement. An inter-German agreement on at least some of the status issues would reduce the East German legitimacy deficit and make the leaders feel more secure. It could also turn the debate over the stability problem towards more openness and less demarcation. Once the SED has realized that the FRG does not question the basis of its rule, it might become less sensitive to Western influences and start behaving in a more self-assured way, like Hungary does.

One could argue that even such concessions would not do away with the more serious challenge to East German legitimacy: the attraction of a larger, wealthier, and more powerful neighbor with the same language and culture. Although it is difficult to prove, there are some indications that this attraction is not as strong as is often assumed. A vast majority of East Germans do not want to leave the country, even if they are dissatisfied with the system. The images from the FRG that are transmitted by West German television are not always so positive: unemployment, youth rebellion, corruption, and inequality often make life in the West seem less desirable. It seems that even the SED overestimates the power of the West German model. Just as more freedom to travel would probably reduce the desire of East Germans to emigrate, more contact with the FRG could make life in the GDR more desirable. Whether and how this deadlock in the thinking of the East German leadership can be broken is not quite clear. However a breakthrough on the status question seems to be the most promising way. Even an agreement on the lesser issues like the dissolution of Salzgitter or the Elbe border could significantly improve the German-German climate and lead to progress in a number of practical questions.

According to this analysis, economic aid also plays a central role for an inter-German rapprochement. However, its main value is not as a bargaining chip (its limited usefulness in this respect has already been discussed), but as a means of reducing the wealth gap between the two German states. Even if economic difficulties will drive the GDR toward closer inter-German relations in the short term, in the long term only a higher standard of living and a more efficient economy will permit a German-German rapprochement.[3]

Due to domestic and constitutional constraints, there is little hope for a change in the West German position on status problems, particularly under the current center-right Democratic government. Still, the policies of the Kohl government illustrate how small a role reunification plays in today's West German politics. Although in the first years of the new *Ostpolitik* the CDU and CSU opposed all retreats from the reunification policy and voted against the Basic Treaty, their attitudes changed in the course of the 1970s. As we will discuss later, by the time Helmut Kohl assumed office in 1982, the Christian Democrats had effectively accepted the permanent division of Germany and have since then continued the social democratic *Ostpolitik*. This does not mean that all CDU members support closer inter-German relations. But the negative attitude of many conservatives toward the second German state seems to be inspired not by an all-German nationalism, but by a separate West German chauvinism that leads to a lack of respect, and even contempt, for a system that is perceived as less wealthy, less efficient, and morally inferior. It is this attitude that the former West German envoy, Günter Gaus, criticized when he called upon West Germans to "accept the GDR emotionally" and to take the country the way it is, with all its faults and problems.[4]

Even more prevalent is a lack of interest in the GDR in the West German population. The attention often given to inter-German relations cannot hide the fact that most West Germans who do not have friends or relatives across the border care very little about the fate of the East Germans, not to mention a future reunification. West Germans do not seem to be willing to make large sacrifices for their brothers in the east. Even the DM 1.5 billion in annual subsidies (approximately $700 million at 1986 exchange rates) that the FRG pays the GDR is small for a country of this economic potential and constitutes only about 0.06 percent of its annual gross domestic product.[5] The media attention given to developments in inter-German relations can be deceiving; while the ties with the GDR occupy a high priority on the political agenda of the government in Bonn, it does not capture the imagination of wide parts of the population. Compared to issues like peace and environmentalism, the German question has a very small mobilization potential in the Federal Republic. It is also advisable to be cautious of poll data that show a vast majority of West Germans in favor of keeping the reunification issue open, or even calling for reunification under neutrality.[6] The fact that reunification is not achievable makes it very easy to support it as a long-term goal. A majority of West Germans, and West Europeans in general, also favor a united Europe, a disarmed world and an end to world hunger, but in all these cases the objectives have little impact on political actions. It is noteworthy that the question of reunification is usually posed in the context of overcoming the division of the whole European continent. Thus it is removed from practical politics and becomes an optimistic utopia that few people could possibly oppose. Just as the West German political parties can safely ignore the constitutional requirement to seek reunification by defining the goal as a "unified Germany within a European order of peace," so people can favor reunification without considering its larger political implications. This objective seems to be rather an expres-sion of the desire to break down the political barriers in all of Europe through detente more than the result of a specific German nationalism.

Still, there exist indications of a renewed interest in reunification. In recent years a group of thinkers who call themselves the "National Left" has begun to emphasize the FRG's withdrawal from NATO and the dissolution of both military alliances as the essential step toward breaking down the division of Europe. These ideas represent a break with the policies pursued by the SPD since the Godesberg Program in 1959, but they contain strong parallels to the social democratic ideology in the 1950s. Once the superpowers have withdrawn, they argue, the German states could dismantle the barriers between them, form a confederation, and ultimately achieve reunification. Similar concepts have been put forward by more conservative nationalist thinkers who demanded West Germany's withdrawal from NATO as a precondition for full national sovereignty. In 1982, an alliance between these groups resulted in a fascinating document. In the book *The German Unity is Sure to Come,* Wolfgang Vernohr brought together writers with very different ideologies who all assert the thesis that the unity of Germany is the precondition for stability in Europe.[7]

The publication of the book, at a time when the peace movement called the FRG's loyalty to NATO into question, caused a strong, mainly negative reaction in the West. The response was largely exaggerated. Forty years after the fall of the Nazi regime, most Germans, and particularly people on the left, are still so suspicious of German nationalism that there exists little desire to reestablish an all-German political entity like Bismarck's Reich. This new German nationalism seems to ignore traditional Pan-Germanic goals of unifying all German people in one Reich; instead, it addresses the alleged limits on German sovereignty imposed by the division of Europe and the hegemony of the superpowers. West German thinkers then become interested in the GDR not only because of the striking parallels between the position of the two German states within their respective alliances, but also because of the belief that the division of Germany constitutes a key element in the subjugation of German independence. One must understand, however, that the ultimate objective of new German nationalists is not German reunification, but a strengthening of German autonomy through the dissolution of both blocs in Europe. Despite its subtlety, this distinction is significant for the understanding of political developments in the Federal Republic.

Even in this limited form, the theoretical objectives of the National Left have little practical significance. More even than a motion toward unification, a dissolution of the European alliance system would not be decided in Bonn or East Berlin but depends on the policies of the superpowers. Obviously, a Soviet withdrawal from Eastern Europe is a futile hope. But even if one assumes that the Soviet Union will one day relinquish its hegemonic control over Eastern Europe, or allow the GDR to gain neutrality and complete political independence, it is not clear that unification would necessarily follow. Although the nature of the current political and economic system in the GDR is largely dependent on the Soviet presence, one can argue that the state's institutions and structures have developed an existence of their own over the last 40 years. Western observers often forget that even the population of a communist dictatorship has vested interests in the politics and economy of its state. Most East Germans have developed some stake in the system, which could be imperiled by reunification. One can easily imagine that the leaders of a neutral GDR, even if they are no longer communist, would prefer to maintain an independent state rather than surrender their power by merging with a far more powerful neighbor — and have their policies dictated by Bonn and Frankfurt instead of Moscow and Leningrad.

Although a confederation model, like the one proposed by Wolfgang Vernohr,[8] seems more realistic than complete reunification because it would reconcile some of these expected conflicts of interest, it is still not a very promising scenario. The example of the European Community illustrates how difficult it is to organize any form of transnational government among sovereign countries, even if they share the same political and economic system. In light of the two German states' different political, economic, and social experiences since World War II, such a plan seems almost illusionary.

The other development that has brought the issue of German nationalism back into the limelight is the sudden GDR preoccupation with German history and German culture. After having insisted for many years that a German nation no longer existed and that the GDR had no connection to the old German Reich, in 1980 the SED began to emphasize its German heritage, particularly its ties to Prussian history. East German journals discussed the positive role in German history of Prussian leaders like Hardenberg, Freiherr von Stein, and Clausewitz.

Even Bismark was commended for his *realpolitik* towards Russia. In December 1980, the statue of the Prussian king Frederick II was put back to its original location in Unter den Linden in the center of East Berlin, reportedly due to Honecker's personal intervention.[9] In a speech in February 1981, Honecker surprisingly brought up again the issue of German reunification under socialism, a term that had been deleted from the official vocabulary for more than a decade: "Be careful. One day, socialism will knock on your door, and when the day comes on which the workers of the Federal Republic undertake the socialist transformation of the FRG, then the question of the unification of the German states will be seen in entirely new light. And there should be no doubt how we will then decide."[10]

This trend reached its climax in 1983, when the GDR celebrated Martin Luther's 500th birthday as a national event. The religious reformer was made a national hero by the atheist state and received far more attention than Karl Marx, who celebrated his 150th birthday the same year. Johann Sebastian Bach's 300th anniversary in 1985 became a similar national celebration. While the surprising turn in the GDR's national ideology was widely perceived as evidence of East Germany's continuing all-German consciousness and its interest in reunification, this view is rather misleading. One possible motive for the GDR's sudden interest in national themes came from the outside: the Soviet attempt to prevent the deployment of new U.S. missiles in the FRG by appealing to the rising nationalism in West Germany. But the much more important reason was East Germany's previous failure to arrive at a separate national consciousness. As discussed earlier, Honecker's demarcation policy in the early 1970s, through which he tried to insulate the country from growing West German influences, also included the "de-Germanization" of the GDR. To destroy all links to the other German state, the SED began to eradicate all references to a German nation from its ideology. It declared the existence of two separate nations, prohibited the singing of the East German national anthem because of its references to reunification, and deleted all references to the word "Germany" in its 1974 constitution.

This strategy had one basic flaw: if the GDR is not German, then what is it? Since it did not want to be German and could not call itself Prussian, it lacked an acceptable definition of nationality. The constitution of 1974 defines the GDR as "a state of workers and peasants" without stating its location or its boundaries.[11] What exacerbated the problem for the East Germans was that the term "GDR" cannot be used as an adjective

— a genuine handicap in day-to-day life. Since the SED refused the expression "East Germans," it had created a people without a name.[12]

By the late 1970s it had become clear that Honecker's de-Germanization had failed. The GDR had acquired a national consciousness which was distinct from the FRG, but which was still inherently German. Indeed, in many respects East Germany showed a stronger affinity for the culture, attitudes, and way of life of the old Germany than the strongly Americanized Federal Republic. Meanwhile, the East German leadership had become self-assured enough that it dared to emphasize its German nature and even compete with the FRG over the claim to the real German heritage. The focus on its German nature strengthened its position in relation to the Soviet Union and improved its reputation in the FRG as well as in other Western countries. Although the GDR still lacks a viable term for its nationality — the FRG had succeeded in monopolizing the term "Germany" for itself — the existence of an East German state consciousness, legitimized by its ties to German history and the stability of the state, can no longer be denied.[13]

At international sporting events, where East and West Germans compete against each other, it becomes particularly apparent to the rest of the world that each German state has its own national consciousness.[14] They still share many common cultural traits and are strongly attracted to each other. Particularly for East Germans, the Federal Republic represents everything that they are missing: wealth, democracy, and the freedom to travel. But this does not mean that East Germans desire reunification; what most of them really want is a GDR with all the advantages, but none of the disadvantages of the FRG. National aspirations for an all-German future seem to have as little relevance in the East as in the West.

Some theorists argue that this is only a short-term phenomenon. In the long run, they say, even centuries of division cannot extinguish the desire of a people for national unity. However, a different example in Central Europe, the case of Austria, suggests the opposite. After World War I, more than 90 percent of all German-speaking residents of the collapsed Austrian-Hungarian Empire supported union with Germany; a national identity did not exist. After seven years of annexation through Nazi Germany and the disaster of World War II, these attitudes had completely changed. Except for an extremely small group of right-wingers, today no Austrians have any interest in a union with the FRG. An open border, free trade, and the multitudes of human contacts satisfy the remnants of desire for a common national identity. The FRG and the

GDR are likely to move in the same direction. Except for a short period between 1871 and 1945, Germany has always been divided. There is no reason why it could not stay divided forever. If one day the GDR is capable of providing its people a standard of living comparable to that in the West, and if it abandoned its policy of demarcation and allowed its people to travel, the German problem will have found a stable solution.

These arguments do not belittle the importance of nationalism in both German states. One cannot deny that nationalist feelings have been on the rise in recent years and will exert an increasingly strong influence on East and West German politics and society, particularly in the FRG. Still, while these developments can influence the domestic climate in these countries and transform their relations to the alliances, they must not be confused with a movement toward or even a desire for reunification on either side of the German-German border. The course of inter-German relations is unlikely to be significantly affected by them.

The belief that reunification is not an issue in inter-German relations is shared today by a vast majority of political commentators, but this analysis tries to emphasize a point that differs from the common views. It is usually argued that (1) Germany cannot be reunited because reunification would upset the balance of power in Europe; or (2) Germany will not be reunited because the Germans do not desire it. Both arguments are unsatisfactory.

The first position is historically correct. It is true that for almost a century, the unified German Reich in the center of Europe had been a destabilizing force. Germany was too strong to be kept in check by the traditional European balance of power and thus caused the downfall of this order in two devastating wars. True, the current European post-war order is based to a large extent on the division of Germany. Yet, it is too simplistic to argue that 80 million Germans in one state would represent a danger to the European political system, while the 60 million people in the FRG do not. One must ask where the limit is. Does there really exist a point at which the number of Germans becomes a critical mass, as the former West German Chancellor Kurt-Georg Kiesinger once suggested? Is then the emigration of East Germans to the West destabilizing because it increases the number of Germans in one state? Although the two German states by themselves constitute a permanent problem for Europe, it is not clear that the unification of the FRG and the GDR would make it any worse. The key to European stability lies in the maintenance of the political status quo, which currently includes the division of Germany, not in the existence of the inter-German border itself. It is not surprising that the warnings about a unified Germany are most loudly voiced by French commentators. France is the country that would lose most through an increase of German power — not so much because of the threat to international stability, but because of stronger German competition.[15]

The second argument, that Germans do not desire reunification, is basically accurate, but it is insufficient to explain the nature of inter-German relations, as well. For according to both of those arguments, the Germans cannot really be trusted. They imply that German nationalism could be a force to be reckoned with, and that left to themselves, the Germans might again pursue the reunification of their country. A striking improvement in the relations between the FRG and the GDR either shows that the two German states have not understood the danger of a unified Germany, or that the lack of interest in national unity is no longer valid. This, then, suggests that the rest of the world has to keep a close eye on inter-German relations, and that the effects of these relations are fundamentally different, more far-reaching, and more dangerous than all other aspects of East-West relations. However, the paradox of rapprochement shows that reunification is inherently impossible to achieve, and that an inter-German rapprochement is moving it even farther away from realization. The conclusion that political leaders in East and West should draw is that there is absolutely no need to worry about an improvement in inter-German relations, such as the thaw of 1984. By necessity, these relations cannot cause a movement toward reunification. Reunification should be an issue for historians and essayists, but not for the policymakers in the inter-German relationship and the European alliances.

The complex nature of the German states' bilateral problems still assigns a unique position to inter-German relations within the larger stage of the East-West conflict. But the relevance of these problems and their resolution is limited to the world between Bonn and East Berlin. They have little impact on the larger political situation on the European continent or on the balance of power between NATO and WTO. Because reunification and the German question do not play an important role in the inter-German relationship, one can gain a much better understanding of this phenomenon by analyzing it as part of the general subject of relations between Eastern and Western Europe. It is undeniable that inter-German relations are different from, for example, relations between France and Poland. Due to historical, geographical, and political reasons, they are more intense and more complex. But because the German national question is not central to the problem, the difference must be seen as one of degree and not of fundamentals. What is at stake in the rapprochement between the FRG and the GDR is the same as between all other West and East European states, the surmounting of the division of Europe without endangering peace on the continent. Accepting this premise, we can now move to an analysis of inter-German relations as a special case within the larger international framework, and evaluate their role in such a setting.

NOTES

1.   At his meeting with Honecker in Werbellin in December 1981, Schmidt addressed this problem: "I believe, Herr Generalsekretär, that the practice of your Hungarian comrades makes many things easier. That should also be possible between you and us, shouldn't it?" Honecker refused to respond. See Klaus Bölling, *Die fernen Nachbarn: Erfahrungen in der DDR* (Hamburg: Gruner & Jahr, 1983), p. 139.

2.   The importance of visitors from the FRG becomes clear when we consider that almost half of the GDR's population come into contact with West Germans during a given year. In contrast, only a small percentage of West Germans ever travel to the GDR. See Mathias Jopp, Berthold Meyer, et al., "Deutsch-deutsche Beziehungen im Ost-West-Konflikt," in Ilse Spittman and Gisela Helwig, eds., *Die beiden deutschen Staaten im Ost-West-Verhältnis,* 15, Tagung zum Stand der DDR Forschung in der Bundesrepublik Deutschland, 1-4, June 1982. (Koln: Edition Deutschland Archiv, 1982), pp. 35-6.

3.   This was also the conclusion of a quasi-official report by the Chancellor's Office in 1976. The report also suggested that the FRG should stop questioning the legitimacy of the GDR, both explicitly and implicitly. See Bruns, *Deutsch-deutsche Beziehungen: Prämissen — Probleme — Perspektiven* (Opladen: Leske & Budrich, 1982), pp. 52-3. For obvious reasons, similar arguments for more economic aid are put forward by East German officials.

4.   Günter Gaus, Interview with *Die ZEIT* (January 30, 1981).

5.   In 1980, the West German GDP was $825 billion.

6.   According to an EMNID poll published in the December 1984 issue of *Geopolitique,* 89 percent doubted that reunification would ever take place, but 73 percent said they nevertheless hoped it would take place. In the same poll, 67 percent of the respondents favored German reunification under conditions of neutrality for Germany and Western Europe. See Jonathan Dean, *Inner-German Relations — Will They Change the Political Map of Europe?* (unpublished manuscript).

7.   Wolfgang Vernohr, ed., *Die deutsche Einheit kommt bestimmt* (Hamburg: Gustav Lübbe Verlag, 1982).

8.   Wolfgang Vernohr, "Deutschlands Mittellage," *Deutschland Archiv* 17 (August 1984): 826-28.

9.   Walter Leisler Kiep, "The New Deutschlandpolitik," *Foreign Affairs* 63 (Winter 1984–85): 316.

10.   *Neues Deutschland,* February 16, 1981. For an analysis of this speech, see Wolfgang Vernohr, "35 Jahre DDR und die nationale Frage," *Deutschland Archiv* 17

(December 1984): 1269; Ilse Spittmann, "Großdeutsche Sprüche," *Deutschland Archiv* 15 (January 1982): 225-7; and A. James McAdams, "Surviving the Missiles: the GDR and the Future of Inter-German Relations," *Orbis* 27 (Summer 1983): 359.

11. Vernohr, "35 Jahre DDR und die nationale Frage," pp. 1267-8.

12. Gebhard Schweigler, "Whatever Happened to Germany?" in Krippendorf, Ekkehart, and Volker Rittberger, eds., *The Foreign Policy of West Germany* (London: SAGE Publications, 1980), pp. 108-9. For an elaboration of Schweigler's views, see his book *West German Foreign Policy: The Domestic Setting* (New York: Praeger, 1984).

13. See Schweigler, "Whatever Happened to Germany?" pp. 110-11. Some opinion polls offer a different picture. According to an informal SED poll in 1979, 75 percent of young people regard themselves as Germans, not East Germans; according to West German data, 50 percent oppose the government. Many observers believe, however, that this result demonstrates dissatisfaction with the SED policies and its definition of nationality rather than a desire for reunification.

14. One of the most striking examples of the German-German alienation occurred during the world championships in ice hockey in the West German town of Dortmund in 1983, where the audience cheered the West German players by shouting "Germany" and threw empty bottles at the East Germans. See Bölling, *Die fernen Nachbarn,* p. 292. Also the often cold reception that East German emigrants receive after moving to the FRG indicates the limits of all-German solidarity.

15. See Henri Menudier, "Das Deutschlandproblem aus französischer Sicht," *Politik und Kultur* 6 (1983): 20-37.

PART TWO
The Germanies Between East And West

4 THE ERA OF CONSENSUS: 1945–79

It could be misleading to define the years between 1945 and 1979 as an era of consensus for NATO and the Warsaw Treaty Organization. Many of the most severe crises in both blocs occurred during this period. However, in respect to the fundamentals of East-West relations, and particularly in respect to the position of the two German states in the alliances, these years are marked by considerable agreement. This chapter will first analyze the interplay between general East-West relations and inter-German relations before 1979. It will then discuss the degree and nature of alliance integration of the FRG and the GDR, and will look at the situation within both alliances at the time of the invasion of Afghanistan in December 1979.

FROM COLD WAR TO DETENTE

Despite differences in their political and economic systems, one can find more parallels between the FRG and the GDR concerning their place in their respective alliances than the two German states like to admit. Both states owe their existence to the development of the blocs, and their formation was linked chronologically and causally to the formation of the two military and economic alliances in Europe. In their first decade, both the Federal Republic and the GDR perceived their membership in their respective alliances as their main source of legitimacy; thus, alliance integration became the most important political goal of both.

But integration was not only a desire, it was also a necessity. The surprisingly swift reconstruction and rearmament of the Federal Republic after the Reich's defeat, in contradiction to allied wartime plans, was acceptable to the other European nations only because of certain restrictions on West Germany's sovereignty. The FRG had to renounce the possession of nuclear weapons and accept the indefinite deployment of foreign troops on its territory. Despite these limitations, Western integration was an excellent solution for the FRG, allowing it to become an equal member of the international community and experience a phenomenal economic recovery in a very short time.[1] Similarly, for the Ulbricht regime in the GDR complete loyalty to the Soviet Union was the only condition under which it could remain in power. The alliance with Moscow also helped it to obtain a coloration of legitimacy despite its lack of popular support and the refusal of the West to recognize it as a second German state.

The security provided by alliance integration was the precondition for the rise to economic and political prominence of both German states. By the 1960s, the West German *Wirtschaftswunder* had already made the FRG one of the world's foremost industrial powers. Fueled by an export-oriented economy and aided by the freedom from trade barriers in the Common Market, West Germany regained the economic strength that it had enjoyed since the late nineteenth century, and soon dwarfed most other West European states in respect to industrial output and per capita income. Following its rearmament program after 1955, the West German army became the strongest military force in Western Europe and the cornerstone of NATO's conventional defense. While the presence of U.S., British and French troops on West German territory imposed some restrictions on the autonomy of the Federal Republic, the exposed military position of the FRG and the permanent threat to West Berlin contributed to its influence within the Western alliance.

However, this powerful economic and military position did not translate into an equivalent political status. Although in the 1950s, the FRG was not a major actor in European politics, it was at the center of East-West relations and could count on its allies' full cooperation. But when, after the building of the Berlin Wall and the Cuban missile crisis, West Germany's allies attempted to bring the Cold War to an end and arrive at detente with the Soviet Union, its exposed position turned from an asset to a liability. Bonn's refusal to recognize the partition of Germany or Poland's post-war borders, as well as its clinging to the Hallstein Doctrine, paralyzed West German foreign policy. The Hallstein

Doctrine also facilitated Soviet attempts to isolate Bonn from its allies by allowing Moscow to focus its Cold War rhetoric against the FRG as the last country that demanded a revision of the status quo in Europe. As NATO increasingly shifted toward a policy of detente with the East, a policy that became official doctrine with the Harmel Report in 1967,[2] West German unwillingness to abandon its revisionist positions began to strain the relations with its allies.

Even in areas where the FRG possessed potential political power, such as in its relations to Western Europe and the Third World, the leadership in Bonn chose intentionally to keep a low profile lest the specter of renewed German hegemony would be conjured up. Instead, Bonn decided to subordinate its foreign policy to the alliance, and particularly to its relationship with the United States and France. West Germany's political aspirations were transferred to the goal of European integration and the development of the European Community; the Bonn-Paris axis became the most important instrument for that purpose.

In contrast, the GDR's lack of political power was hardly voluntarily; it was a consequence of West German policies and challenges to the legitimacy of the East German regime. Although the building of the Berlin Wall allowed the GDR to consolidate its economy and to soon achieve a similar economic status in the East as the FRG enjoyed in the West, in the international arena it remained emasculated. Not only did the Western nations treat East Germany like a pariah and refuse any diplomatic relations, but the Hallstein Doctrine kept the emerging Third World countries from establishing diplomatic relations with East Berlin.

The international situation was highly biased in favor of the FRG. Although both states were excluded from membership in the United Nations, Western pressure also prevented the GDR from participating in international organizations in which the FRG was a member, such as UNESCO, the World Health Organization, the International Atomic Energy Agency, the World Bank and to the International Monetary Fund.[3] Although both German states were shut out of relations with the other bloc, the FRG enjoyed political and economic relations with most countries; the GDR was restricted to the comparatively small community of socialist states.

Still, as the 1960s progressed, many West Germans realized that their country would also become increasingly isolated if it did not establish relations with the Eastern bloc. Given Germany's central location and its historical orientation toward East and West, the lack of a viable policy toward the Eastern bloc was a major handicap. But only the change in government in Bonn brought about the beginning of a new *Ostpolitik*. Aided by overwhelming support for a new approach to the East from the West German public, the government of Willy Brandt succeeded in ending the paralysis from which West German foreign policy had suffered for so many years.

Brandt was fully aware the German problem was not isolated, but was deeply rooted in the East-West conflict. His first overtures to the East were not directed toward East Berlin, or even toward the other East European states as former Foreign Minister Gerhard Schröder and U.S. foreign policy expert Zbigniew Brzezinski had proposed, but toward the Soviet Union. The agreements that were reached in the Moscow Treaty of August 1970 were primarily of symbolic value: the two states committed themselves to cooperation and detente on a range of issues and renounced the use of force for the settlement of bilateral problems. Most importantly, the FRG affirmed its recognition of the European post-war borders.

The Brandt government then began to fulfill these commitments in its relations with Eastern Europe. In the Warsaw Treaty with Poland of December 1970, the FRG recognized the Oder-Neiße line as Poland's inviolable western border and abandoned its claims to former German territories.[4] By 1973, the FRG had established diplomatic relations with Bulgaria, Czechoslovakia, Hungary, and Romania.

A central aspect of the new *Ostpolitik* was the recognition of the GDR. As discussed earlier, a condition for the establishment of inter-German relations was a regularization of the status quo of West Berlin, which depended on the cooperation of the four powers. Fortunately for the inter-German relationship, in early 1970 both superpowers were eager for this outcome. The Nixon administration had become somewhat suspicious of the ultimate goals of West German *Ostpolitik* and feared that Brandt would weaken the Atlantic alliance by offering unilateral concessions to the Soviets. Through the Berlin negotiations, Henry Kissinger, Nixon's national security advisor, believed the United States could get more closely involved with Bonn's *Ostpolitik* and gain more control over its future development.[5] The Soviets, meanwhile, realized that concessions on the Berlin question were the only way it could induce the West to agree to a Conference on Security and Cooperation in Europe (CSCE) that would permanently ratify the European post-war territorial order.[6] After SED leader Walter Ulbricht's opposition was broken through his forced resignation, the Quadripartite Agreement over Berlin was signed in the fall of 1971.

Ulbricht's successor, Erich Honecker, completely followed Moscow's line in the detente process. Just as the Soviets made significant compromises to achieve recognition of the status quo in Europe and then shifted toward a much more restrictive detente policy, Honecker made the concessions needed to gain West Germany's recognition of East German statehood, but subsequently pursued a policy aimed at minimizing Western influence in his country. This loyalty to the Soviet Union, impressive even by Eastern standards, became most apparent in the subsequent CSCE negotiations, where the GDR never once swerved from Moscow's line.

The CSCE talks also affirmed West Germany's loyalty to the West, not because the FRG subordinated its own interests to those of the alliance, but because the conference set Bonn's *Ostpolitik* into the framework of European East-West relations. As the West Germans assured that the accords would not serve as a quasi-peace treaty for Germany that would codify the partition,[7] the results of the Helsinki Accords for Western Europe resembled the results of the Eastern Treaties for the FRG: they confirmed the political and territorial status quo in Europe while calling for measures that would ease the division of the continent. Thus, Brandt's initiative was no longer an isolated move that could have aroused suspicion among the allies, but part of a larger European and even global movement.[8]

The Helsinki Accords of 1975 marked the peak and beginning decline of both East-West detente and inter-German relations. Both the Soviets and East Germans had achieved their main goals, and their incentive to cooperate with the West subsequently declined. The Soviet Union increased its activities in the Third World and continued its military build-up through the deployment of SS-20 medium-range missiles. Western public opinion grew increasingly disillusioned with detente.

One can argue that the very success of detente, particularly of the human rights provisions in the Helsinki Accords, accelerated its downfall. The Eastern commitment to human rights in the final document led to a wave of dissidents demanding the implementation of those provisions. As the country most exposed to Western influence, the GDR was most fearful of this creeping subversion from the West. In the short term, the Basket Three provision concerning family reunification and human contacts between East and West induced the SED to make some concessions in these areas. However, the fear of destabilization through the onslaught of millions of West German visitors and the daily flow of information through West German television also reinforced the turn toward increased demarcation from the FRG.[9] The SED leadership reacted by repressing all internal dissent, refusing to relax travel restrictions for East Germans, fortifying the inter-German border with automatic shrapnel guns, expelling West German journalists, resisting cooperation in a range of inter-German issues, and intensifying its hostile rhetoric toward the Federal Republic. Early hopes of a change in the policies of the East German regime and a subsequent genuine inter-German rapprochement were soon shattered.[10]

Also, the West German interest in the German-German relationship declined to a certain extent. Helmut Schmidt, who became chancellor when Brandt resigned in 1974 over the Guillaume affair, was notably less committed to the pursuit of all-German ideals than was his predecessor. His initial lack of respect for Honecker, which became most apparent at their first meeting at the CSCE meeting in Helsinki, contributed to Schmidt's indifferent attitude.[11] Still, the inter-German relationship functioned on a routine basis and even yielded some progress in limited areas. The border commission continued its work, and the number of West German visits and telephone calls to the GDR increased steadily. Critics charged that inter-German relations were only administered, but no longer actively pursued. While this assertion might have been exaggerated, the relations were undoubtedly in a phase of stagnation compared to the atmosphere of awakening in the early 1970s.

ALLIANCE INTEGRATION OF THE FRG AND THE GDR

Although this deterioration of inter-German relations was not caused by any direct superpower intervention (even in the case of the GDR, it was more an expression of self interest than obedience toward Moscow), inter-German relations were fully in harmony with the policies of the superpowers during most of the 1970s. To some extent, they followed the fluctuations of U.S.-Soviet relations. While detente had strengthened the position of both German states within their respective alliances, it had not called into question their loyalty to the blocs. One can argue that detente actually reinforced these ties, since both states gained more political and economic prominence and their status as the main pillars of the alliances was confirmed.

The central role that the alliances play in the politics of the FRG and the GDR become most apparent in their extraordinarily high degree of economic integration. Despite all the attention given to West Germany's

Eastern trade, and inter-German trade in specific, the inter-German border still constitutes the dividing line between two largely separate economic spheres. The FRG, with an annual foreign trade volume of about $200 billion making it the world's third largest trading power, conducts 75 percent of its foreign trade with OECD countries; only 5.4 percent of its exports are sent to the East. Although West Germany's Eastern trade doubled during the 1970s, as a share of total foreign trade it actually declined.[12]

The GDR demonstrates a similar economic dependence on the Eastern bloc. Two-thirds of its foreign trade is conducted with members of CMEA, one-third with the Soviet Union alone. It receives 80 percent of its oil supplies and 100 percent of its natural gas from the Soviet Union. This dependence is far greater than Western dependence on OPEC has ever been and constitutes a severe restriction of East Germany's scope for maneuver in its Western trade. Particularly since 1982, the Soviets have used the threat of reduced oil shipments to make the GDR deliver more of its industrial goods to the Soviet Union instead of exporting them to the West for convertible currency.[13]

The dense net of economic interdependence between each German state and its alliance is reinforced by an equally high level of military integration. Not only do both states depend for their defense on the military alliances, but they also are the principal military partners of the superpowers on the European continent. West Germany's armed forces were established as a condition of the FRG's membership in NATO. The West German rearmament program after 1955 was only acceptable to its European neighbors because it was firmly integrated into NATO. Even today, the FRG seeks to avoid independent military initiative lest it raise fears of German militarism in both East and West. The low profile it has kept in multilateral negotiations, such as the Mutual Balanced Force Reduction (MBFR) talks in Vienna, and its reliance on a Franco-German axis for any European defense initiative, illustrate this hesitance.[14]

This policy does not negate the FRG's central role in the European defense system. With 500,000 troops, almost half of NATO's forces in Europe, the West German *Bundeswehr* today constitutes the largest and best trained army in Western Europe.[15] As NATO's front-line state, West Germany's defense is the most important aspect of West European security. This contrast between military potential and necessary political restraint creates a dilemma for West Germany's defense policy that was best expressed by Egon Bahr: "The German *Bundeswehr* must be strong enough to hold the Russians in check, but not strong enough to threaten Luxemburg."[16]

Even more important for West Germany's Western integration is its reliance on the U.S. extended nuclear deterrence. After the traumatic experience of the conventionally-fought World War II, the West German public rejected the idea of basing the defense of the FRG solely on conventional forces. Arguing that nothing would be worse than a replay of that war, Bonn's leaders welcomed the nuclear deterrence which was provided through the U.S. superiority in strategic nuclear forces. When in the late 1950s the commitment was called into question by the growth of the Soviet nuclear arsenals, and Britain and France built their own deterrent force, some politicians in Bonn floated the idea of German access to nuclear weapons. The ill-fated Multilateral Force, a plan to deploy nuclear missiles on surface ships that would be manned by crew members from various NATO countries, was a result of these demands. But the thought of German nuclear weapons struck a sensitive nerve in almost every European capital. Even today that topic remains a taboo, a sign of the special status that Germany still occupies in the world. Although the decade-long debate over NATO's military strategies was laid to rest by the doctrine of flexible response in 1967 and did not reemerge until Helmut Schmidt's London speech ten years later, the continuing bickering between Americans who demand a conventional defense buildup and West Germans who insist on strengthening the United States' nuclear commitment has become a permanent feature of intra-NATO politics.[17]

The integration of the GDR into the WTO is dictated at least as much by internal as by external requirements. While the belief that the purpose of the 19 Soviet divisions on East German soil is to suppress popular unrest is probably a myth, these troops still represent a key element for the viability of the East German regime. Regardless of whether or not the GDR could remain independent if the Soviet withdrew (I have suggested earlier that it could), the very existence of the second German state has always been based on military and political integration into the Eastern bloc.

Just as the West German *Bundeswehr* is the cornerstone of NATO's defense, so are the 213,000 troops in East Germany's *Nationale Volksarmee* (NVA) the most important non-Soviet section of the WTO forces. The GDR is the only state of the Eastern alliance that grants unlimited stationing rights to Soviet troops, and its army is fully subordinated to the Soviet command even in peace time.[18] But despite this ostentatious loyalty, East German defense interests do not necessarily coincide with Soviet military goals. Just as the FRG has a stronger interest in avoiding war in the European theater than any other NATO member, so also the GDR, which would inevitably be the first victim of such a confrontation, is more sensitive to any policies that increase the likelihood of war.

Contrary to its Western counterpart, the GDR seems to have little chance to pursue these interests. Practically all decisions regarding doctrine, armaments and even defense spending are routinely made in Moscow. The only time when the East German leadership was known to criticize Soviet military planning was when Moscow responded to NATO's INF deployment by stationing new Soviet nuclear missiles in the GDR and Czechoslovakia, a case that is the subject of a later discussion.

The high degree of economic and military integration of both German states into their alliances creates fundamental political constraints. Despite calls for a West German withdrawal from NATO from the Green party and the left wing of the SPD, such as from the Saarland's charismatic prime minister, Oskar Lafontaine, such policy does not seem feasible. Not only would NATO collapse, but West Germany's independent national existence would be in jeopardy. Since the rise of the FRG to independence and power was so closely linked to its membership in NATO, a withdrawal would force the other European powers to deal again with the first and most urgent post-war problem: how to control Germany. A nonaligned or neutral Federal Republic would be economically fully viable and, save a full-scale attack from the WTO, probably even able to defend itself; but it would lack the prerequisites for finding a stable place in the European political system.

The underlying problem is that the "German question" was never fully addressed after World War II but found a temporary solution in the division of Germany and the integration of its parts into the European security alliances. The FRG's withdrawal from NATO would bring the underlying ambiguities and dilemmas back into the open. Nobody can predict the impact of such a development on the European balance of power, but its effects could be disastrous. Given these constraints and the strong support for the alliance among the West German public, debates about withdrawal has never been a salient issue in West German politics.

Despite these limits, the FRG has considerable scope for maneuver in foreign policy. This ambiguous amount of political power became most striking in the 1970s, when Bonn's influence in Europe vastly increased. The French retreat from NATO, Britain's decline as a world power and the prospering of detente made the FRG the strongest country in Western

Europe and the United States' most important ally.[19] Bonn's relationship to Washington was also no longer one of submission, but one of strong and sometimes highly competitive partners who clashed repeatedly over military and economic issues. This trend was reinforced by Soviet strategy. As the Kremlin leaders began to see the United States as an increasingly unreliable interlocuter, they turned the focus of their detente policy towards the FRG and induced Bonn to assume a central role in East-West relations.[20]

This somewhat involuntary leadership role in Western Europe conflicted with West Germany's continuing desire to maintain a low political profile in the alliance lest it arouse fears of German unilateralism or even German desires for hegemony on the continent. The historical analogy regularly conjured up is Rapallo, where Germany and the Soviet Union signed a treaty of cooperation in 1922. A repetition of the seesaw policy that Germany conducted in the 1920s in order to strengthen its position *vis-à-vis* the victor nations of World War I is still an anathema to many West European countries. Ironically, it is the Soviet Union that would have most to fear from an assertive and unpredictable Germany in the center of Europe. Thus, any movement toward neutrality would not only upset the Western allies, but would also greatly disturb the Soviets and thus hurt the prospects of detente.[21]

The FRG's most successful strategy for assuming its leading role in Europe while avoiding the impression of unreliability has been to emphasize its close relationship with France. The Franco-German axis strengthens Bonn *vis-à-vis* the United States and bestows more legitimacy on its European leadership role. Since the late 1960s, the FRG has tried to tie France closer into the Western alliance and the EC; in return, France has received vast economic benefits from its more prosperous and efficient neighbor, particularly through the unequal distribution of payments and benefits in the Common Market.[22]

While the autonomy of the GDR cannot be compared to that of the FRG, East Germany seems to enjoy more freedom in its foreign policy than is sometimes assumed. Although the GDR follows Soviet policies more loyally than any other East European country, this course is not always based on coercion, but on the ideological preferences and interests of the East German leadership who sees loyalty to Moscow as their most important goal in foreign policy. As will be discussed later, the East German leeway has actually grown in recent years. Although the Soviets still enjoy veto power over all foreign policy decisions, East Berlin can decide its own course in more marginal issues. East German assertiveness has been strongest in the CMEA, where it has occasionally voiced strong criticism of Soviet economic policies, and weakest in the WTO.[23]

THE TWO GERMAN STATES AND
THE SUPERPOWERS IN 1979

By 1979, the state of relations between the two German states and their alliances was still characterized by a basic agreement on the central aspects of East-West relations. In both alliances, however, the seeds for coming conflicts had already been planted.

In the Western alliance, U.S.-European relations had deteriorated since Carter's assumption of office. West European leaders, particularly Helmut Schmidt, were appalled by Carter's seemingly uncertain leadership of the alliance, by his evident naiveté in the foreign policy area, and by his economic policies. For example, they criticized the continuous decline in the value of the dollar, which jeopardized the stability of the world currency system. Also, politicians like Schmidt and France's President Valers Giscard D'Estaing, who were interested in nonideological and pragmatic relations with the Soviet Union, rejected Carter's attempt to infuse East-West relations with a missionary concern for human rights while seemingly to sacrifice European security needs in the SALT II negotiations. This conflict over the rhetoric of East-West relations became most apparent at the CSCE review conference in Belgrad in 1977-78. To the chagrin of the West European governments, the Carter administration attempted to turn this meeting into a tribunal on Soviet human rights abuses, an act they claimed hurt the detente process.[24]

It was the concern over Carter's apparent neglect for the United States' nuclear commitments to Europe that fueled the trans-Atlantic debate most intensively. Helmut Schmidt expressed this fear in his Alastair Buchan Memorial Lecture at London's International Center for Strategic Studies in October 1977, when he argued that the forthcoming SALT II treaty would exacerbate the military imbalance on the European continent.

> SALT neutralized [the superpowers'] strategic nuclear capabilities. In Europe, this magnifies the significance of the disparities between East and West in nuclear tactical and conventional weapons. . . . We are not unaware that both the United States and the Soviet Union must be anxious to remove the

threatening strategic developments from their relationship. But strategic arms
limitations confined to the United States and the Soviet Union will inevitably
impair the security of the West European members of the Alliance *vis-à-vis*
Soviet military superiority in Europe if we do not succeed in removing the
disparities of military power in Europe parallel to the SALT negotiations.[25]

This speech represented a major challenge to the U.S. government
since it questioned the strength of the U.S. commitment to defend
Western Europe. The Carter administration reacted by initiating a plan to
modernize NATO's intermediate range theater nuclear forces in Europe,
which ultimately led to NATO's double-track decision of December
1979. In this landmark decision, NATO's member states vetoed to
deploy 576 Tomahawk ground-launched cruise missiles and Pershing II
ballistic missiles by the end of 1983, but to pursue arms control
negotiations with the Soviet Union simultaneously.[26]

It is interesting to note that NATO strategists were never clear
about the military rationale for this project; its main, and perhaps only,
value was its confirmation of the U.S. nuclear commitment to Europe
and of the political unity of the alliance.[27] As will be discussed later, it
was the political nature of the double-track decision that made it turn
from a support for NATO solidarity into a major threat to this very
concept of alliance unity. Former National Security Adviser McGeorge
Bundy's prediction at the time of the decision proved to be frighteningly
correct:[28] "If West Europeans' willingness to deploy these essentially
irrelevant missiles becomes a test of alliance unity, we'll be handing the
Soviets a splendid bludgeon with which to split the alliance." Instead of
subduing the fears of nuclear coupling, the decision actually reinforced
uneasy feelings about the viability of NATO's defense doctrine. And
perhaps most important, by creating the impression that the FRG was
forced to accept missiles that only served U.S. interests, the decision
jeopardized the popular concensus on defense matters in the West
German polity.

By 1979 large parts of the European political establishment had lost
faith in the United States' leadership of the alliance. Europeans were
angered by Carter's unilateral cancellation of the neutron bomb, and grew
concerned over the declining support for detente and arms control in the
U.S. Congress. When the nonissue of a Soviet brigade in Cuba almost
induced Carter to withdraw SALT II from ratification, and the White
House saw the need to introduce the MX missile system in order to
garner sufficient support for the treaty in the Senate, it became apparent

that the domestic political base for an active arms control policy had vanished in the United States.[29]

As U.S. legislators drifted away from detente and began to favor a strong arms buildup, they also grew impatient with the alleged European unwillingness to make sacrifices for NATO's military needs. Western Europe, they argued, had become addicted to detente, Eastern trade, and arms control, and preferred to let the United States pay for its defense rather than shoulder the financial burdens themselves. It was most symptomatic of the growing gap between the psychology of the United States and of Western Europe that the U.S. president had to agree to a major arms buildup in order to achieve ratification of SALT II, while West European leaders needed a U.S. commitment toward arms control negotiations with the Soviet Union in order to sell the INF deployment to their own population.[30]

The Eastern alliance had also undergone significant changes during the era of detente, causing some tension between the Soviet Union and its East European allies. Eastern Europe was more strongly affected by the sudden rise of Western influence than was the Soviet Union, both by its positive and negative aspects. The surging of East-West trade contributed to a significant increase in the standard of living, but it also made Eastern Europe increasingly dependent on its Western trading partners. Poland and the GDR used Western credit and technology for a rapid modernization of its industries, while Hungary and Bulgaria introduced a series of economic reforms that included the decentralization of industry and the privatization of agriculture. Romania pursued a very independent foreign policy since 1967 and relied heavily on Western trade for its industrialization drive. Since the Soviets engaged in East-West trade as well, the divergence in interest with Eastern Europe was not over goals, but over priorities. With the exception of grain purchases from the United States, foreign trade never did play the central role in the Soviet economy that it did in the export-oriented economies of the small East European countries.

Also, the domestic policies of the East European states differed from Soviet practices. Faced with an increase in human rights activities that was fueled by the Helsinki Accords and Western influences, countries like Poland and Hungary relaxed political controls, allowed their citizens more freedom to travel, and sought a reconciliation with the Catholic Church and other noncommunist institutions. Even the SED attempted to gain popular support by offering a rising standard of living and maintaining relations with the FRG. Only in Czechoslovakia did the continuing trauma of the 1968 invasion prevent a relaxation of the domestic climate.

Generally, one can speak of a new era of relations between the East European governments and their citizens which developed during the 1970s. Faced with the knowledge that neither could escape Soviet hegemony nor stray too far from the Soviet political model, the two sides agreed to a form of internal peaceful coexistence: the population refrained from challenging the political rule of the party, while the leaders provided them with an ever increasing standard of living. This "new social contract," as it is frequently called, led to an unprecedented domestic consensus in some of the countries. However, this consumer communism depended to a large extent on the performance of the economy. And in a country like Poland that failed to institute economic reforms, the emphasis on consumer goods over capital investments and sound economic policies led to economic crisis and the breakdown of the social contract in 1980.

In conclusion, detente was already on its decline in 1979 and was constantly undercut by the rhetoric and the policies of the two superpowers, but it still served as an operational framework for East-West relations. The United States and the Soviet Union had just signed their first arms control agreement since 1972 and were cooperating on a range of international issues. Although the United States had few stakes in East-West trade, most of the EC pursued aggressive export strategies toward the East European countries and aided their economic development with large loans.

At that time, inter-German relations were in tune with both the general state of East-West relations and the conditions in both alliances. The two German states built an intricate web of political and economic cooperation, but reached no consensus on the more principal questions in their relationship. The GDR strengthened its efforts to ward off Western influence through its demarcation policy and made only few concessions with respect to human rights. The FRG continued its policy of small steps toward human benefits and steadily increased its financial payments to the East German government in exchange for often small returns. Its *Deutschlandpolitik* was imbedded in alliance politics and was void of any plans for a separate inter-German role in European politics. The stability of orderly bilateral relations between the two German states had muted most of the allies' fears of an all-German conspiracy in pursuit of national reunification or even of neutralist tendencies on either side of the inter-German border.

NOTES

1. Edwin Fedder, "Transformations in the Alliance," in Edwin H. Fedder, ed., *Defense Politics of the Atlantic Alliance* (New York: Praeger, 1980), pp. 8-11.
2. Klaas De Vries, "Security Policy and Arms Control: A European Perspective," in Marsha McGraw Olive, Jeffrey D. Porro, eds., *Nuclear Weapons in Europe: Modernization and Limitation* (Lexington, Mass.: Lexington Books, 1983), p. 53.
3. Wilhelm Bruns, *Deutsch-deutsche Beziehungen: Prämissen — Probleme — Perspektiven* (Opladen: Leske & Budrich, 1982), p. 94.
4. For the text of the Eastern treaties, see Helmut Kistler, *Die Ostpolitik der Bundesrepublik Deutschland 1966-1973* (Bonn: Bundeszentrale für politische Bildung, 1982), pp. 73-8.
5. Henry Kissinger, *White House Years* (Boston: Little, Brown, 1979), pp. 529-30.
6. See Gerhard Wettig, "Das Problem der Bindungen West Berlins bei der Anwendung des Viermächteabkommens," *Deutschland Archiv* (Sept. 1979): 936-37, and *Instrumentarien der Entspannungspolitik* (Köln: Berichte des Bundesinstitutes für internationale und ostwissenschaftliche Studien, 1981), pp. 29-35.
7. Angela Stent, *From Embargo to Ostpolitik: The Political Economy of West German-Soviet Relations 1955-1980* (Cambridge: Cambridge University Press, 1981), pp. 197-98.
8. Mathias Jopp, Berthold Meyer, et al., "Deutsch-deutsche Beziehungen im Ost-West-Konflikt," in Ilse Spittmann and Gisela Helwig, eds., *Die beiden deutschen Staaten im Ost-West-Verhältnis*, 15, Tagung zum Stand der DDR-Forschung in der Bundesrepublik Deutschland, 1-4, June 1982. (Köln: Edition Deutschland Archiv, 1982), pp. 29-30.
9. Stent, *From Embargo to Ostpolitik*, pp. 197-8.
10. Christian Hacke, "Soll und Haben des Grundlagenvertrages," *Deutschland Archiv* 15 (December 1982).
11. Klaus Bölling, *Die fernen Nachbarn: Erfahrungen in der DDR* (Hamburg: Gruner & Jahr, 1983), p. 179; and *Der Spiegel,* 20 (May 12, 1980).
12. All figures from *Zahlenspiegel: Bundesrepublik Deutschland/Deutsche Demokratische Republik — Ein Vergleich* (Bonn: Bundesministerium für innerdeutsche Beziehungen, 1983).
13. Michael Schmitz, "Das Beste für den großen Bruder," *Die ZEIT* 4 (Jan. 25, 1985).
14. Reimund Seidelmann, "Möglichkeiten und Grenzen der MBFR-Politik der BRD und der DDR," in Spittmann and Helwig, eds., *Die beiden deutschen Staaten im Ost-West-Verhältnis*, pp. 124-8.
15. Helmut Schmidt, "A Policy of Reliable Partnership," *Foreign Affairs* 59 (Spring 1981): 746.
16. Philip Windsor, *Germany and the Western Alliance: Lessons from the 1980 Crises,* Adelphi Paper No. 170 (London: International Institute for Strategic Studies, 1981), p. 8.

17. See David Schwartz, *NATO's Nuclear Dilemmas* (Washington, D.C.: Brookings Institution, 1984).

18. Angela Stent, "Soviet policy toward the GDR," in Sarah M. Terry, ed., *Soviet Policy in Eastern Europe* (New Haven: Yale University Press, 1984), p. 48.

19. Fedder, "Transformations in the Alliance," in Fedder, *Defense Politics,* p. 17.

20. Windsor, *Germany and the Western Alliance,* pp. 5-7.

21. Stent, *From Embargo to Ostpolitik,* p. 260.

22. Windsor, *Germany and the Western Alliance,* p. 8; and Pierre Lellouche, "Europe and her Defense," *Foreign Affairs* 59 (Spring 1981): 827.

23. See Stent, "Soviet policy towards the GDR," in Terry, *Soviet Policy,* p. 41, and David Buchnan, *Western Security and Economic Strategy toward the East,* Adelphi Paper No. 192 (London: International Institute for Strategic Studies, 1984), p. 42.

24. Stent, *From Embargo to Ostpolitik,* p. 235.

25. Quoted after Schwartz, *NATO's Nuclear Dilemmas,* pp. 214-15.

26. On the origins of the NATO deployment decision, see Strobe Talbott, *Deadly Gambits* (New York: Knopf, 1984), pp. 27-39.

27. Joseph Joffe, "Allies, Angst, and Arms Control," in Fedder, *Defense Politics of the Atlantic Alliance,* pp. 33-34.

28. Talbott, *Deadly Gambits,* p. 43.

29. Windsor, *Germany and the Western Alliance,* pp. 19-20.

30. Joseph Joffe, "American-European Relations: The Enduring Crisis," *Foreign Affairs* 59 (Spring 1981): 842.

5 A EUROPEAN DETENTE?

THE EUROPEANIZATION OF DETENTE

A series of events in late 1979 and 1980 destroyed this consensus and brought about the biggest challenge to the European post-war order since its inception 35 years before. First came the breakdown of U.S.-Soviet relations, caused primarily by the Soviet invasion of Afghanistan; then the Polish crisis; then these events triggered a crisis of unprecedented magnitude in the Western alliance. As Europeans and Americans increasingly disagreed over the correct response to the Soviet military adventures and domestic crises in the Eastern bloc, the intra-NATO debate began to overshadow even these initial events. The experience was unique because it was the first time that an East-West crisis did not lead to more solidarity, but to more friction within the Western bloc. Particularly with the debate over the INF deployment, which threatened the domestic consensus over Western integration in the Federal Republic and other European states, the viability of the whole Western security system was called into question. Since these events directly affected the two German states and shaped inter-German relations in the following five years, it is worth discussing the crises of 1980 at some length.

It is difficult to assign the blame precisely for the breakdown of detente in 1979. As mentioned before, detente had already been under severe strain both in the United States and the Soviet Union and had lost the momentum of the early 1970s. Especially in the United States, the political establishment had grown disillusioned with detente. Through its policy of linkage, Nixon and Kissinger had hoped to induce the Soviet

Union to modify its foreign policies, slow down its arms buildup, and refrain from aggressive military initiatives in the Third World, thereby freezing the political and military status quo not only in Europe, but on a global basis.[1] This situation, the Nixon administration believed, would allow the United States to retreat from its role of "world policeman" after the sobering experience of the Vietnam War, and to drastically reduce its defense expenditures without risking a deterioration of U.S. or Western security.

This goal was never achieved, however. While the Soviet Union willingly cooperated in the stabilization of the political status quo in Europe, it did not follow the U.S. guidelines for detente in other areas. Instead, it continued its rapid military buildup, introduced a new generation of SS-20 long-range theater nuclear missiles in Europe and East Asia, and engineered military interventions in Angola, Ethiopia, and South Yemen. As Americans perceived their global power and credibility to be dwindling, many arrived at the conclusion that the decade of detente and arms control had not benefitted them, but only the Soviets. It was therefore not surprising that when for the first time the Soviet leaders sent their troops to a country outside the Eastern bloc, the U.S. government preceived this as the right moment to switch to a course of confrontation with Moscow. In response to the invasion of Afghanistan in December 1979, President Carter essentially declared the end of detente. In the following months, he withdrew the SALT II treaty from ratification in the Senate, embarked on a major military buildup, and imposed a trade embargo on the Soviet Union. With these tough measures Carter actually adjusted to the mood of the U.S. populace, which was wary of humiliations like the Iranian hostage crisis and desired a reassertion of U.S. military and political power in the world. The election of Ronald Reagan confirmed the abandonment of detente and the return to a policy of military strength and global containment of Soviet expansionism.[2]

To the dismay of the U.S. government, most European governments did not accept this new policy. With the exception of Britain's Prime Minister Margaret Thatcher, the political leaders of France, West Germany, Italy, the Netherlands, and most other European states rejected Carter's analysis of the nature of the conflict and criticized his harsh response to the Soviet invasion of Afghanistan. In contrast to the U.S. administration, which perceived Afghanistan as a first step toward a Soviet expansion into the vital Persian Gulf region and therefore as a major threat to Western energy supplies and Western security, most Europeans regarded the conflict as a regional issue. In the comments by politicians and newspaper editorials the Soviet invasion, though dangerous and unjustified, was still described as a defensive reaction to a regional problem. Few Europeans agreed with the U.S. analysis that the invasion was part of a Soviet grand design against the Persian Gulf or any other strategic region in the world.[3] Also, when Europeans looked at the results of detente on their continent, they saw a decline of ideology in Eastern Europe and pragmatic communist leaders who were more interested in the modernization of their economies than in the spreading of socialism in the West. Thus they no longer accepted the notion of the inherently expansionist nature of Soviet foreign policy and of the importance of ideology in the East-West conflict.

Underlying the difference in analysis between Europe and the United States was a conflict of interest that had evolved during the 1970s. In contrast to the United States, the decade of detente had brought the West European states significant benefits, benefits that they were now unwilling to abandon for the sake of an almost uninhabited country in Central Asia. Trade with the East had acquired a central role in their economic calculations, particularly for the FRG, which conducted almost half of all East-West trade in the world. The intensification of personal relations between East and West mitigated the harshest aspects of the division of Europe and raised the hope that the "iron curtain" would one day wither away. Again, the FRG was the main beneficiary of this development, particularly through the humanitarian and political benefits of the accommodation with the GDR after 1971.

Most important, however, had been the effect of detente on the psychology of the continent. A decade of relaxation of tensions had changed Europe from a tension-ridden region to one of the most stable regions in the world. Despite the continuing existence of two hostile military and political blocs, Europe was perceived to be on its way to normalization. Since all these achievements were jeopardized by the renewed superpower confrontation, many European leaders felt that Europe should be insulated from the global crisis. Their analysis of Afghanistan as a regional conflict, though correct in many respects, was also motivated by self-interest. Once detente failed on a global basis, European leaders came to share the Soviet goal of making detente divisible so that it could be maintained on the European continent.

While this attitude was plausible in some respect, it conflicted with the requirements of the U.S. confrontation strategy. The Carter administration needed European solidarity in order to lend credibility to its policies, and it needed European cooperation to make its boycott measures effective.[4] The refusal of practically all European governments to support the U.S. demands led to a previously unknown degree of bitterness and antagonism in the alliance. European politicians and commentators criticized the alleged abuse of the alliance for the United States' global aspirations as a world power and its neglect of Europe's needs and interests. U.S. leaders could not understand why Western Europe began to emphasize the regional nature of NATO just when the United States needed its allies most in other parts of the world. They charged that Europe had become so dependent on detente that it had lost the ability to assert itself against the Soviet Union. Western Europe's failure to criticize even a blatant violation of international law like the invasion of Afghanistan was perceived as *prima facie* evidence for Europe's "self-Finlandization" about which conservatives have warned since the dawn of detente.[5] This assessment of Europe's psychological state strengthened isolationist and unilateralist tendencies in the United States and fueled the call for a reduction of U.S. troops in West Germany. A growing number of congressmen and senators asked themselves whether the United States should spend billions of dollars and risk the destruction of its homeland for the defense of people who were unwilling to defend themselves.

While the rather low-key reaction of most European governments, especially West German Chancellor Schmidt, to the military crackdown in Poland in December 1981 reinforced these U.S. views, the European objections to U.S. policies grew stronger with the advent of the Reagan administration and its hawkish rhetoric. References of key officials to fighting and winning a limited nuclear war in Europe particularly aroused new anxieties in wide parts of the public. The old fear that the United States would not fight a war in the case of a Soviet attack on Western Europe was overshadowed by a new sentiment: that the United States would risk fighting a war – even a nuclear war — through a reckless foreign policy, but that it would attempt to limit it to the European theater. Europe's opposition to U.S. policy was no longer seen as only a question of its political and economic interest; its physical survival was now at stake. The touchstone of alliance solidarity changed from whether the United States would have to sacrifice Chicago for the defense of Europe to whether Europe would have to sacrifice its own cities for the sake of U.S. great power politics.

The simultaneous debate over the INF deployment, the rise of the peace movement in practically every European country, and the growing neutralist sentiments among leftist elites increased the pressure on

European government to put more distance between themselves and the United States. Many European governments were faced with two contradictory requirements. They had to preserve the unity of the alliance lest they jeopardize the basis for Europe's security. But they also wanted to advance their own independent interests more strongly than in the past and had to accommodate popular demands to refuse cooperation with the arms buildup and the "policy of strength" of the U.S. government. This dilemma was most pertinent to Helmut Schmidt. The FRG not only had the biggest stakes in both a strong defense and the continuation of detente, but it was also most closely watched by the superpowers. Although the FRG showed more loyalty to the U.S. than most other allies, as evidenced by its boycott of the Olympic games in Moscow, it had to bear the main thrust of the U.S. frustration with the alliance. And although it worked harder to maintain detente than any other state, it became the main victim of Soviet pressure against Western Europe. The need to cope with this dilemma was the most critical problem of both Schmidt and Helmut Kohl throughout the INF debate.

This situation led a number of European theorists to develop a new mode of thinking about Europe's position in the East-West conflict. Since the United States with its erratic public opinion on foreign policy issues could no longer be trusted to guide Western Europe's relations to the East, Europeans had to take their Eastern policy into their own hands. Dependence on the United States had to be reduced by strengthening the European leg in the alliance. Then, Europe could pursue a more independent policy toward the Soviet Union and Eastern Europe even if that conflicted with U.S. foreign policy goals.

These concepts were encouraged by developments in the WTO that indicated a more independent approach to East-West relations by some East European governments. After Afghanistan, Eastern Europe seemed to show little enthusiasm for the confrontational policies of their Soviet ally. Just like most West European governments, the party leaders in Hungary, Poland, and even East Germany went to great lengths to confirm their commitment to a continuation of detente and the lessening of international tensions.

Based on this common goal, a number of theorists and political leaders suggested that, without breaking either of the alliances, Europeans in East and West could still find a way to resist U.S.-Soviet fluctuations and put detente on a more stable basis. These concepts found their strongest articulation in West Germany. In particular, leading thinkers in the SPD like Egon Bahr, Horst Ehmke, and the former envoy to the GDR, Günter Gaus, espoused various ideas which all had at their core the concept of the "Europeanization of detente."[6] The most complete and provocative account of this outlook was given by Peter Bender, a social democratic journalist and columnist, in his book *The End of the Ideological Era: The Europeanization of Europe*.[7] Bender's thesis is already summarized in the title of his book. With the demise of the ideological fervor in the communist bloc, the East-West conflict had changed from an ideological to a purely political conflict in which the interests of the European nations no longer coincided with that of the superpowers. Not the ideological gap between East and West, but the global aspirations of the United States and the Soviet Union and their rivalries constitute the principal threat to peace and stability in Europe. Hence, East and West Europeans have to join forces to prevent conflicts on their continent and save their common cultural heritage.

It is worth developing Bender's rich and controversial argument here in more detail. Bender's main premise is a pessimistic view of the viability of the communist system and ideology. While in the first years after the end of the war, communism still showed the ideological fervor and aggressive missionary spirit that scared the West into forming defensive alliances for the containment of Soviet expansionism, the requirements of a modern industrial society soon turned the attention of the leaders to more practical issues. During the 1960s and 1970s, communist parties became less concerned with changing the nature of man or building a better society, but instead concentrated more on improving the efficiency of their economies. Economic pragmatism superceded ideological purity as the driving force behind the policies of the party leaders. Stuck with an economic system that did not work, Eastern Europe increasingly turned to the West for credit and technology as a compensation for domestic deficiencies. But along with Western machinery and Western consumer goods, Western values entered as well and forced the pragmatic East European leaders to tolerate an increasing level of pluralism in their societies. The GDR accepted that three-quarters of its population watched West German television every night, Poland permitted the Catholic Church to function as an autonomous and highly powerful force in the country, and Hungary did away with many more remnants of a repressive regime. Eastern Europe turned from a totalitarian to a nonideological, authoritarian system that tried to gain popular support by promising a rising standard of living and a relaxation of social restrictions.

As the East-West conflict lost its ideological component, the Western fear of falling victim to communism faded as well. In the arena where the conflict was now carried out — the sphere of economics and popular support — the Western democracies were vastly superior to the East. But also the goals of the conflict had changed: the aim of the European states was no longer victory over the other system through persuasion or force, but the creation of a stable political balance in Europe. The era of detente, the new West German *Ostpolitik,* and especially the Helsinki Accords marked the end of ideological crusades in European East-West relations. East and West European states bridged their ideological gaps and linked the continent with a growing net of economic and human interdependence.

As the European states arrive at a new, higher level of European awareness, their interests increasingly diverged from that of the superpowers. Both the United States and the Soviet Union are global powers, the interests of which lie increasingly outside the European arena. Not constrained by the lack of power that inhibits small states, the two nations are more likely to pursue reckless and dangerous policies in the pursuit of their own interests while ignoring the needs of their European allies. These dangerous strands in their foreign policies are reinforced by the influence of an erratic public opinion with strong idealistic tendencies in the United States and by an exaggerated desire for absolute security among Soviet leaders. As the alienation grows between West Europeans and Americans on one side and East Europeans and Russians on the other, Eastern and Western Europe move closer together. Although the countries belong to opposing military blocs, their cultural heritage creates a common tie that is stronger than their loyalty to their non-European, or in the case of the Soviet Union semi-European, allies. As the superpowers become preoccupied with the global competition between them, their rivalry constitutes the main problem for Europe. Not the prospect of a Soviet invasion or of Soviet political blackmail, but the chance of military escalation in a U.S.-Soviet conflict is the most serious threat to peace and stability in Europe of today.

It is therefore in the interest of Europeans, both in East and West, to insulate the continent from the continuing arms race between the two superpowers, and to reduce the danger of nuclear war by decoupling themselves from their nuclear strategies. Since in contrast to the United States, Western Europe has benefitted enormously through detete, it is also in its interest to strengthen the net of economic and political interdependence with Eastern Europe. These developments should not destroy the structure of NATO; however, the alliance must adjust to the divergent interests of its members and focus on the common goals of its members. A similar development could occur in the Eastern bloc, where it becomes increasingly difficult and costly for the Soviet Union to impose its will on its client states and to stall overdue economic reforms. These trends could ultimately lead to the partial democratization of Eastern Europe and make the military presence of the United States and the Soviet Union in Europe obsolete.

Neither Bender's arguments nor the concept of an autonomous European detente policy are new; but because of the political circumstances under which they were publicized, they are more relevant than earlier concepts. A long tradition of neutralism and opposition to NATO has existed in the FRG since the beginning of Western integration. Before 1959, the SPD was the major protagonist of this position, which is currently carried on by the Greens. But in contrast to these notions, the concept of a Europeanization of detente does not advocate the dissolution of the Western alliance. Instead, it attempts to adapt the alliance to the changes in the international arena which have occurred since its establishment 35 years ago by reconciling alliance integration with European detente.

Regardless of whether one accepts Bender's ideas, views of this nature have dominated the intra-alliance debate and the policies of most West European governments since 1980. Whether it was the strengthening of Europe's political influence within NATO, the debate over the INF deployment, the attempted resurrection of the West European Union (WEU) in 1984, or the lively exchange of high-level visits between Western and Eastern European states in 1983 and 1984 despite growing Soviet reclusiveness, those policies can be explained or justified by these ideas. Although most European leaders would not go as far as Bender, the concept of a special "security partnership" between Eastern and Western Europe has become generally accepted.

The development of inter-German relations since 1980 must also be viewed within the context of a Europeanization of detente. Both West German and East German leaders defied their allies at some point in order to maintain detente between the two German states. Lest such a development arouse fears of German separatism in both alliances, it had to be integrated into a larger European movement toward an autonomous detente. To answer the question of whether inter-German relations can flourish independently of U.S.-Soviet relations, we must therefore first evaluate the chances of success for such a Europeanization of detente.

The following chapter will analyze a range of different issues in order to arrive at a satisfying answer to this question. First, we must establish the magnitude of the conflict between the United States and Western Europe. Do there really exist separate West European and U.S. interests in the East-West conflict? Also, even if the interests of West Europeans diverge, do they have a chance to pursue these interests while their defense depends on the U.S. nuclear umbrella? Is Western Europe's military self-reliance feasible, or will it remain wishful thinking due to economic constraints and the lack of unanimity among European states? To what extent can political relations between Eastern and Western Europe improve while the armament policies of the superpowers jeopardize East-West relations? Finally, would Western Europe be able to stand alone against the Soviet Union, or does a European detente mean the "Finlandization" of the continent?

Similar questions concern the developments in the Eastern alliance. Is there a real conflict of interest between the Soviet Union and Eastern Europe or do they all essentially share the same goals? Can East European states gain any independence in their foreign policies at all? Were the signs of discord in 1983 and 1984 only a reaction to the lack of leadership in Moscow, or were they even part of a grand Soviet "dual-track" strategy? Finally, is Eastern Europe able to reform, or will liberalization inevitably lead to instability and subsequently to more repression, as it did in Poland after 1981?

THE GERMANIZATION OF DETENTE

In analyzing the prospects for a European detente, inter-German relations can serve as an insightful example. The special German case, however, has some features that make it more complex than general East-West European relations. For the two German states are in a position to pursue not only larger European interests, but also specific German interests. The German interests, which are unique to inter-German relations, include the issues that were discussed in Part I of this study: national or nationalistic sentiments in both states (to the extent to which they are still relevant today), the special stakes the GDR has in inter-German trade and the associated economic benefits, and the humanitarian interests of the FRG. Other, less central issues in this set are environmental protection and cultural exchange.

In contrast, the European interests of the two German states are more closely related to their political and military security. As the front-line states of the alliances, the FRG and the GDR would be the first to suffer from an armed conflict. Since East German concerns about war are usually expressed within the context of Soviet propaganda, we do not know how genuine is the fear of war of the East German people and the leadership beneath the official rhetoric. West Germans, in contrast, have been much more outspoken about their discomfort with their exposed position. However, West German concerns are twofold and contradictory in themselves. Traditionally the FRG has feared a lack of resolve of their Western allies to defend them in a case of Soviet attack. In recent years, however, fear of the Soviet military has subsided and has been replaced by fear of nuclear war and aggressive U.S. policies. The pacifist sentiments that dominated much of the domestic debate in the 1950s and that have always flourished in Scandinavia and the Netherlands have returned as an increasingly important factor in West German politics.

The potential interests arising from this situation include not only all measures leading to a reduction of the threat of war, such as arms control and confidence-building measures, but also the confirmation of the political and territorial status quo in Europe. In the most extreme case, the pursuit of these interests could lead to a withdrawal from either German state from its respective alliance in order to escape the confrontational course of their allies. These interests are not uniquely German. Only the two Germanies extremely exposed position makes them a more salient issue for the FRG and the GDR than for most of their neighbors.

This is not to say that both German states always share the same interests. On the contrary, some of these interests are contradictory in themselves, and the choice of which interests to give priority can also become a point of controversy between the two German states. Still, these two sets of interests are an appropriate characterization of the dual nature of the inter-German relationship, and are particularly useful for establishing a model for the evaluation of inter-German relations in the context of European alliance politics.

One can argue that the fear of the implications of inter-German relations among Eastern and Western allies is not rooted in the realization of only one of the two sets of interests alone. If the allies can be sure that the FRG and the GDR will remain loyal members of their respective alliances, then the pursuit of their national interests should not raise any extraordinary concerns. Similarly, when either of the German states — and here only the Federal Republic is a realistic example — grows so disillusioned with its membership in the alliance that it moves toward neutralism, such a step becomes a particular "German" problem only through the simultaneous pursuit of national interests. Otherwise, it would not differ fundamentally from neutralist tendencies in the Netherlands or from France's withdrawal from the military organization of NATO in 1966; it would only be more disturbing because of West Germany's central position in NATO. However, when the pursuit of "national" interests also involves the pursuit of "European detente" interests, or vice versa, then the "German question" with all its negative connotations becomes again a problem.

Following are some examples of scenarios in which these two sets of goals interact in a way that would threaten the structure of the alliance system:

1. A surge of nationalist feelings in the Federal Republic, fueled by similar tendencies in the GDR, induces the West German government to abandon its loyalty to the Western alliance and to seek an accommodation with the Soviet Union in the pursuit of its national goals. After Moscow responds with a tempting offer of reunification, or even the prospect of unity in the future, Bonn withdraws from NATO.

2. After years of a hardening of Soviet policy toward the West and simultaneously a creeping disintegration of the WTO, severe economic difficulties confront the East German government with two alternatives. It can maintain its loyalty to the Soviet Union and jeopardize economic relations with the FRG, thus risking economic collapse and popular unrest, or it can denounce the Soviet policies and arrive at a separate accommodation with the West, particularly with the FRG. While the SED would still resist unification, it would move toward democratization and seek a quasi-neutral status between the blocs, similar to the "Austrian model" that Adenauer proposed for the GDR in the late 1950s.

3. In the Federal Republic, a left-leaning SPD forms a coalition government with the Greens. Under their joint program, the coalition partners prepare the withdrawal from NATO and the neutralization of the FRG. In order to maximize the pacifist effects of this move and to rally popular support behind its policies, the government proposes that the GDR undertake a similar step and subsequently forms a confederation with the FRG as a first step toward reunification.

Although none of these scenarios is likely to occur in the foreseeable future, it is in this context that most of the debate over the larger political implications of inter-German relations takes place. As we showed in the first part of this study, reunification is neither a realistic possibility nor a serious aspiration of either German state. Contrary to the impressions created by peace demonstrations, the majority of West Germans is still strongly committed to the Western alliance and would resist any neutralist tendencies. What is at stake is not the Federal Republic's membership in NATO but its attitudes and policies within the alliance. Finally, not even the most severe economic crisis would ever induce the East German government to abandon its alliance with the Soviet Union lest it jeopardize the strongest guarantee for its own existence. A scenario in which the GDR would withdraw from WTO in the pursuit of disarmament is so unrealistic that it is not even worth discussing.

What these scenarios show is that in popular political thought the danger of the "German question" is almost always based on the link between German nationalism and defection from the alliances. Hence, in order to evaluate the relevance of the "German question" and the impact of a German-German rapprochement on the alliance structure in Europe, one of the issues that will be examined in the following discussion on inter-German relations after the breakdown of detente is how the "German" and "European" interests of the two German states have interacted since 1979. The most fascinating question is whether the FRG and the GDR will ever want to collude against their alliances in any of these areas of interests.

NOTES

1.   Henry Kissinger, *White House Years* (Boston: Little, Brown, 1979), pp. 114-30.

2.   See Joseph Joffe, "European-American Relations: The Enduring Crisis," *Foreign Affairs* 59 (Spring 1981): 840; and Pierre Lellouche, "Europe and her Defense," *Foreign Affairs* 59 (Spring 1981): 820.

3.   For a good discussion of the intra-NATO crisis in 1980 see Philip Windsor, *Germany and the Western Alliance: Lesson from the 1980 Crises,* Adelphi Paper No. 170 (London: International Institute for Strategic Studies, 1981).

4.   Although Schmidt promised not to undercut the United States' trade embargo, he refused to participate in it. While U.S. trade with the Soviet Union declined from 1979 to 1980 from $3.6 billion to $900 million, West German trade rose from $3.66 billion to $4.4 billion in the same period. See Joffe, "European-American Relations," p. 841.

5.   The term "Finlandization" was coined by the German political scientist Richard Löwenthal in 1966; in 1978, U.S. national security advisor Brzezinski used "self-Finlandization" in reference to the FRG. Pierre Hassner defined it as the "constant need to adopt the most reassuring interpretation of Soviet behavior because one cannot face a more disquieting one or one cannot afford to take actions that would follow from

it." See Werner Link, "The Coordination of Detente Policy," in Edwin H. Fedder, *Defense Politics of the Atlantic Alliance* (New York: Praeger, 1980), pp. 92-4.

6.   See Egon Bahr, *Was wird aus den Deutschen? Fragen und Antworten* (Hamburg: Rowohlt, 1982), pp. 22-7; Günter Gaus, *Wo Deutschland liegt: Eine Ortbestimmung* (Hamburg: Hoffmann und Campe, 1983), pp. 285-90.; and Horst Ehmke, "Überlegungen zur Selbstbehauptung Europas: Ein Diskussionspapier," *Politik* 1 (January 1984).

7.   Peter Bender, *Das Ende des ideologischen Zeitalters: Die Europäisierung Europas* (Berlin: Severin und Siedler, 1981).

6 EUROPEAN DETENTE AND INTER–GERMAN RELATIONS: 1979–85

A GERMAN SPRING AND POLISH SUMMER

For the two German states, the second Cold War started by the super-powers in the wake of the invasion of Afghanistan had little resemblance to the first Cold War. Instead of spearheading their allies' political campaigns, the FRG and the GDR succeeded in continuing inter-German relations as if nothing had changed. In fact, both Schmidt and Honecker indicated their intentions to strengthen inter-German ties in order to help maintain detente in Europe. Honecker joined the Soviets in denouncing NATO's double-track decision, but his attacks against the FRG were much milder than Moscow's. And just as Schmidt openly criticized Carter's harsh reaction to Afghanistan, Honecker quietly communicated his displeasure about the Soviet invasion and its consequences to Moscow.[1]

Only two weeks after the invasion, the East German leader invited the West German envoy in East Berlin, Günter Gaus, to an extensive conversation in which they discussed the international situation. When Honecker asked Schmidt for a personal meeting, however, his Soviet allies intervened; an unofficial meeting between the two men in East Berlin had to be cancelled. Also, an official visit by Honecker to the FRG that was planned for February 27, 1980 was indefinitely postponed when the Soviets demanded stronger adherence by the GDR to their confrontational course. Yet Honecker announced the cancellation in such a low-key manner and confirmed so strongly his interest in a continuing thaw that the inter-German relationship was hardly damaged.[2]

A stream of prominent West German visitors to the spring fair in Leipzig in early April initiated a series of high-level exchanges between the officials of the two German states, which climaxed with the visit of Politbureau member Günter Mittag at the Hannover Fair on April 17. During this period, East and West German officials signed a new traffic treaty and opened negotiations on a number of large-scale economic projects. Bonn agreed to pay DM 2.4 billion for the electrification of five railway lines leading to Berlin and DM 2.1 billion for the construction of a soft coal power plant near Leipzig. The GDR would pay back these loans by supplying the FRG with electricity. In addition, Honecker offered a surprising concession: in contrast to the East German policy of severing the ties between West Berlin and the Federal Republic, he offered to link the city to the West German electricity net, thus making Berlin less dependent on East German energy supplies.

At Yugoslav leader Tito's funeral in Belgrad in early May 1980, Schmidt and Honecker finally met. In contrast to the stiff and cold atmosphere of their first and only encounter at the Helsinki conference in 1975, the talks were cordial and friendly. In the course of the preceding six years, Schmidt had changed his negative attitude toward Honecker and had developed some respect for the East German leader. Both men confirmed their common interest in insulating inter-German relations from the global crisis and promised to use their influence within the alliance to improve U.S.-Soviet relations. Honecker urged Schmidt to abstain from the Olympic boycott, while Schmidt suggested that Honecker intervene against the Soviet armament policy.[3] Honecker also encouraged the West German chancellor to go ahead with his planned meeting with Soviet leader Leonid Brezhnev in Moscow, suggesting that this trip would increase the leeway of the East Europeans in the detente process. But to Schmidt's disappointment, the SED leader failed to give any indication about possible Soviet concessions on INF negotiations.

At first, Schmidt postponed his visit to Moscow in order to consult with U.S. President Carter, who had not attended Tito's funeral and who was not enthusiastic about friendly talks with Soviet leaders during the Afghanistan crisis. Schmidt's position vis-à-vis the United States was strengthened when French president Giscard D'Estaing suddenly decided to meet with Brezhnev in Warsaw in late May. On July 30, Schmidt finally went to Moscow. Although the German chancellor told Brezhnev that he could not serve as a mediator between the blocs, he achieved an important success for East-West detente. He persuaded Brezhnev to agree to INF negotiations with the United States, which began in November 1981.[4]

On August 13, Schmidt announced that he would visit the GDR in September. Since East German Prime Minister Willy Stoph's visit to Kassel in 1970, no state visit had taken place between the two German states. In contrast to earlier plans, the Soviet leadership, which had rediscovered its interest in relations with Western Europe, did not oppose a German summit. Brezhnev had already indicated his approval for the meeting during Schmidt's visit in Moscow.

However, by the time of this announcement, the atmosphere between the two German states was already deteriorating. This became apparent when Honecker visited Brezhnev in his summer resort on the Crimea on August 1. Not only was Brezhnev disappointed that Schmidt had remained loyal to the United States by boycotting the Olympic games in Moscow, but he was even more disturbed by the unrest that had started in early August at the Lenin shipyard in Gdansk, Poland, which was rapidly spreading throughout the country. These events made the Soviets increasingly concerned over West German influence within the Eastern bloc. Two previous revolts in Poland had erupted a few days after Willy Brandt's visit to Warsaw in 1970 and shortly after the signing of the Helsinki Accords in 1975. At the time, the Soviets suspected that subversive Western influence had passed from the Federal Republic through the GDR into Poland. Isolating the GDR from the West was therefore seen as a crucial step toward a restoration of order in Poland. Hence, after his meeting with Brezhnev, Honecker no longer emphasized the positive aspects of inter-German relations, but stressed his demands for sovereign relations between the two German states.[5]

As the situation in Poland deteriorated, Soviet tolerance for the inter-German thaw rapidly declined as well. The strongest sign for this new attitude was the growing anti-West German rhetoric in the Soviet media. Already during the crackdown against internal dissidents in early 1980, when the Soviets banished Andrei Sakharov to Gorky and staged nine trials against dissidents within six weeks, Soviet newspapers had stepped up their attacks against the FRG, charging it with "revanchism" against the East European nations and criticizing West German support for the INF decision. That these attacks were aimed not only at Bonn but also at the "doves" in East Berlin became apparent with an article by two Soviet journalists, Vladimir Lomejko and Oleg Prudkov, about their experiences in the GDR, which was published in the literary magazine *Literaturnaya Gazeta*. It sharply attacked the habit of millions of East Germans of watching West German television: "The enemy enters the house at night and sits at the fireplace. And many let him willingly in."[6]

For a few months, East German officials seemed to resist these pressures. But as the strikes in Gdansk intensified, GDR officials became less cooperative and began to obstruct the planned Honecker-Schmidt summit. First the meeting was moved from the Baltic Sea resort of Dienhagen to Werbellin, north of Berlin. In mid-August, the East German media joined the Soviet propaganda campaign when an article in the East German party newspaper, *Neues Deutschland,* attacked the Federal Republic for initiating the NATO double-track decision and encouraging revanchist and fascist activities. After the East Germans cancelled Schmidt's planned visit to Rostock, a port on the Baltic Sea that was only a few miles away from the centers of the Polish strikes, under the pretext of a Cuban-German youth meeting, the West German chancellor regarded that as evidence that he was not welcome in the GDR. On August 22, he called Honecker to cancel his visit.

Schmidt's cancellation was also motivated by his reluctance to be in the GDR while Soviet, and possibly even East German, troops intervened in Poland. In light of U.S. suspicions about West German reliability, he did not want to take this risk. Some commentators in the United States and Western Europe had already charged the FRG with denying support to the Polish opposition in order to safeguard its interests in inter-German relations. A visit at that time, Schmidt feared, would have aroused fears of German separatism.[7]

There has been considerable debate over Honecker's personal reaction to the cancellation. At the time, the West German government assumed that he was actually relieved, but later some commentators argued that the cancellation had deeply offended Honecker and had contributed to his decision to change his policy toward the FRG.[8] Retrospectively, it is not clear whether Schmidt's visit could have prevented the following events. On September 9, 1980, the GDR announced an increase in the minimum currency exchange, the entrance fee for West German and West Berlin visitors, from a daily rate of DM 12 to DM 25 and abolished all exemptions for children and senior citizens. West German officials were aghast. The move not only broke an informal agreement that the countries had reached in the course of swing negotiations in 1974, but the currency to be exchanged for residents of West Berlin had been explicitly determined in official agreements that were attached to the Quadripartite Agreement on Berlin.[9]

Although East German officials justified the measure by citing the need to protect their currency from illegal speculation, the real motivation was obviously the crisis in Poland.[10] East Berlin had grown particularly nervous over the Polish situation after the government signed the accords of Gdansk, in which it yielded to practically all workers' demands and permitted the establishment of an autonomous trade union. The SED took the lead in the East European attacks against the Polish party. In order to protect itself against the "Polish bacillus," the GDR even reversed its 1972 decision to permit East Germans to cross the border to Poland without special permission or visa, which had been the first measure of this kind in Eastern Europe. It was not surprising that the GDR also desired to insulate itself from West German influence by reducing the flow of visitors.

Four days later, Honecker intensified his demarcation policy against the Federal Republic with his widely noted speech in Gera, in which he made the solution of all inter-German status problems the precondition for further progress in inter-German relations.[11] The West German government reacted with anger to these signals from East Berlin. Schmidt demanded that the GDR rescind the increase of the minimum exchange and refused to compensate West Germans for their increased expenses to keep the responsibility for this move with the East Germans. However, other than a freeze on all new economic projects, the government decided against economic sanctions. As discussed earlier, a cutback in inter-German trade would have destroyed the last functioning area in inter-German relations and would have hurt West German economic interests. It was widely believed that the SED would not yield in exchange for economic incentives; its move had been motivated not by pecuniary interests, but by vital political concerns. As the East Germans reached their goal of severely reducing the number of West German visits to the GDR, inter-German relations dropped to their lowest point since the signing of the Basic Treaty.

The most interesting question to be asked is whether the sudden termination of the inter-German thaw was Moscow's doing or an autonomous East German decision. For many observers, the reversal supported the notion that inter-German relations could only flourish with Moscow's explicit consent and therefore only in times of friendly relations between the United States and the Soviet Union. As FDP member of the *Bundestag* Hans-Günter Hoppe said after the increase of the minimum currency exchange: "This measure was no autonomous decision by the GDR, but a contribution to the demarcation of the whole bloc that was demanded by Moscow."[12]

A closer look at the chain of events shows that the situation was more complex. In many respects, the intervention of the Soviets was obvious. So long as Moscow approved, albeit grudgingly, the inter-German thaw until the summer, East German officials showed eagerness to cooperate with the FRG. But immediately after Honecker's meeting with Brezhnev on the Crimea, the East German attitude underwent a radical transformation that climaxed with the speech in Gera. The conclusion that Moscow had given new instructions to its German client was supported by a *Pravda* editorial that asserted, "Relations between the GDR and the FRG cannot be governed by nonexisting inner-German interests, but represent a coordinated course of the Warsaw Pact."

However, Poland was as much a problem for the SED as it was for the Kremlin, and perhaps more so. East German officials feared spillovers from the Polish strikes, particularly in the regions of the Baltic Sea, as it had happened during similar strikes in 1970. These fears never materialized, but the concessions made by the Polish party and the subsequent rise of Solidarity also constituted a major threat to the SED. A victory of liberal forces in Poland would have surrounded the GDR with two challenges to its rule: the destabilizing attraction of the FRG in the West, and a reformed communist system in the East. The democratization of Poland, East Germans feared, would geographically cut off the GDR from its Soviet protectors and threaten the SED's monopoly of power. Also, the party saw its balancing act of allowing limited contacts with the Federal Republic while maintaining an orthodox socialist regime at home imperiled by turmoil in Poland. This concern also explains the restriction of privileges that the regime had previously granted the Protestant churches and a crackdown on contacts between East and West German artists in the fall of 1980.[13]

In the early days of the strike, Honecker still supported an "administrative solution" for Poland — a Soviet invasion into Poland, just as Ulbricht had done during the Prague Spring in 1968. But when he began to realize that the strikes would remain limited to Poland and not spill over to his own state, he apparently changed his mind. In his meeting with Brezhnev on the Crimea, Honecker is said to have strongly discouraged military intervention, warning that such a step could destroy the last remnants of detente and poison the atmosphere in East-West relations for years. Signals coming from Bonn reinforced this attitude.

An East German participation in an invasion of Poland, so Schmidt warned in a letter to Honecker, would make continuation of inter-German relations almost impossible.[14]

Caught between its concern for internal stability and its interest in protecting the benefits of detente and inter-German relations, the GDR carefully steered a middle course. Honecker discouraged a Soviet invasion, but contributed to the overall Soviet attempts to stabilize the East through his own demarcation policy with the FRG. This course was reflected in Honecker's decisions of September 1980. By sending a strong signal to Bonn, Honecker satisfied the hardliners within his own party and in Moscow, but he did not preclude future cooperation with the FRG. Thus the increase of the currency exchange and the speech in Gera constituted a compromise between conflicting factions within the SED, between the GDR's need of alliance unity and the economic dependence on detente with the West, and between pressures from Moscow and the desire of the East German population to increase relations with the Federal Republic.

THE ROAD TO WERBELLIN

As this analysis suggests, the inter-German chill lasted only through the fall. When the WTO meeting on December 5 in Moscow, in which plans for intervention in Poland were apparently cancelled, signaled an end to the state of emergency in the Eastern bloc, Honecker immediately began to make new overtures to Bonn. In a period of a few weeks, the newly appointed West German envoy Klaus Bölling, a close Schmidt confidant, was invited to two meetings with Honecker. In an interview with the English publisher Robert Maxwell in mid-February, the East German leader emphasized the positive contribution that inter-German ties had made to detente and lamented the fact that "these relations are presently not as good as they could be." Two days later, he made the sensational speech in which he raised the prospect of German reunification under socialism. In his keynote address at the Tenth Party Congress in April, the SED leader emphasized the dependence of inter-German relations on the state of relations between United States and Soviet Union, but he also mentioned the positive influence that inter-German relations could exert in the international sphere.[15]

Although Honecker still rejected any reduction of the minimum currency exchange and insisted on the four demands of Gera as a condition for further progress, in early summer East and West German officials resumed the preparations for a visit by Schmidt to the GDR. Still fearing a spill over from Poland, Honecker requested a more modest and inconspicuous meeting than had been planned in 1980. That these moves enjoyed Moscow's support became apparent after Honecker's annual visit to Brezhnev's summer cottage on the Crimea in August. The two leaders published a joint statement in which they emphasized that present world tensions made "broad international exchanges as well as regular political contacts between leaders of countries with differing social systems" both valuable and necessary. Surprisingly, the statements did not include the familiar attacks against West German revanchism and militarism.[16]

The renewed inter-German thaw can be explained by a number of facts. The East German leadership had realized that the biggest threat to stability in the GDR was not Solidarity, which had little attraction for the GDR population, but its own internal economic situation. Although the East German economy had grown by a brisk 4.1 percent in 1980, the GDR needed continuing West German economic support to sustain this performance in the face of the worldwide recession. Particularly important was the renewal of a swing agreement, which was bound to expire at the end of 1981. Without a new agreement, the interest-free loan would have fallen from a high of DM 850 million to a base level of DM 200 million.[17]

The Soviet Union had also reduced its emphasis on intra-bloc solidarity as it came to understand that the threat of the "Polish disease" to other East European countries was smaller than expected, and would disappear once the movement had been crushed. East German workers especially strongly resented the developments in their neighboring countries and the economic sacrifices they had to make in order to keep the Polish economy afloat. But the most obvious reason for the change in tone in East Berlin was the beginning debate over NATO's double-track decision on the INF. As the Soviets observed the growing resistance to this decision in Western Europe, the rise of the peace movement in the summer of 1981, and a trans-Atlantic rift heightened by Reagan's election as U.S. president, they began to focus their strategy on a propanganda war directed at the Western European public opinion. Since the FRG played a central part in this strategy, it was logical for Moscow to use inter-German relations as a lever on West German policies.

The new role was apparently assigned to inter-German relations at Honecker's meeting with Brezhnev in August 1981. Soon afterwards,

East German officials suggested ways of intensifying inter-German ties through high-level consultations and the conclusion of a treaty on economic cooperation. These offers were explicitly linked, however, to the West German renunciation of the deployment of new U.S. missiles in Europe.

Due to these stipulations, Schmidt's reaction was far from enthusiastic. In a letter to Honecker on July 24, he confirmed his interest in increased cooperation between the two German states, but rejected East German attempts to influence the West German deployment decision: "The building of trust is necessary to secure peace, but it is only possible if every state can decide itself over its internal affairs," he wrote. Schmidt also warned Honecker not to press Moscow toward a tougher policy against Poland.[18]

West German officials were suspicious about the sudden shift of the SED's emphasis away from the sovereign recognition by the FRG to questions of disarmament. Although disarmament had always had a high priority in communist propaganda, the sudden preoccupation with arms control issues was startling. On the surface, it only seemed logical that the two front-line countries of the alliances would include military questions in their bilateral negotiations. Even Article 7 of the Basic Treaty called for consultations on peace and disarmament. But because of the structure of the two military blocs, arms control had never been an area to which inter-German relations could make substantial contributions. As discussed earlier, nuclear issues were decided by the leading powers, and decisions concerning conventional forces were the multilateral responsibility of the two alliances and could not be the subject of bilateral negotiations. While the West German government could exert some influence on defense matters and arms control, the GDR always adopted Soviet positions and repeated almost verbatim their arguments in international forums. Even when there arose an opportunity for German-German cooperation on arms control, it was never used effectively. On disarmament resolutions in the U.N. General Assembly, the two German states had voted only 3 out of 24 times on the same side. And neither in the MBFR negotiations in Vienna nor in the CSCE talks in Belgrad or Madrid did the FRG and the GDR ever arrive at a common position that diverged from that of their allies.[19]

West German officials also perceived the East German emphasis on disarmament as a way of diverting attention from more important humanitarian issues, such as the minimum currency exchange and travel restrictions for East Germans. Still, during the low point in inter-German relations in early 1981, the Schmidt government agreed to German-German arms control consultations in order to resume some kind of contact with the other side. On July 3, 1981, the arms control expert of the West German government, Friedrich Ruth, met with the East German disarmament expert, Ernst Krabbatsch, in East Berlin. Several more meetings of this kind took place in the following months, culminating in a conversation between Egon Bahr, then chairman of the disarmament committee in the *Bundestag*, and Honecker. None of these talks yielded any concrete results, but they improved the atmosphere between the two German states. Bonn valued the meetings as the potential beginning of a new thaw, and for the East Germans, it gave them an opportunity to demonstrate the usefulness to the Soviet Union of inter-German relations.[20]

For Schmidt, talks of this kind served an additional purpose. They showed his commitment to the pursuit of arms control talks to the left wing within his own party and helped him to diffuse the growing opposition against the INF deployment. The INF debate constituted perhaps the most difficult problem that Schmidt ever faced during his years in office because it threatened to thwart his efforts to maintain a balance between his loyalty to the West while continuing detente with the East. After the new *Ostpolitik* had permitted a policy in which these two goals could be pursued simultaneously,[21] Bonn was again forced into a position of having to choose between the East and West. Schmidt realized that the FRG could escape this dilemma only through the cooperation of the superpowers on the issue of INF negotiations. He began to lobby for these talks in both Washington and Moscow.

In a letter to Reagan in the spring of 1981, Schmidt warned that he would be unable to keep his commitment to deploy the proposed missiles unless the United States started serious negotiations on INF by the end of the year. Despite opposition within his own administration, Reagan reacted positively. At the annual summit of the Western industrial powers in May, the U. S. president declared that he was now ready to negotiate with the Soviets over the INF. Then, in a widely publicized speech on November 18, Reagan proposed his "zero-zero option," which called for the dismantling of all Soviet SS-20 missiles in exchange for the cancellation of NATO's INF deployment. Although the proposal was highly unrealistic, its simplicity and pacifistic tone appealed to the West Germans, who had originally conceived of a similar option.[22]

A few days later, Brezhnev visited Bonn and presented his own INF proposals, which included a moratorium on medium-range missiles and the postponement of the NATO deployment beyond 1983, even if the talks in Geneva yielded no agreement. Although most NATO officials regarded Brezhnev's offer as unacceptable since it would have required the cancellation of NATO's deployment plans without equivalent Soviet concessions, it created sufficient good will in the FRG to weaken West German support for the double-track decision.[23]

Given the prominence the INF issue enjoyed both in the East and West, it was not surprising that it also dominated the German summit in Werbellin, just north of Berlin, from December 11 to December 13, 1981. Honecker essentially repeated Brezhnev's proposals and added further suggestions for a complete ban on nuclear weapons and a breakthrough at the lagging MBFR talks in Vienna. Schmidt urged the East German leader to exert some pressure on Moscow to compromise more strongly on the INF issue. "We are involved," he told Honecker, "and it is my urgent desire that you do the same. We both have signed the nuclear non-proliferation treaty. The world powers have an obligation towards us. We must exert pressure on them." In their final speeches, both statesmen repeated their concern about nuclear missiles in Europe — however, each meaning primarily the missiles on the other side.[24]

Although Honecker would have preferred to limit the Werbellin summit to disarmament issues, on Schmidt's insistence the two leaders achieved some progress in practical inter-German issues. The final communiqué, which was published uncensored in *Neues Deutschland,* called for good-faith efforts in all important questions in the inter-German relationship, including controversial issues like "family reunification, the lessening of hardships, and other humanitarian questions," and even mentioned differences over "the situation in Afghanistan" and the "raising of the minimum currency exchange." Thus Honecker implicitly abandoned his position to make the fulfillment of his demands at Gera a condition of further progress in inter-German relations.[25]

Ultimately, Honecker gained more from the meeting than Schmidt. Although it facilitated the chancellor's balancing act between the alliance, relations with the East and his leftist critics at home, he did not gain any major concessions from the GDR, in particular on the central issue of the minimum currency exchange. The subsequent negotiations on the swing showed that in contrast to the similar situation in 1974, not even economic levers could induce the GDR to abandon a policy that had become a prestige question. In June 1982, the swing was extended for three more years with a limit of DM 600 million although East Berlin made only minor humanitarian concessions.[26] For Honecker, the official summit meeting with one of the world's most respected statesmen and the agenda dominated by international issues vastly increased his reputation abroad and at home. It helped him to reconcile the conflicting goals of loyalty to the Soviet Union and progress in inter-German relations for the sake of the economy and the popular morale in the GDR.

Werbellin marked the end of the inter-German chill that had set in after the Polish crisis and the beginning of a gradual improvement in the relations that lasted until the eventful summer of 1984. According to the description by the then-West German envoy Bölling, the meeting was characterized by both men's concerns over the tense international situation and their frustration over their limited influence on the super-powers. This feeling of common experience, which reflected the popular notion of a German-German "community of fate," undoubtedly influenced Schmidt's decision not to interrupt his visit when Polish leader Wojciech Jaruszelski declared martial law on December 13. Intended as a gesture to emphasize the special ties between the two German states in the face of outside turmoil, it aroused severe criticism in Bonn and in other Western countries.[27]

THE IMPACT OF POLAND

The Polish crackdown was ironically in the interest of both German states. Although the suppression of Solidarity was perceived as a violation of human rights and the spirit of detente by many West Germans, it lowered Soviet anxieties over Western influence in the East and permitted better relations between the FRG and Eastern Europe. It also confirmed the political status quo on the continent, the prerequisite for any detente in Europe. For the GDR, just as for most of Eastern Europe, martial law was a major relief. Though in the course of 1981 it had become clear that Solidarity was a much smaller threat to the other East European regimes than was initially believed, only the eradication of the movement could safeguard the stability of the bloc. The crackdown did not constitute a defeat for the reformist forces in the alliance. On the contrary, Solidarity's more radical demands had jeopardized the success of evolutionary change in other East European countries. Its defeat allowed reformers, particularly the Hungarian leadership, to proceed with their program without arousing Moscow's fears of another Poland. The fact that Poland was able to "solve" its crisis without Soviet intervention actually strengthened the position of other East European governments *vis-à-vis* the Soviets.

It was Moscow's decision not to intervene directly that had perhaps the most profound impact on the future of the Eastern bloc. Twelve years earlier, Moscow had sent its tanks to crush a Czech reform movement that represented less of a challenge to the communist system than Solidarity did. Although the Prague Spring cast doubt on the reliability of the Czech party, the dominant role of the Communist party itself, the pillar of any communist system, was never called into question. In contrast, in 1980 and 1981 not only was the reliability of the Polish party cast into doubt, but the party was in severe danger of losing control over the country and society. Still, the Soviets refrained from sending their own troops, and instead solved the crisis with the help of the national army, which subsequently replaced the party as the center of power.

This decision was not part of a well-planned strategy in Soviet policy towards Eastern Europe. According to some reports, in early December 1980 the Politbureau fell only one vote short of deciding in favor of an invasion.[28] But the fact that Moscow ultimately rejected the option illustrates the new restraints that a decade of detente had imposed on Soviet foreign policy. At the time of the Polish crisis, the Soviet Union was involved in a frustrating war in Afghanistan and was facing U.S. economic sanctions and a military buildup. It participated in two international conferences, the CSCE review conference in Madrid and the INF talks in Geneva, and would have risked losing all positive results of these meetings by an invasion. Moscow was bent on continuing detente with Western Europe for the purpose of Western credit and technology and wanted to influence its public opinion to prevent the INF deployment.[29] The Soviets had reason to believe that the timid Western response after the invasion of Czechoslovakia could not be expected this time. In contrast to the 1968 campaign, a military crackdown in Poland was bound to lead to a prolonged civil war with a well-organized and spirited indigenous population. In times when the Eastern bloc increasingly depended on relations with the West to keep its economies afloat, an invasion would have been a foolish enterprise.

Even more important than the Soviet's concern for Western public opinion were intra-bloc considerations. The Polish crisis was primarily a consequence of misguided economic policies. To prevent such a development in the future, the communist leaders had to improve the economic performance of their countries — a goal that could only be achieved in cooperation with the population of Eastern Europe. A repetition of the Czech solution, the "graveyard peace" that has been paralyzing that country for more than a decade, was no longer appropriate. For the sake of Soviet relations with Western Europe, Eastern Europe, and possibly even Poland, martial law was by far the more skillful and adroit measure than a military invasion. It also had its costs, however. In contrast to 1956 in Hungary and 1968 in the CSSR, Moscow had little control over the process of normalization. Instead, it had to rely on a regime with its own agenda, an agenda that included more tolerance toward the political opposition and the Catholic Church than the Soviets preferred.[30]

Moscow had to accept similar developments in other East European countries. The Polish crisis confirmed the need of East European governments to maintain the "social contract" with their populations, to put more emphasis on the performance of the economy and to tolerate a limited degree of political pluralism. Hungary's experiments in decentralization and a partial free market system constituted the most vigorous pursuit of this strategy. That these reforms enjoyed the support of a powerful faction in the Kremlin became apparent when Yuri Andropov succeeded Brezhnev as general secretary of the Soviet Communist Party in November 1982. In his drive for limited economic reform, Andropov repeatedly suggested during his short tenure that the Soviet Union emulate some of the economic practices of Hungary and Bulgaria, particularly in agriculture.[31]

The country that profited most from the lessons of the Polish crisis was the GDR. Because of East Germany's strategically central role in the WTO, the Soviet leaders realized that similar signs of instability in the GDR would constitute a critical threat to the whole alliance. Thus the Soviets gave the SED the freedom to take appropriate measures in the interest of domestic stability, as long as the dominance of the Communist party and the loyalty to the WTO were not called into question.[32] In the opinion of the moderate wing of the SED, this task could be best achieved through closer relations with the Federal Republic. Inter-German relations not only funneled large financial resources into the country and sustained its economic growth, but the regime's popularity came to depend to a large degree on the state of relations with the FRG. Many East Germans perceived Honecker as the man who had given them West German television, West German visitors, West German consumer goods, and at least a psychological escape from the seclusion of the GDR. Not surprisingly, it was the East German population that suffered

most under the new demarcation policy of 1980 and the decline of West German visitors.

Equally important was the changed status of the GDR within the Eastern alliance. As the largest and economically most powerful country in Eastern Europe, Poland had been Moscow's main ally before 1980. The rise of Solidarity changed this situation. Not only had Poland become politically unstable and unreliable, but the frequent strikes in 1980 and 1981, the effect of wasteful investment projects, and the lack of cooperation by the population after the declaration of martial law between 1980 and 1983 almost destroyed the Polish economy. Only large-scale subsidies by the Soviet Union and other East European countries, particularly the GDR, kept Poland from going bankrupt. Thus in the wake of the Polish crisis, the GDR, which had always occupied a unique position in the Eastern alliance, became Moscow's principal ally. This became apparent at the CPSU congress in 1981 in Moscow, when Honecker was the first East European party leader to speak, an honor that had traditionally been reserved for the Polish party chief. Also, the prestigious role of launching disarmament proposals for the Western audience was subsequently moved from Warsaw to East Berlin.[33] In the economic division of labor within the CMEA, the GDR was given the central task of supplying investment goods and machinery. As the United States tightened the restrictions on high technology exports to Eastern Europe, East Germany's strong exposure in foreign trade and its special trade relations with the FRG made it Moscow's main window to Western technology.

The GDR also grew increasingly important as a political aide, since it was the only East European country that combined orthodox communist ideology and strict loyalty to the WTO with active relations with the West. After having served as Moscow's main aide in Soviet policies toward the Third World, including military adventures, in the late 1970s, the GDR also assumed the role of an envoy for the Eastern bloc in the West. The strengthened East German position *vis-à-vis* the Soviet Union became apparent in early 1983 when Honecker asked Andropov to dismiss the Soviet ambassador to the GDR, Pjotr Abrassimov, who had influenced East German policies in a heavy-handed manner for almost two decades. The Soviet leader, who wanted to maintain friendly ties with Honecker, almost immediately recalled Abrassimov and replaced him with a far more malleable and accommodating diplomat.[34]

The rising status of the GDR in the Eastern alliance was accompanied by a growing reputation in the Western world. As described before, the

GDR was isolated internationally until the Basic Treaty and did not establish diplomatic relations with most countries in the world before 1974. The Helsinki conference in 1975 was the first major international event in which the GDR took part. Still, for a few more years it did not participate in the exchange of high-level visits of political leaders between East and West. The GDR first sought closer relations with neutral countries like Austria and Sweden. In March 1978, Austria's chancellor Bruno Kreisky was the first Western head of government to visit East Berlin, and also Honecker's first trip abroad was to Austria. But soon after his meeting with Schmidt in December 1981, Honecker launched an impressive diplomatic offensive to establish closer relations with other Western states. His personal diplomacy reached its climax in early 1984, when a series of politicians from NATO countries visited East Berlin. This policy not only enhanced Honecker's popularity among his own people and increased his room for maneuver with the Soviet Union, but also served concrete economic interests.

Honecker's intensified relations with the West had a profound impact on inter-German relations. Since the beginning of *Ostpolitik,* the inter-German relationship had suffered under a fundamental asymmetry. While the Federal Republic enjoyed considerable autonomy in its foreign policy, the GDR was highly dependent on the Soviet Union. And while the FRG was regarded as a formidable opponent and an important partner by the Soviets, the GDR played hardly any role in U.S. foreign policy.[35] Many of the central issues in inter-German relations were negotiated between Moscow and Bonn, while the GDR was relegated to the humiliating status of a passive observer. Egon Bahr, in particular, emphasized the Soviet role in the German-German relationship as he grew increasingly frustrated with Honecker's limited room for maneuver.[36] As the GDR assumed a more independent voice for its foreign policy after the invasion of Afghanistan and the Polish crisis, the focus of West German *Ostpolitik* also shifted. Moscow still exerted considerable influence on East Berlin's foreign policy and maintained *de facto* veto power over all aspects of inter-German relations, but the level of cooperation and the atmosphere between the two German states was now determined as much in East Berlin as in Moscow. And as the East Germans began to develop a keener interest in inter-German relations, dealing with Honecker often yielded better results than negotiations with the Soviets.

This development even led to some movement in U.S.-East German relations, the most underdeveloped aspect of East German foreign policy. U.S. policy has always differentiated between the countries in Eastern

Europe. In the late 1960s, Zbigniew Brzezinski was the first one to suggest that the U.S. should encourage and reward any signs of independence from the Soviets among East Europeans,[37] a policy that was rediscovered in a very undiplomatic manner by Vice President George Bush in a speech in Vienna after his visit to Eastern Europe in 1982.[38] Due to their excessive loyalty to the Soviet Union and their involvement in military adventures in the Third World, the GDR was always put in the category of "bad" East European countries, which also included Bulgaria and the CSSR, and was never granted economic benefits like the most favored nations (MFN) status. Relations with East Berlin were left to the West German allies.

Only in the 1980s, after the GDR began to demonstrate more assertiveness *vis-à-vis* Moscow, did the U.S. State Department begin to see the GDR as an important actor outside the framework of inter-German relations and became interested in establishing contacts to East Berlin that were independent of Bonn's *Ostpolitik*. Yet a number of unresolved problems have hindered this rapprochement. The United States still claims compensation for U.S. property that was seized on the current East German territory in 1945, and U.S. Jewish organizations have opposed any economic concessions to East Berlin because of the GDR's refusal to pay compensation to victims of the Holocaust. Also, in accordance with the Jackson-Vanik Amendment, Congress refuses to grant MFN status until the GDR relaxes its restrictive emigration policies. Recently U.S. officials have proposed an agreement in which the U.S. would lower duties for specific East German goods while the additional East German revenues would be used to settle the U.S. claims. So far, the East Germans have rejected these and similar proposals.[39]

West German officials have been divided over these signs of East German independence. On the one hand, they hope that a more autonomous East German foreign policy could help insulate inter-German relations during periods of U.S.-Soviet tensions. On the other hand, they believe they may derive certain benefits from their dominating position in the inter-German relationship. As long as the GDR depends on Bonn as her only access to the West, it would be more willing to make concessions in practical and humanitarian issues, West German officials have sometimes argued. However, this position is difficult to defend. In light of our earlier analysis, it is more plausible that a stronger integration of the GDR into the international system will strengthen the self-esteem and the legitimacy of its leadership and thus facilitate an inter-German rapprochement.

THE INF DEBATE

In the course of 1982, the rift in NATO seemed to widen even further. The Reagan administration clashed with most West European governments over the correct response to the declaration of martial law in Poland as Western Europe refused to join U.S. sanctions against Poland and the USSR. Many West European leaders were reluctant to criticize the Jaruszelski regime, and refused to abandon the construction of a gas pipeline from the Soviet Union to Western Europe with European loans and technology. The most divisive issue remained the debate over the INF deployment and the associated rise of the European peace movements.

Most disturbing was the situation in the FRG, the country that would have to bear the brunt of the missile deployment. In 1981 and 1982, more than 3.5 million West Germans, including a number of the country's leading intellectuals, signed the Krefeld Appeal that called for the banning of both U.S. and Soviet nuclear missiles in Europe. In October 1981, 300,000 people protested in the first of a number of large West German antimissile demonstrations. Opinion polls showed that a majority of West Germans opposed the deployment of new U.S. missiles, even in the event that the negotiations in Geneva failed. The new Green party, which advocated unilateral disarmament and West German withdrawal from NATO, scored impressive electoral successes in state elections and threatened to replace the FDP as the country's third largest party. And Schmidt, whose 1977 speech had initiated the double-track decision, was gradually abandoned by his own party. Only with tactical maneuvering could he prevent the SPD from adopting an antideployment resolution at its party congress in April 1982.[40]

This critical situation was aggravated by the intransigent negotiation strategies of both the United States and the Soviet Union. While the United States refused to consider any alternative to the zero-zero option, the Soviets rejected all proposals that included the deployment of *any* new U.S. missiles. West German officials, particularly Friedrich Ruth, constantly pressured the Reagan administration toward adopting a more flexible position at the talks. These efforts yielded few results. When the Reagan administration rejected the "walk in the woods" proposal that the U.S. negotiator Paul Nitze had worked out with his Soviet counterpart Yuli Kvitzinsky in informal talks in July 1982, the West German government was not even consulted about the existence of the plan. After the Kohl government learned about this proposal in the following year, it regarded it as an acceptable compromise and attempted unsuccessfully to bring it back to the negotiating table.

The West German position *vis-à-vis* the Reagan administration was weakened by the widespread belief in the West that the peace movements were engineered by the Soviet Union. The extent of Soviet influence on the West European peace movements has never become completely clear. U.S. officials and conservative Europeans repeatedly asserted that the peace demonstrations were staged by communist organizations such as the World Peace Council and the West German Communist Party. These accusations, which often smacked of McCarthyist rhetoric, failed to take into account the genuine fear and aversion against the U.S. missiles in large segments of the population. It also failed to see that most peace protesters were concerned about the security interests of the West and had rational grounds to believe that the INF deployment would make both Eastern and Western Europe less secure. Soviet support for the peace movement only showed that East and West Europeans had certain common interests when it came to security and survival.

Yet the Soviet interest in the peace movement was indisputable. At the beginning of the INF debate, the Soviet Foreign Ministry created the new Department for International Information which was headed by two of the most prominent Soviet experts on the FRG, Leonid Zamyatin and Velantin Falin. These and other officials used every chance to voice their views in the West German press.[41] The main test for the ability of the Soviets to influence West German policies, and for the West German INF policy in general, came with the West German parliamentary elections in March 1983. In the previous fall, the SPD/FDP coalition had fallen apart and Schmidt was ousted from office. Under their new, more leftist leadership, many Social Democrats stepped up their opposition to the INF deployment. Thus the elections in March turned into a vote over the missiles and were anxiously monitored by the rest of the world. In contrast to the Reagan administration, which tried to disassociate itself from the campaign, the Soviets made several blatant attempts to aid the SPD. This tactic backfired, as heavy-handed Soviet interference actually aggravated the defeat of the Social Democrats.

The Soviets failed in their campaign to prevent the INF deployment because they had misread West German public opinion. Just like many Americans, the Kremlin leaders overestimated the intensity of antinuclear and anti-American sentiments in West Germany. They observed hundreds of thousands of people protesting on the streets and assumed that this represented the majority of Germans. They did not see the hundreds of thousands of people who strongly supported the double-track decision nor the millions of people who, though against new missiles, never took a strong stand on the issue and ultimately favored Kohl's policy regarding the deployment.

The main reason for the wide-spread silent support for the INF deployment was the nature of the debate. The main issue of the INF was not military doctrine. Few people knew about the esoteric questions concerning the strength of NATO's deterrence, the fear of decoupling, and the need for escalation dominance to pursue a "flexible response to a Soviet attack." Since its conception in Schmidt's 1977 speech, the INF debate had been a political fight over the unity of the Western alliance. Proponents defended it primarily as a necessary symbol for NATO's unity, while most opponents demonstrated an anti-American and anti-NATO attitude. The Soviet aim was not only to prevent the deployment of the missiles, but also to sever the ties between the United States and Western Europe. The fight in the streets and in the Budestag ultimately turned into a struggle over West Germany's future in the alliance. And on this question, the majority of West Germans were firmly on the side of the West.

Instead of detaching West Germany from NATO, the Soviet strategy had two very different and unintended effects: it contributed to the new surge of nationalism both in East and West Germany, and it introduced a new quality into the inter-German relationship. For the Soviet strategy to influence West German public opinion, the unique characteristics of the German-German relations represented the most effective instrument. Thus Moscow did not hesitate to play the "German card": it encouraged closer relations between the GDR and the FRG and even suggested that this relationship could ultimately result in confederation between the two German states if the FRG rejected the missiles.[42] But as the GDR assumed the central role in the new Soviet approach toward the "German question," this strategy unleashed forces in both German states that soon came to jeopardize Moscow's control over the GDR.

When the East German government intensified its offensive against the INF deployment in 1982, it added a strong national component to its peace propaganda. The two German states, Honecker argued, had a special responsibility for maintaining peace in Europe and should avoid becoming pawns in the hands of belligerent allies, such as the Reagan administration. The saying, "never again must a war start from German soil," became the standard phrase in almost every address that Honecker made on international issues. In his new year's article in January 1983,

Honecker tied the disarmament issue to progress in inter-German relations: "We proceed from the assumption that both German states are obliged to a special degree to make constructive contributions to peace and security. Corresponding good-neighborly relations between the GDR and the FRG serve the transformation of Europe from a continent of tensions and wars to an area of peaceful cooperation to the benefit of all parties involved."[43]

The intensification of inter-German relations in this period must be seen in connection with these joint Soviet and East German aims. It is not clear to what extent the prevention of the INF deployment was a genuine concern for Honecker or if it was primarily his contribution to the Soviet propaganda campaign. On one hand, one can note that the NATO deployment did not add a military threat against the GDR. The main difference between the existing Pershing I and the new Pershing II missiles was the range: while the Pershing I could only hit East German territory, the new missiles could reach the Soviet Union.[44] On the other hand, the GDR undoubtedly shared many security interests with the Soviets and did not want to see a change in the military balance. It also had reason to fear that the Soviets would demand a severe restriction on inter-German relations after the INF deployment. Honecker expressed this view in his remark to Schmidt in Werbellin: "Good-neighborly relations between the GDR and the FRG cannot prosper in the shadow of new American missiles." Although this linkage between two disconnected issues was widely perceived as arbitrary, most West Germans expected a rapid deterioration in inter-German relations once the deployment was scheduled to begin.[45]

East German support for the West German peace movement, however, had some unintended effects in the GDR. Outside of the official peace movement, which staged massive demonstrations in support of the Soviet and East German official positions, an unofficial peace movement came into being in the GDR and steadily gained popular support. The attraction of this movement, which operated primarily under the auspices of the Protestant church, was two-fold. As the church was the only major institution that enjoyed a certain degree of autonomy in the GDR, it allowed disillusioned young people to find a niche in society that was not dominated by the party apparatus. And because the Protestant church had found a *modus vivendi* with the regime, this involvement did not require outright opposition to the communist system.[46]

The church had also traditionally been in opposition to the growing militarization of East German society. The rise of the peace movement in the West and the intensive peace propaganda of the GDR government fueled the pacifist sentiments in the East German population. Since an involvement with peace activities was in tune with the proclaimed ideals of SED, the autonomous peace movement allowed a growing number of people to develop independent ideas and express their dissatisfaction with the system without challenging the communist ideology itself. With the biblical proverb "swords into ploughshares" as their slogan, East Germans began to stage spontaneous peace demonstrations in which they protested against nuclear missiles in East and West, demanded unilateral disarmament and the demilitarization of society. In February 1982, 5,000 people gathered in Dresden; in June, 3,000 participated in a protest rally in East Berlin; and a few days later 3,500 followed that example in Potsdam.

The SED leadership was caught in a severe dilemma. On one hand, it loathed any spontaneous political activities, feared a repetition of the events in Poland and did not want East Germans to criticize the defense policies of their Soviet ally. On the other hand, a crackdown against the peace activists would have destroyed the credibility of the GDR's commitment to peace and would have undercut its campaign against NATO's missile deployment. At first, the government wavered. While it tolerated some peace marches, it dissolved them with force at other times and even prosecuted people who were only wearing the "swords into ploughshares" signs.

But the nervousness of the SED grew when West German peace activists began to establish contacts with their Eastern counterparts. Encouraged by the apparent similarities in the goals of the East and West German organizations, some activists developed the notion that an all-German peace movement could not only reduce the chances of war, but also surmount the division of Germany. When the East German government realized that it contributed to this development itself through its flirtation with the West German peace movement, it soon reversed its course. An all-German movement not only challenged Eastern defense policies, but called into question the GDR's very existence. In its opposition to the all-German peace movement, the SED was joined by many observers in Western and Eastern Europe who feared the explosive force of a combination between German nationalism and pacifism that is described in an earlier chapter.

The SED decided on its own double-track policy: The indigenous peace movement was allowed to carry on its activities but was put under increasingly strict surveillance. Meanwhile, all contacts with West

German peace activists were prohibited. This policy led to some embarrassing situations, though. In October 1983, Honecker met with Petra Kelly and Gert Bastian, two leading representatives of the West German Green party. Although Kelly and Bastian demanded unilateral disarmament measures and the release of imprisoned peace activists, Honecker reacted positively throughout the meeting.[47] But when a week later, members of the Green party staged a joint rally with East German activists, the GDR broke all relations with the Greens and even kept party members from crossing the border.

Ultimately, it seems that observers in East and West overestimated the significance of this phenomenon. Few exponents of the peace movements in the FRG and GDR were driven by national aspirations. Instead, they were looking for allies in their struggle and found them across the inter-German border. Even within the Green party, the "all-Germans" were in a constant struggle with other members who perceived the interest in national unity as dangerous and destabilizing.[48]

The dilemma lessened after the *Bundestag* elections in March 1983. As the Soviets realized that the peace movement would not be able to prevent the INF deployment, they gradually abandoned their efforts to influence West German public opinion and shifted their attention toward the arms control talks in Geneva. This shift was welcomed by the East German leadership, for it permitted a crackdown on the indigenous peace movement without sacrificing the political interests of the alliance.[49] The crackdown proved effective, and after the emigration wave in early 1984, during which many of the leading peace activists left the country, the movement soon returned to obscurity.

A CHANGE IN BONN

The demise of the SPD/FDP coalition in the fall of 1982 after 13 years in power presented the GDR with completely new circumstances in its relations with the FRG. The FDP deserted the coalition government over severe disagreements about economic policy and fiscal austerity and joined forces with the conservative opposition. On October 1, Helmut Schmidt was ousted by a no-confidence vote in the *Bundestag* and Helmut Kohl, the leader of the CDU, became the new chancellor of a coalition government of CDU/CSU and FDP.

The East German leadership had reason to be concerned about this development. The Christian Democrats had never accepted the social democratic *Ostpolitik* and had deplored practically every inter-German accord, including the Basic Treaty. Many of the party's leading figures, particularly Franz Josef Strauß and the new CDU/CSU parliamentary leader, Alfred Dregger, still seemed committed to the radical anti-communism of the Adenauer years. Thus the SED had tried to aid the SPD in every parliamentary election. In 1972, the GDR agreed to the final version of the Basic Treaty a few days before the parliamentary elections in which Brandt gained a majority in the *Bundestag*. In 1980, it delayed the raising of the minimum currency exchange until a few days after the national elections. Even during the hectic days before Schmidt's ouster, Honecker sent signals to Foreign Minister and FDP leader Hans-Dietrich Genscher that the GDR would reward a continuation of the coalition with humanitarian concessions.[50]

To the surprise of East and West Germans, the Christian Democrats who assumed office seemed to have undergone a radical transformation since the days when they labelled the Basic Treaty and the *Ostverträge* as a national sellout and treason. The new government still emphasized the all-German aspects of the FRG's national ideology and included the theme of reunification and self-determination of the German people in most of its official statements. But it also accepted all inter-German agreements and committed itself to the continuation of the social-liberal *Ostpolitik* in all practical aspects.

This surprising about-face in the CDU/CSU was mainly a consequence of the lack of a viable alternative. Although many Christian Democrats were still emotionally opposed to the recognition of the GDR and of the Oder-Neiße line, their leaders had come to realize that the SPD/FDP *Ostpolitik* was irreversible. Neither the West German public nor the rest of the world would have accepted a radical change in the FRG's relations to the East. The first signs of this new approach came in 1981, when the CDU assumed governmental responsibility in West Berlin, the center of inter-German relations, and the newly-elected mayor, Richard von Weizsäcker, fully endorsed the SPD/FDP policy toward the GDR.[51]

Once in office, Kohl continued all on-going inter-German negotiations and even developed new initiatives. One of his first official acts was the opening of the Berlin-Hamburg highway that had been financed mainly with West German capital. In a series of meetings between high-level East and West German officials, new areas of economic cooperation were discussed. In the first half of 1983, the number of East Germans who were allowed to travel to the FRG for "urgent family affairs" rose to 46,000, twice the number of 1982.[52] In his desire to maintain continuity in his *Ostpolitik,* Kohl decided to keep Hans Bräutigam as the West German envoy in East Berlin. Bräutigam, a nonpartisan diplomat, had succeeded Bölling in 1982 after Schmidt called his former chief aide back to the chancellor's office. The bipartisan consensus on inter-German relations in the FRG reached its climax in early 1984, when the government and the SPD passed a joint declaration for the Federal Republic's *Ostpolitik.*

Kohl's focus on an improvement of inter-German relations, which even went beyond Schmidt's efforts, was motivated by several circumstances. First, the rise of Solidarity had aroused new hopes among West Germans of all political parties that intensified contacts with the West would be able to affect profound changes in the communist systems. Second, Kohl was also faced with a rising national consciousness in the FRG and a growing interest in the life of the "other Germans." Finally, the chancellor hoped that an improvement in inter-German relations could deflect some of the opposition against the imminent INF deployment. By demonstrating that the deployment would not lead to a "palisade of missiles" through Germany, as Soviet leaders had warned, but instead result in achieving progress in inter-German relations, Kohl hoped to strengthen the West German loyalty to the Western alliance.[53]

Also the GDR had strong, mainly economic, interests in a continuing inter-German thaw. The worldwide recession and a mounting foreign debt had led to a further deterioration of the East German economy in 1982. The Soviet Union reduced its oil shipments by 10 percent and significantly raised its prices, thus aggravating the GDR's balance of payments deficit. For the first time, the GDR was no longer able to obtain a sufficient amount of loans on Western credit markets. In order to cope with the foreign debt of $12 billion that it owed to Western banks, the GDR drastically reduced its imports and launched an unprecedented export campaign. Indeed, the debt burden dropped by a third by the end of 1983, but this result was only achieved at the cost of fewer imports of essential industrial and consumer goods.[54] East German agriculture, which was once a showcase of the Eastern bloc, had deteriorated in the late 1970s due to disastrous large projects that were planned by Gerhard Grüneberg, the agricultural expert in the Politbureau.[55] The crisis in food supplies peaked in the fall of 1982, when for several months there was neither meat nor butter on the market. Finally, the GDR was burdened by the need to provide economic aid to Poland, whose economy was still on the verge of collapse.

The new flexibility in East Berlin was also fueled by the SED's surprise over the continuity in Bonn's *Ostpolitik*. For the first time since the beginning of inter-German relations, the East German leadership could be certain that no opposition would undercut these relations or challenge the legitimacy of its rule. Although East German officials still criticized the nationalist rhetoric in Kohl's "Sunday speeches" and his uncompromising position on status problems, they repeatedly praised his "reasonable policy" on practical issues. However, the GDR was still under severe restraints in its policies to the FRG. Domestic unrest, the challenge from the peace movement, and insecurity about the future course of the Soviet leadership allowed it only little room for humanitarian concessions and created a strong incentive to continue its demarcation policy.[56] These limits to the inter-German rapprochement became apparent in an incident in April 1983, shortly after a large number of high-ranking West German visitors at the trade fair in Leipzig had created new hopes for these ties. When a West German citizen died of a heart attack on the East German border, West German papers immediately speculated that East German border guards had killed the man, and Bavarian Prime Minister Franz Josef Strauß lost no time accusing East Berlin of murder. Citing this anti-GDR campaign, Honecker cancelled his plans to visit the Federal Republic in April. Probably the more important reason for Honecker's cancellation, however, was Soviet pressure again. Shortly before his recall, Soviet Ambassador Abrassimov had reportedly told the East German leader that a visit to the FRG in the year of the INF deployment would not be welcomed by Moscow. Similar to 1980, Honecker emphasized his continuing interest in inter-German relations and asked for Bonn's understanding for his need to cancel the trip.[57]

The next stunning turn in the German drama involved the most ardent opponent of *Ostpolitik*. In July of 1983, Franz Josef Strauß surprised his foes and followers with the announcement that he had engineered an unrestricted West German loan to the GDR for more than $380 million. It was financed by several West German banks, was guaranteed by the Federal Republic's government, and exceeded all previous financial concessions to the GDR. Contrary to the CDU/CSU's political principle of demanding an East German quid pro quo for every service, the loan had absolutely no conditions attached. Strauß contended that the GDR had committed itself to relax border control on the transit routes, but this was never officially agreed upon. The CDU/CSU did just what it had accused the SPD of doing for more than a decade: it made a unilateral concession in the hope of future rewards.

What induced the patron of the German right to turn around so radically? Strauß had previously lost his fight against FDP leader Genscher over the post of foreign minister and yearned for influence on West German foreign policy. Indeed, with this initiative, the Bavarian prime minister took a leading role in the FRG's relations to the East. The loan was also a profitable deal for West German banks, particularly for the Strauß local bank, the Bayrische Landesbank. The interest rate was set at 1 percent above Libor, a rate that was low for the East German credit rating, but very high in light of the West German guarantee.[58]

Aides to Kohl and Genscher later suggested that the chancellor had tricked Strauß into this policy in order to co-opt him for his German policy. Regardless of whether or not this was true, the inclusion of Strauß put the conciliatory policy toward the GDR on an even wider political basis. The loan helped the East German government over a time of severe financial strains and allowed it to consolidate its economy. It created the atmosphere that allowed inter-German relations to prosper despite the looming INF deployment.[59] The number of West Germans visiting the GDR steadily increased, as did the volume of inter-German trade. In mid-1983, negotiations on nine different issues were held between the FRG and GDR, including river pollution, air pollution, the safety of nuclear reactors in border areas, science and technology,[60] cultural exchanges, and the upgrading of transit routes. After decades of quarrels, the problem of the *Schnellbahn* in West Berlin was finally resolved when the GDR transferred authority over the railroad to West Berlin. Just as it had been promised to Strauß in the loan negotiations, East German customs officials at the transit routes became noticeably more polite and cooperative. And the GDR accelerated the dismantling of the automatic shrapnel guns along the inter-German border.[61] A mass movement of prominent West German politicians visited East Berlin, including former Chancellor Helmut Schmidt; new SPD leader Hans-Joachim Vogel; Bahr; the Berlin mayor, von Weizsäcker; and Strauß. East German officials expressed their interest in an economic skeleton agreement and abolished the minimum currency exchange for children under age 15. The family reunification program was reorganized so that a larger number of individuals could move to the West. Even the West German rock star Udo Lindenberg, who had ridiculed Honecker in a popular song after having been denied permission to perform in the GDR, was finally allowed to play in East Berlin. The inter-German thaw also seemed to enjoy Moscow's blessing. Whether it was as a last-minute effort to halt the INF deployment or sympathy for East German needs, Andropov had reportedly given Honecker more freedom to conduct inter-German relations during the meeting in Moscow in the summer of 1983.[62]

However, there was little progress on most of the fundamental issues. The CDU/CSU rejected any compromises on status questions; not even the Elbe border or the documentation center in Salzgitter were subject to negotiations. Similarly, Honecker did not abandon his demands of Gera and showed little willingness to revoke the increase of the minimum currency exchange. A second West German loan for $300 million, promised to the East Germans by Strauß, was cancelled when Kohl insisted on more significant East German concessions. As the date of the INF deployment approached in late 1983, the earlier enthusiasm for inter-German relations gave way to a more sober realism. Although Honecker made no indication about a dramatic change in his policies towards the FRG, most people doubted that inter-German relations could weather the impending international crisis.

DISCORD IN THE EMPIRE

In November 1983, the West German *Bundestag* approved the deployment of Pershing II and cruise missiles, with the SPD and the Greens voting against it. When the first missiles arrived in Britain and the FRG, the Soviet Union walked out of all arms control talks with the United States and announced the beginning of a new chill in East-West relations. While Moscow startled the West with increasingly hawkish rhetoric, the East German leadership offered a different kind of surprise. At the seventh plenum of the SED Central Committee (CC), which convened a few days after the *Bundestag* vote, Honecker refused to join Moscow in its harsh condemnation of the United States and the Federal Republic and instead expressed his desire to "limit the damage" to detente through its relations with the FRG.[63]

In the following months, Western observers witnessed a unique case of open conflict in the Eastern bloc — a bitter and often vicious fight over the future of detente that forced every East European country to take sides. For years the Soviets had warned that the deployment of a single U.S. nuclear missile in Europe would disrupt East-West relations and spell an end to detente. When that situation finally became a reality, Moscow tried to make true on its threats. It broke off most negotiations with the United States and embarked on a sharp propaganda campaign against the West. Moscow's main target became the Federal Republic, which had to be punished for disappointing Soviet hopes and following the United States in its aggressive policies. But just as Carter came to realize that the West European states did not want to go along with his punishing campaign against the Soviets after Afghanistan, the Soviet Union was deserted by some of its East European allies who refused to abandon detente with the West. Particularly bitter for Moscow was the behavior of the GDR, the country central to the Soviet policy toward the FRG. Despite the deployment of the U.S. missiles, Honecker refused to freeze inter-German relations and even developed these relations to an unprecedented degree.

These signs of resistance were only a symptom of a trend toward more independent foreign policies in the East, and the inter-German thaw of 1984 must be analyzed in this context. In the course of the INF debate in 1982-83, Eastern Europe had intensified its desire for improved relations with the West. The Soviet peace offensive directed at Western Europe created the ideal forum to pursue East-West economic relations and develop a more accommodating attitude toward the West. Thus Eastern Europe willingly cooperated in the peace campaign, the "carrot" aspects of the Soviet strategy. Hungary continued its economic reform and took increasing advantage of Western credits and loans, the GDR intensified its inter-German trade relations, and even Poland actively attempted to improve relations with the West in the wake of the lifting of martial law in late 1982.[64]

But when the failure of this policy became apparent in 1983 and the Soviets began to put the "stick" of their strategy into effect, the East European countries balked. Romania was the first country to criticize Soviet policies. In tune with its independent foreign relations, the Romanian government sponsored an official peace movement that called for a withdrawal of *all* Soviet and U.S. missiles from European soil, thus implicitly endorsing the Western demand for the dismantling of the SS-20. Also, the other WTO members were no more cooperative. In May 1983, the Soviets publicly announced plans to deploy a new generation of intermediate-range missiles in the GDR and Czechoslovakia as a counter-measure against the NATO weapons. These missiles included the SS-21 and SS-22, two upgraded versions of older systems, and the SS-23, a more advanced, highly accurate missile. However, the meeting of the WTO in June did not produce the official announcement of the deployment. The Bulgarian party leader Todor Zhivkov even proposed a nuclear-free zone for the Balkans, thus suggesting his opposition to new Soviet missiles plans, and assured the Turkish and Greek governments that Bulgaria would not station any Soviet missiles on its territory. Even the CSSR, traditionally Moscow's most stalwart ally, showed signs of dissatisfaction. A letter to the editor in the Czech party newspaper *Rude Pravo* voiced doubts about the necessity of the deployment decision at that early date.[65] In November 1983, the Czech Federal Assembly called upon the superpowers to continue their negotiations despite NATO's missile deployment. This resolution stood in clear contradiction to a Soviet statement published the same day in Andropov's name that precluded a continuation of negotiations once a single U.S. missile was deployed.[66] Also, the December meeting of the WTO in Sofia failed to endorse the new missiles, despite the fact that the Soviets had already officially announced the deployment decision. The East European countries could not prevent the deployment with these moves, but at least they demonstrated their opposition to the missiles.

East European leaders also became increasingly concerned over concrete Soviet deliberations to prepare a preventive nuclear strike once the Pershing II were deployed.[67] To the dismay of the Soviets, Eastern Europe seemed more worried about Soviet missiles and Soviet defense plans than the new weapons in the West. This attitude reflected growing fears of nuclear war among large segments of the population — a sentiment that was fueled by the official peace propaganda against the West — and their resistance to the financial burdens that the arms race imposed on their economies.[68]

The main critic of the new missiles was the GDR, the Soviets' most important ally in their policies toward the West. As early as October 1983, *Neues Deutschland* had taken a dramatic step of dissent by publishing two letters from church groups in East and West Germany that deplored the deployment of new missiles in the GDR and proposed unilateral disarmament as the only way to end the arms race. In a meeting with his Swedish colleague Bodström, East German Foreign Minister Oskar Fischer remarked that the East European states were "forced to take measures that they do not want." In his speech before the CC plenum in November, Honecker defended the deployment of Soviet missiles but admitted that they "evoked no joy in our country." During the visit of Austrian President Rudolf Kirchschläger in East Berlin, Honecker was even reported to have said, "We'd rather not have this piece of devilry here." East Germany had good reason to oppose the deployment. Although the weaponry itself was supplied by the Soviet Union, the

GDR had to pay for the missile bases and all support installations. In addition, East Germans disliked the idea of deploying potential first-strike weapons that could induce NATO to launch a preemptive strike on their territory.[69]

But East German resistance to the Soviet policies went beyond the missile deployment. What was at stake was the survival of detente, which had served the GDR so well in the 1970s, in the face of Soviet attitudes that neglected Eastern Europe's economic and political interests. The theoretical basis for East Germany's position was provided by Hungary, which had traditionally pursued a liberal domestic policy while completely adhering to Moscow in foreign policy issues. In a widely noted lecture in October 1983, the Hungarian Central Committee secretary for international affairs, Matyas Szüros, developed the thesis of a reciprocal relationship between "national" and "international" interests in the Eastern bloc, in which small and medium-sized countries could pursue an independent policy toward the West and still advance the interests of the socialist camp as a whole. When in the following months the GDR put this theory into practice, a strange alliance developed between East German and Hungarian leaders, who had been fierce ideological rivals in the past.[70]

Refuting the Soviet warnings that the deployment of U.S. missiles would lead to a breakdown of inter-German relations, the GDR embarked on the most striking improvement of inter-German relations since the signing of the Basic Treaty in the early 1970s. As both sides made significant concessions, the inter-German relationship assumed a new quality and raised both hopes and fears about the prospects of a German-German rapprochement. East Berlin's first initiative in its relations with the FRG was a relaxation of its emigration policy. In the first half of 1984, 31,000 East Germans were allowed to move to the FRG. Until the end of the year, more than 40,000 people had left the country legally, four times the number of legal emigrants in the years before. During the height of the emigration wave in mid-March, more than 300 people arrived daily in the West German reception camp in Giessen. The emigrants not only included political prisoners and dissidents, but people who had never before come into conflict with the East German state.[71]

The reasons for the sudden about-face in the GDR's emigration policies can only be surmised. One can assume that Honecker regarded the lessening of emigration restrictions as a contribution to the inter-German thaw, as well as a means to extract West German economic concessions. In addition, allowing citizens to leave has always been a very advantageous arrangement for the GDR, since Bonn financially rewards family reunification and the release of political prisoners. But retrospectively, it seems that the emigration wave was not a well-planned policy, but the consequence of specific circumstances and the dynamics of the East German bureaucratic process.

The triggering event occurred on January 20, 1984 when six East German citizens sought refuge in the U.S. embassy in East Berlin and refused to leave until they were granted exit visas. This was not the first time that East Germans had used embassies as a gateway to the West; in almost every case, Wolfgang Vogel (the East German lawyer and Honecker confidant who dealt with most of the sensitive emigration cases) induced the refugees to return silently to their homes by promising exit permits. This time, however, the case could not be handled as discreetly. The refugees had called a West German television station, and the same evening both West and East Germans knew about the incident. East German officials reacted quickly. French Foreign Minister Claude Cheysson and Canadian Prime Minister Pierre Trudeau were expected to visit the GDR, and Honecker did not want the incident to overshadow these prestigious diplomatic events. After a mediation effort by Wolfgang Vogel, within two days the six refugees were deported to West Berlin.

This lesson was not missed by other East Germans. Two days later, 12 people requested asylum in the West German mission in East Berlin. Again, they were allowed to leave within a matter of days. Apparently, these incidents sparked a discussion in the Politbureau and Honecker requested a full-scale report about the problem of visa applicants. The results shocked the SED leaders: several hundred thousand, possibly as many as half a million GDR citizens had applied for exit permits, and some had been waiting for years. Although the problem must have been familiar to Politbureau members, they may not have been aware of the huge number of applicants. Exit permits are the responsibility of regional authorities who often file the applications without ever processing them. At least the issue had never been thoroughly discussed by the most powerful body of the GDR. Now, both moderates and radicals within the leadership arrived at the same conclusion. The former group argued that it did not make sense to hold back people who had burned all their bridges behind them. Since they had lost their jobs, they no longer made positive contributions to society and could only damage the morale of the rest of the population. Similarly, the idea of expelling antisocial elements and troublemakers had a strong appeal to the hard-liners. Within a few days, the emigration wave to the FRG began.[72]

Retrospectively, the emigration policy of 1984 must be regarded as a failure for the SED. Indeed, the East Germans disposed of the hardened dissidents and the leaders of the peace movement. Some particularly active Protestant parishes even had to close down because all their activists left for the West. However, the emigration wave did not seem to have increased the stability of the country. To the contrary, the sudden exit of friends and colleagues made individuals consider emigration who had not thought about this before. Since almost every emigrant left family members and relatives behind, thousands of people now became eligible to apply for emigration under the family reunification program.[73]

Since it was widely assumed that the GDR would reimpose tight emigration restrictions in the near future, many East Germans were caught by a last-minute panic and rushed to apply for visas. Not all of them were successful, however. By February, 48 more people had entered the West German mission in East Berlin. Again, they were allowed to leave. But when 58 East Germans requested asylum in the mission in June, the SED grew tired of this game. With the consent of the FRG, the building was closed for five weeks and reconstructed so as to deter people from seeking asylum. Although the West Germans felt embarrassed about collaborating with the East Germans in making their borders impenetrable, they knew that these incidents damaged inter-German relations and reduced the chances for people to leave the GDR legally.

Meanwhile, the embassy problem had shifted to a neighboring socialist country. In February, Inge Berg, the niece of East German Prime Minister Willy Stoph, requested asylum with her family in the West German embassy in Prague. Again, Vogel negotiated an agreement and the Bergs were given an exit permit after they returned to the GDR. And again, the example spread. When the West German television news reported these incidents, hundreds of East Germans made the trip to the CSSR and settled in the loft of the West German embassy. In October, the embassy housed 160 people; by Christmas there were still 50 people in the building.

The series of refugee dramas, nevertheless, did not stop the German-German rapprochement. In one of the largest economic joint ventures, the Volkswagen Corporation agreed to construct an auto engine factory in the GDR for $200 million. East and West German negotiators came closer to an agreement on environmental protection, and in July the GDR attended the International Environmental Protection Conference in Munich. Talks on a cultural agreement, which had been resumed in 1983 after an interruption of eight years, gained new momentum. And due to the elimination of the minimum currency exchange for children in 1983, the number of West German visits rose to 9 million in early 1984, the same volume as before the 1980 crisis.[74]

West German enthusiasm surrounding the rapprochement led to a genuine mass migration of representatives from all West German parties to the annual spring fair in Leipzig, which had often served as the best gauge for the state of inter-German relations. Political figures like Strauß and FRG Minister of Economics Erich Graf Lambsdorf visited Leipzig in order to meet with Honecker and other East German officials. Soon afterwards, the West German national airline Lufthansa announced an agreement with the GDR to establish regular flights to the fall fair in Leipzig — a decision that was perceived as a major step toward creating the first regular flight connection between the FRG and the GDR.

In July the FRG granted a second guaranteed $380 million loan to the GDR that it had denied in November 1983. Although it was officially presented as an unrelated decision, East Germany announced a number of concessions concerning travel restrictions at precisely the same time. The minimum currency exchange for senior citizens was reduced from DM 25 to DM 15, and their maximum length of stay extended from 30 to 45 days. The number of days that East German senior citizens were permitted to stay in the West was raised from 30 to 60 annually. Finally, the maximum stay permitted in the "small border traffic," an arrangement that allows residents of the West German frontier areas many short visits to East German towns close to the border, was extended from one to two days.

This last stipulation caused a major embarrassment for the Kohl government, and particularly for its main negotiator, Phillip Jenninger, when the GDR later declared that the new provisions were not valid for West Berlin. Not only do the large majority of "border tourists" come from Berlin, but this exclusion also violated the principle of equality between the city and the FRG that had governed most inter-German agreements since 1969. The GDR also refused to yield to Bonn's urgent demand to reduce the minimum age at which East German senior citizens are allowed to travel freely to the FRG, currently set at 65 for men and 60 for women.

It has never become quite clear whether or not the East German concessions were motivated solely by the loan. Naturally, the GDR welcomed West German credit as a boon for its economy. While in 1983 the first West German loan was urgently needed by the GDR to manage its foreign debt, the East German foreign exchange situation was no longer that critical in 1984 that the government would have sacrificed essential political interests in return for financial concessions. According to the Bank for International Settlements in Basel, in 1983 the GDR had reduced its foreign debt by $1.8 billion to $8.5 billion due to large trade surpluses with the West. In the same period, the balance of savings accounts held by the GDR in Western banks almost doubled to $3.8 billion. This development helped improve the GDR's credit rating, but it also indicated that the GDR was not in desperate need for additional loans. Finally, the conditions of the West German loan were not much better than conditions which the GDR could have received on international financial markets.[75] It seems that the East German humanitarian concessions were motivated at least as much by a political interest to advance the German-German rapprochement as by urgent financial need. However, this does not explain why the GDR gave the appearance of a linkage between humanitarian concessions and loan negotiations, although it had always tried to avoid yielding to financial pressures or inducements.[76]

Throughout 1984, Honecker pursued an active policy of personal contacts with Western leaders. In February, U.S. Assistant Secretary of State for European Affairs Richard Burt came to East Berlin, and in the course of the summer Canadian Prime Minister Pierre Trudeau, Swedish Prime Minister Olof Palme, Greek Prime Minister Andreas Papandreou and Italian Premier Bettino Craxi visited the GDR. But the event that received most attention was Honecker's planned visit to the Federal Republic, which was scheduled for the following September. Although this trip had been on the inter-German agenda since 1980 and had to be cancelled twice because of international tensions, never before had so many expectations been attached to such an event. Honecker's first visit to the FRG and his journey back to his place of birth in the Saarland was widely perceived as the highlight of the German-German thaw. Honecker himself fueled these hopes with an interview with the Italian daily newspaper *Il Messagero* on July 8, shortly before the visit of Italian Prime Minister Bettino Craxi to the GDR. In his strikingly conciliatory remarks, Honecker confirmed his visit, expressed his interest in discussing disarmament measures with Kohl, and emphasized the importance of the German-German dialogue for peace and security in Europe.[77]

However, in the following two months Honecker's policies and plans encountered severe opposition as the Soviet Union stated a massive propaganda campaign aimed at disrupting the inter-German relationship. Although the Soviet media attacked the West German government, the real target was clearly Honecker and his detente policy. What was surprising about this media campaign was not only the bluntness with which the Soviets criticized their most loyal ally in the eye of the public, but the stiff resistance they encountered in the East German media. A stunned Western audience was able to observe a genuine conflict between two Eastern countries firsthand, a conflict that soon came to involve the whole communist bloc. None of the attacks and counterattacks were carried out directly. Instead, both East German and Soviet writers used phrases that indicated their position in the dispute, and the newspapers of various East European countries demonstrated their approval or disapproval by choosing to publish or to neglect these articles. The analysis of this newspaper feud offers a fascinating insight into the inner workings of Warsaw Pact politics.

Accusing the FRG of revanchism, militarism, and Nazism had been a common way to attack West German policies and positions for the Soviet press, particularly before 1969. Even in the 1970s and 1980s it had been the standard terminology for Soviet propaganda against the FRG. The Soviets had also used it in early 1980 to express their disapproval of an inter-German rapprochement during the Afghanistan crisis. And it had proven to be a useful instrument to rally other East European states closer to the Soviet Union, particularly the alleged victims of West German revanchism, Poland and Czechoslovakia. The Soviet revanchism campaign was closely coordinated with Moscow's attempts to intensify East-West tensions in early 1984.

The first signs came in February, when TASS wrote that West German schools used maps showing Germany within the borders of 1937 as an example of West German revanchism, and Soviet magazines reported on the glorification of Nazism and fascism in West German books and movies.[78] However, this first campaign petered out after a few weeks. The next major wave of attack against inter-German relations was spearheaded by a Soviet ally. On March 30, the Czech party paper *Rude Pravo* printed an editorial attacking "particularistic and separatist tendencies" on the part of "some fraternal parties" who attempt to gain financial advantages. Although the "brother parties" remained anonymous, the targets were obviously Budapest and East Berlin. The editorial explicitly rejected Szüros' thesis of an "independent course in foreign policy" for small states and warned that "fundamental socialist interests" must not be sacrificed for a "momentary 'national' advantage."

The different reactions to this article clearly showed the growing gap between East German and Soviet positions. While *Pravda* reprinted the article in full,[79] *Neues Deutschland* ignored the common policy of East European newspapers to reprint ideologically significant articles. Instead, on April 12 the newspaper published an interview with Szüros that had previously appeared in the Hungarian newspaper *Magyar Hirlap*. Under the title "Common goals — national interests," the Hungarian foreign policy expert carried his previous arguments in favor of detente even further:

> . . . Through dialogue and constructive relations, the small and medium-sized European states belonging to the two alliance systems can exert a favorable impact on the international atmosphere, in which several opportunities could arise for improving relations between the Soviet Union and the United States, which [could] decisively influence the fate of detente. . . . It is a fact that . . . different capitalist countries show varying degrees of interest toward certain socialist countries. Austria, Finland and the FRG, for instance, show more interest and are more active in [developing relations with] Hungary than [with certain] other socialist countries. This is not, however, a privilege unique to us, since the same special attention is received by Bulgaria from its two neighbors in the Balkans, Turkey and Greece, or by Cuba from Spain, or by the GDR from the FRG. This works the other way around, as well. It is not only our conviction but also our experience that these individual possibilities can be exploited for the cause of common goals while also implementing national interests. . . . [80]

Not only were the East German readers presented with a forceful defense of Honecker's foreign policy, but they were also reminded of the "special nature" of inter-German relations, a notion which even the SED had previously rejected. Not surprisingly, *Pravda* never published this interview.

It was not until mid-April that the Soviet Union began to crack down seriously on inter-German relations as part of a general hardening of its policies toward the West. On May 8, the Soviet Union announced its boycott of the Olympic games in Los Angeles; all WTO countries except Romania followed Moscow's lead, though somewhat grudgingly. Soon afterwards, Moscow cancelled the visit of a high-level official to China. When West German Foreign Minister Genscher met with his Soviet colleague Andrei Gromyko, in Moscow on May 21, he received no positive signals about an improvement in East-West relations. When Genscher mentioned the "constructive development in the relations between Bonn and East Berlin," *Pravda* suppressed this passage.[81] Even more ominous was Gromyko's reference to the Potsdam Agreements while criticizing the planned revival of the Western European Union (WEU) as the cornerstone of a European defense. These agreements prescribe the four allies' control over Germany, and thus Soviet control of the GDR.[82] Now Moscow launched the progaganda campaign against Bonn with full force, accusing the West Germans of revanchism, warmongering and aggressive designs against Eastern Europe at every occasion. Still ignoring these attacks, the SED Politbureau strongly supported Honecker's policy of "limiting the damage" at the CC plenum in May, while East German theorists attempted to lend legitimacy to this policy in a series of academic debates and articles.[83]

It soon became apparent that the Soviet leadership itself was divided on the issue of inter-German relations. Alexander Bovin, a Central Committee member and a confidant of the late Andropov, commended the SED for improving inter-German relations in an article in the Soviet government paper *Istwestija* on July 12. A few days later he told an East German newspaper in an interview that the GDR should "take advantage of every opportunity for a constructive dialogue." This was now of "double and triple importance," he added.[84] This contrast between *Pravda* on one side and *Istwestija* on the other characterized the Soviet propaganda campaign throughout 1984. Just as the Soviets vacillated on proposed space weapons talks with the United States in Vienna during the summer, which ultimately never took place, these differences indicated a power struggle between different factions in the Kremlin over detente.

The campaign in *Pravda* gained new momentum with the second West German loan to the GDR. Two days after the announcement of the loan on July 25, Lev Bezymensky, a Soviet expert on German issues, published an article entitled "In the Shadow of American Missiles" in *Pravda* in which he harshly attacked the Kohl government of pursuing an aggressive policy against the East designed "to change the present-day social and political face of Europe," and contended that Bonn used "both economic levers and political contacts" to "impose 'patronage,' fan chauvinist sentiments, and solicit concessions on matters of principle that affect the republic's sovereignty." To bolster his claims, Bezymensky cited the demands Honecker had defined as a condition for progress in inter-German relations in his speech in Gera in 1980, and his 1981 warning that "good-neighborly relations cannot flourish in the shadow of new American nuclear missiles." He deliberately ignored the profound transformation that Honecker's public pronouncements and East German policy had undergone since that time. The article concluded that "relations between the two German states cannot be viewed in isolation from the entire international situation," a clear condemnation of the basis of East German policy toward the West.[85]

East Berlin responded to this massive attack on its policies by reprinting an editorial from the Hungarian newspaper *Nepszava* that praised East German foreign policy and specifically inter-German relations. On July 32, *Neues Deutschland* summarized an article by *Isvestija* that advocated an intensification of East-West trade. In an editorial commemorating the ninth anniversary of the Helsinki Accords, a date that is usually not mentioned in the communist press, *Neues Deutschland* offered another vigorous defense of Honecker's policies and the benefits of detente.[86]

An editorial in *Pravda* on August 2 escalated the Soviet attacks even further. Although the Soviets seemingly still targeted the FRG, the main thrust of the criticism was now openly directed at East Berlin. For example, the newspaper called alleged West German attempts to "limit the damage" of the INF deployment to inter-German ties a "pharisaical logic." As *Pravda* was undoubtedly aware, this term had never been used by Kohl, but was coined by Honecker. The editorial then criticized the West German loan and the humanitarian concessions that the GDR had made in exchange: "All this resembles not so much an expansion of contacts for humanitarian purposes, which people in the FRG are so fond of talking about, as an attempt to obtain new channels for exerting political and ideological influence."[87]

The East German response was both simple and effective: *Neues Deutschland* did not reprint the editorial and published instead an article by the chairman of the Soviet Committee for European Security and Cooperation, Lev Tolkunov, who supported Honecker's ties with the FRG and claimed that "the policy of detente is not part of the past. It belongs to the future." At that point it became clear that the division ran right through the Eastern bloc. While the Hungarian weekly *Magyaroszág* published another article that emphasized the role of the small European nations in detente, the Polish party paper *Trybuna Ludu* and the Czech *Rude Pravo* reprinted *Pravda's* attack.[88]

In August, the East Germans offered the first signs of yielding to Soviet pressure. On the occasion of the 14th anniversary of the Moscow Treaty between the FRG and the Soviet Union on August 12, the Soviet press continued its propaganda campaign and accused Bonn of violating the agreement on the renunciation of force through its revanchist policies. While *Neues Deutschland* cited Politbureau member Herbert Häber who confirmed the SED's commitment to a dialogue with the FRG, an East German military magazine followed the Soviet lead and charged Bonn with a "revanchist military policy."[89]

Honecker had remained silent throughout most of the controversy. It was not until August 19 that he gave his first interview since the beginning of the revanchism campaign. In this interview, the East German leader steered a fine line between his loyalty to the Soviet Union and his interests in inter-German relations. At first, Honecker confirmed the GDR's unconditional loyalty to the alliance and its friendship with the Soviet Union. He went on to attack extremists in the West German government who cling to nationalist and revanchist aspirations, and accused the United States "and some of her allies" of preparing an imperialist war. He even restated his demands of Gera, emphasizing the unqualified recognition of GDR citizenship. But despite these harsh statements, Honecker indicated his interest in continuing his dialogue with the FRG. "The struggle for peaceful coexistence requires the continuation of our policy of an active dialogue with all forces that show reason and the willingness to contribute to the securing of the peace," he said. "For there exists no justifiable alternative, neither to peaceful coexistence nor to the political dialogue."[90] To Bonn's disappointment, Honecker failed to mention his planned visit to the FRG.

Officials in Bonn were struck by the difference in tone between this interview and Honecker's more conciliatory statements earlier that year. The SED leader had essentially adopted the Soviet arguments on West German revanchism and militarism and had put the demands of Gera again on the top of his agenda. The Kohl government still expected him to visit the FRG, but it no longer hoped for any impressive results. That the dispute with the Soviets was far from over became apparent in the way *Pravda* and TASS reported his interview. First TASS published an English version which reflected accurately Honecker's remarks, but in the subsequent Russian version it deleted all positive references to inter-German relations or East-West relations and published only his attacks against the FRG. *Neues Deutschland* then reprinted this censored version, demonstrating to East Germans how little Moscow valued their national interests. Since East Germans were informed about the background and details of the campaign through West German television, these distortions of their chief's words came as a shock to them. To stress the East German insistence on its national interests even more, *Neues Deutschland* published a Hungarian article that emphasized

Hungary's need to pursue its own economic and political interests in East-West relations.[91]

Honecker also demonstrated his independence by being the only East European party leader to attend the celebrations in Bucharest for the 40th anniversary of the liberation of Romania. This was a blatant affront to the Soviets who had apparently pressured their allies to stay away from the event in order to isolate the Romanian leader, Nicolae Ceausescu, within the alliance. Through a joint East German-Romanian communiqué on foreign policy issues, Honecker lent his support to Ceausescu's idiosyncratic policy toward the West and endorsed the Romanians' call for the withdrawal of *all* nuclear weapons from European soil, implicitly including the SS-20.[92]

Throughout most of the Soviet-East German conflict, the Kohl administration was at a loss as to how to react. All it did was reject the charges of revanchism and militarism and encourage Honecker to maintain his travel plans. Meanwhile, Bonn's political and media scene became seemingly preoccupied with a guessing game: "Will he come or will he not?" Some West German officials, however, suggested that the FRG should stop creating exaggerated expectations for a possible German-German breakthrough at the meeting. The huge attention given to Honecker's trip, they warned, would only raise suspicions in the East and thus damage inter-German relations. Instead of calming down the debates, the Kohl government managed to stir up an additional controversy. In an interview with the conservative West German daily *Die Welt* on August 23, the CDU/CSU parliamentary floor leader, Alfred Dregger, remarked sarcastically that "the future of the Federal Republic does not depend upon whether Herr Honecker pays us the honor of his visit." He added in a later television interview that West Germans should not even urge Honecker to come because "it is a great uplifting for the general secretary and the GDR that Herr Honecker is welcomed here in the Federal Republic."[93]

Dregger, an exponent of the CDU's right wing, was probably trying consciously to undercut Kohl's *Ostpolitik;* in this task he succeeded. Although the chancellor distanced himself from this statement immediately and confirmed his interest in the German-German summit, the damage had already been done. Regardless of whether or not Honecker was still committed to the visit, Dregger's remarks gave him a pretense to extricate himself from his difficult situation. East German officials sharply attacked Dregger and suggested that Honecker himself was not that eager to visit the FRG. As Kohl urged Honecker to give a firm confirmation of his trip, rumors spread in East Berlin that the SED leader would postpone his trip, possibly until the end of the year.[94]

One more time, the West and East German public witnessed the conflict between Eastern doves and hawks. Responding to a speech by Kohl at the meeting of expellees from the German Eastern territories, *Pravda* reiterated its charges of revanchism and accused the FRG of intending to "annex the socialist GDR." *Neues Deutschland* failed to reprint this article, and instead reported the remarks of Soviet Deputy Prime Minister Leonid Kostandow who praised the GDR as "the reliable bastion of peace and socialism in Europe."[95] But if this induced some West Germans to maintain their hopes for Honecker's visit, these illusions quickly faded at the fall fair in Leipzig. In contrast to the spring fair, when Honecker had spent several hours at the West German booths and had met with a number of prominent guests, this time he only stopped for a few moments at the booth of the chemical company BASF. When journalists asked him about his upcoming visit to the FRG, Honecker turned around and walked away. According to some reports, the East Germans had originally planned a longer stop at BASF, but changed the schedule at the last moment. On September 4, the East German envoy in Bonn, Ewald Moldt, told West German officials that "the current date was no longer realistic," citing the "style and public discussion in the FRG in connection with the visit" as the cause.[96] The German summer drama had come to an end.

The events of the summer of 1984 startled observers all over Europe. Some were surprised at the degree of independence that the GDR had demonstrated, while others were disillusioned by the heavy-handed intervention which the Soviet Union had used to discipline its ally. Actually, none of these phenomena should have been too surprising; they were both a logical consequence of long-term trends within the Eastern bloc. The first thing to note is that the debate over the right approach to East-West relations was not a one-time dispute limited to Moscow and East Berlin. For many years, theorists and political leaders had debated the value of "soft" and "hard" policies toward the West. This debate grew more intense through NATO's INF decision. East European strategists were now caught in the dilemma between blocking the deployment of the missiles by exerting pressure on Western Europe, and maintaining good relations with these countries in the economic sphere. This dilemma became most critical regarding Eastern Europe's relations to the FRG, and particularly in inter-German relations. How to punish the FRG without hurting themselves was an almost unsolvable problem for both Soviet and East German policymakers.

This debate was carried out in East German and Soviet academic journals between 1979 and 1984, and different opinions cut through the scholarly community in both countries.[97] The best gauge of the writers' attitudes to relations with the FRG was their evaluation of Schmidt's role in the double-track decision. While proponents of a hard-line towards Bonn emphasized Schmidt's 1977 London speech and called him "the whip of NATO's double-track decision,"[98] others suggested that the FRG was only following the U.S. lead. Until 1979, the number of positive and negative articles on the FRG was rather balanced in both East German and Soviet journals. While Soviet publications maintained this balance after 1979, in the period of the inter-German chill of 1980, East German journals began to emphasize the negative role of the FRG. This trend was reversed in 1982 and 1983, when most East German articles adopted a more positive attitude and began to focus on disagreements between the FRG and the United States. East German scholars also grew more concerned about "national" interests in the context of East-West relations, while Soviet writers continued to emphasize "proletarian internationalism" and the need for bloc loyalty.

Thus the East German-Soviet conflict of 1984 was as much a national conflict as an ideological conflict between hard-liners and moderates in all Communist parties. It was partly coincidental that in 1984 the East German and Soviet parties were dominated by different wings. In East Berlin, the moderate faction around Foreign Minister Oskar Fischer and Politbureau members Günter Mittag and Herbert Häber had the upper hand against traditional hard-liners Paul Verner, Hermann Axen, Albert Norden, and Defense Minister Heinz Hoffmann. Apparently, this moderate wing also enjoyed Honecker's support.[99] In Moscow, meanwhile, a faction around Foreign Minister Gromyko and Defense Minister Ustinov appeared to have pressed successfully for a confrontational post-INF strategy toward the West, while proponents of detente like Prime Minister Tikhonov (and perhaps Mikhail Gorbachev) were in the minority.[100]

Under normal circumstances, the dominant Soviet position would have determined the policies of all of Eastern Europe. However, the lack of effective Soviet leadership in the Warsaw Pact since Brezhnev's last years changed this situation. Andropov had also been severely ill since August of 1983, when he appeared in public for the last time; he died in February 1984. His successor, Konstantin Chernenko, was widely perceived as a transitional leader and was in poor health throughout his tenure. Between mid-June and September, at the height of the intra-bloc debate, Chernenko made not one single public appearance. Not even interviews were published in his name. The Kremlin leaders meanwhile could not decide on a viable policy toward the West after the failure of their campaign against the INF deployment.

In the midst of the overall confusion over Soviet intentions and plans, it was not surprising that East European leaders took advantage of this leadership vacuum and advanced their interests in detente. For the East German leadership, the case for stepping up its Western policy was even more compelling. A sustained period of domestic stability and Honecker's unchallenged leadership position within the party had decreased the risks that the SED traditionally associated with an opening up to the West. After overcoming the debt crisis of the early 1980s, the East German economy was now in a better position to take advantage of Western trade and technology than it had been in the past. And just as Szüros suggested, the breakdown in communication between the super-powers opened up an opportunity for the small East European states to increase their own weight in international affairs by fostering East-West contacts. Regardless of whether or not Honecker's talks with Western leaders activities actually reduced global tensions, they definitely enhanced his reputation as a respected statesman, both in the West and at home. This quest for respectability and legitimacy was probably the driving force behind his intended trip to the Federal Republic. Being received with all the honors of a foreign statesman in the country that for decades had refused to recognize the existence of the GDR was for Honecker the final step to full political emancipation of his country. And just as Brandt's *Ostpolitik* vastly increased the weight and influence of the Federal Republic in the Western alliance, Honecker's Western policy was designed to strengthen his position and maneuverability within the Eastern alliance without diluting his bloc commitment in any way.[101]

Honecker had good reason to believe that he would succeed in resisting the Soviet crusade against his trip. Not only was the GDR Moscow's most important ally, but the emerging axis with Hungary and Romania and the support that detente enjoyed in Bulagaria and Poland had strengthened the East German power bases in the alliance. Some articles in the Soviet press also indicated that Honecker could count on support in Moscow. Some observers even suggested that Honecker was supported by Chernenko, who had endorsed the East German policy at the CMEA meeting in June. The key attacks in the Soviet press appeared while Chernenko was away from Moscow, either on vacation or in a hospital, and the Soviet rhetoric against the West softened somewhat once he returned. It is likely that Honecker was holding out against the attacks from Moscow while he hoped for Chernenko's intervention and only cancelled his trip after realizing that the Soviet party chief's influence was weaker than expected.[102]

Moscow had often been worried about the lack of discipline in the Eastern bloc but this time this concern was exacerbated by the involvement of the GDR, strategically and politically the pillar of its empire. It was also disconcerting for the Soviet leadership to see the beginnings of an axis between East Germany, Hungary, and Romania. Hungary and Romania were the two countries that had developed the most independent policies in certain fields — the Hungarians through their economic reforms and the Romanians through their foreign policy. That these three countries, the only non-Slavic states in the East, also represented the forces that had fought against the Soviets in World War II was an additional source of anxiety for the history-conscious Soviet leadership. A related problem for Moscow was the expiration of the Warsaw Pact on June 4, 1985. Although the renewal of the treaty was never really in doubt, some East European states indicated their intention to use their formal voting right as a political lever for more equal military arrangements. Romania in particular planned to block the renewal unless the structure of the alliance was reformed.[103]

These concerns were reinforced by the traditional Soviet fear of German reunification. Although the Soviets had repeatedly made proposals of a neutralized and unified Germany, and had made use of the "German question" in their anti-INF campaign, the fear of German reunification seems to be more deeply engrained in the Soviet psyche than in that of any other country. Not even 30 years of East German loyalty to the Soviets could do away with their deep-seated suspicions about ultimate East German motives. The fact the SED had not followed Soviet foreign policy at a crucial moment only fueled Soviet fears and strengthened their incentives to hinder an inter-German rapprochement.

These observations can largely explain the Soviet revanchism campaign. The campaign was intended to evoke traditional fears of German expansionism among the other East European states and rally them around the Soviet Union. Since the WTO had been founded as a response to the rearmament of the FRG in 1955, it revived the original *raison d'être* for the Eastern alliance. It served as a reminder of the dangerous consequences of too much rapprochement between the two

German states for the SED leadership. By demonstrating the dependence of inter-German relations on Soviet approval of the FRG, the Soviets hoped the campaign would deter the West German government from continuing its nuclear buildup. Finally, the campaign was a means to end the embarrassing impression that Moscow was unable to deliver on its threats of a freeze in East-West relations. Even if the deployment could no longer be reversed, the Soviets still hoped to avoid looking like paper tigers.[104]

During the campaign some observers suggested that the attacks were actually a strategy to strengthen Honecker's position during his meeting with Kohl. Honecker could point to his limited leeway with the Soviets, they argued, and then request more West German compromise and offer fewer concessions himself.[105] In light of the final cancellation of his visit, it is doubtful that such "good guy/bad guy" techniques were consciously intended. Yet one of the less ambitious Soviet aims could have been to force Honecker toward a less forthcoming position *vis-à-vis* the FRG, even if he did not cancel his visit. As Honecker's interview in August showed, the Soviets reached this goal at a relatively early date.

Honecker's cancellation was also caused by mistakes by both East and West German officials. The vastly exaggerated media attention that was given to the visit in the West raised unnecessary suspicions among both Eastern and Western allies. And as Dregger's remarks showed, Kohl was unable to control hostile sentiments within his own party. Similarly, the East Germans did not refrain from confrontational statements that in turn provoked negative reactions by West German conservatives. Most important was the inability of both sides to decide on an agenda for the talks. The GDR focused on disarmament and demanded a language that was unacceptable to Kohl because it would have raised Western suspicions about West German neutralism. Similarly, Kohl announced early that he would not negotiate over any status problems, including the Elbe border and the documentation center at Salzgitter. Instead, he wanted to focus the discussions on environmental issues and travel relaxations, none of which were of any interest to Honecker. At one point, West German officials suggested that the two leaders discuss a joint initiative on the renunciation of force at the Conference on Confidence-Building Measures and Disarmament in Europe (CCDE) in Stockholm. Since the Soviets strongly supported such a resolution, this initiative would have strengthened Honecker's position *vis-à-vis* Moscow.[106] But Kohl abandoned this idea in order to avoid criticism from the Reagan administration. In an interview with the

Austrian television network ORF on August 14, 1984, he explicitly rejected a joint initiative, citing the FRG's loyalty to NATO as the reason. "The Federal Republic is tied to the West, it is not a wanderer between the blocs," he said.[107]

Honecker's preoccupation with prestige and symbolism was also neglected by the West German officials. All meetings with West German leaders were set up in places outside Bonn lest Kohl be faced with the sensitive question of whether to visit East Berlin at a later trip to the GDR. This itinerary struck Honecker as a diminution of his own status as a respected leader of a sovereign country. He was also offended by Kohl's attempt to exclude issues of international importance like disarmament from the agenda and limit the talks to practical issues like environmental protection. "But for these questions we have our departmental ministers," he purportedly remarked indignantly once.[108] Thus there was little that Honecker could have gained from the visit. That the decision for the cancellation was made only in the last minute was suggested by East Berlin's long refusal to give a definite answer and by the sudden change of schedule at the Leipzig fair. Many observers contended that a more forthcoming attitude on the side of the Kohl government, and particularly a willingness to discuss the Elbe border with its strategic interest for the Soviets, could have saved the summit. Kohl's failure to do so, however, was not only his personal choice, but also a consequence of the political constraints that the chancellor faced within his own party.

Ultimately, the revanchism campaign constituted a loss for all sides. The FRG had to postpone its hopes for a future German-German rapprochement and for further human concessions. Honecker lost both in prestige and substance. His courageous fight against Soviet intervention was widely applauded by the East German population, but his defeat also demonstrated the limits of his power. Although the cancellation of his visit did not weaken Honecker's position in the SED, his miscalculation about Soviet intentions and Soviet power limited his scope for maneuver in the following months and froze advances in inter-German ties for almost a year. Even for the Soviet Union, the cancellation was a mixed blessing. While it succeeded in disciplining rebellious allies, the month-long media war between various Eastern countries and within the Soviet Union itself demonstrated the weakness of Moscow's leadership to the rest of the world. Its heavy-handed intervention aroused the anger of officials in the GDR, Hungary and other East European states and reinforced anti-Soviet sentiments in the East German population. The campaign violated the lesson that Moscow should have learned from Poland, that problems with East European allies are solved most effectively by the national governments themselves. As discussed earlier, most East European leaders understand today that the political and economic stability of their countries depends to a large degree on a consensus with the population. The Soviet disruption of the inter-German relationship was an example of a policy that ignored this knowledge.

Moscow also lost in its relationship with the West. The revanchism campaign helped rally many West Germans around Kohl's pro-U.S. policy and reduced Soviet leverage over the West German domestic debate on the INF deployment and on defense policy in general. While the FRG still maintained high stakes in East-West trade, the ill feelings caused by the campaign could make economic concessions like loans and the sale of high technology less likely in the future.

In light of these costs, it seems unlikely that the Soviet campaign was motivated by a grand strategy towards the West. Undoubtedly, Moscow was interested in punishing Bonn for the INF deployment and in influencing the 1984 U.S. presidential elections by showing that Reagan's policies lead to global tensions. But these rather secondary goals would not have warranted the costs and efforts of the revanchism campaign. The only interests that are vital enough for the Soviets to justify such an initiative are those that affect the stability of the Eastern alliance itself. One must conclude that Moscow intervened against the inter-German thaw because it feared to lose control over its European empire. While the Soviet leadership as a whole was not so much opposed to the East German foreign policy itself, particularly since it was divided itself, it grew highly concerned that this policy was made without its approval and even against its will. Once the issue was no longer one of policy but of hegemony, it was clear that Moscow would win the struggle. However, on the larger question of relations to the West, it had no viable alternative to offer.

BACK ON THE CHAIN GANG?

The weeks directly following Honecker's cancellation were characterized by confusion and uncertainty over the future course of inter-German relations. East German officials reassured their West German counterparts that the cancellation was only a postponement and should not constitute an impediment to the bilateral relationship. The day after the

East German announcement, Honecker met with a West German environmental group, led by the prominent activist Jo Leinen. The meeting received prominent coverage in *Neues Deutschland*.[109] As Moscow continued to rally the states of the WTO behind its hard-line policy toward the FRG, however, the prospects for a continuation of the inter-German thaw deteriorated. Accusations of West German revanchism remained a central part of the official vocabulary of most East European states and Soviet pressure forced other states to reconsider their relations to Bonn. A few days after Honecker's decision, the Bulgarian leader Todor Zhivkov announced the cancellation of his own visit to the FRG. Only Romania's Nicolai Ceausescu followed through on his plans to visit Bonn that fall.

Even more detrimental to the inter-German relationship was the breakdown of the domestic consensus that had characterized the West German *Ostpolitik* since the early 1980s. After Honecker's cancellation demonstrated the failure of Kohl's policy toward the GDR, the SPD abandoned its support for the chancellor's *Ostpolitik* and began an aggressive campaign of criticism against the government. Former Chancellor Willy Brandt's comment about the CDU's "garrulous dilettantism" in handling the Honecker visit was the most publicized, but not the harshest, accusation.[110] While the rhetoric of the Kohl government moved increasingly to the right in the coming months, the SPD began to develop its own distinct policy toward the GDR. As with the collapse of the West German consensus on its policy toward NATO, which was undercut by the SPD's vote against the INF deployment, the bipartisan support for West Germany's *Ostpolitik* was now in danger of breaking down.

The increasing self-assertion of the left concerning *Ostpolitik* was accompanied by a resurgence of rightist rhetoric within the CDU/CSU. A small but vocal group on the right wing of the coalition, led by Dregger and the leaders of associations of Germans expelled from Eastern Europe, Herbert Hupka and Herbert Cjaja, had always emphasized West German claims to sole representation of the German people and to all former German territories east of the Oder-Neiße line. And just as the dogmatic statements by some CDU officials had undermined inter-German relations during the summer, the revisionist rhetoric concerning the eastern borders imperiled West Germany's relations with the whole Eastern bloc. Especially an ongoing debate over a seemingly academic question served as a constant irritant for Poland. While the West German government was committed to the recognition of Poland's western border by the Warsaw Treaty of 1970 and other documents of the detente period, leading conservatives such as Minister of Interior Friedrich Zimmermann and Dregger had repeatedly contended that his obligation was only valid for the FRG in its current political configuration. Once Germany was reunited, they insisted, it would also be permitted to reclaim its eastern territories. Given the constitutional requirement to always seek reunification, this hypothetical claim actually voided West Germany's recognition of the Polish borders. In his first two years in office, Kohl's commitment to continuity in the West German *Ostpolitik* and particularly Strauß's support for inter-German relations had muted this conservative rhetoric. Once Kohl's pragmatic course had experienced its first severe setback, supporters of a hard-line toward the East became more assertive. As if to validate retroactively the Soviet charges against West German revanchism, all-German rhetoric gained a new momentum in the fall of 1984 and caused suspicion about West German intentions in the East and West. Even pragmatic politicians like Italian Foreign Minister Gulio Andreotti felt compelled to warn of "pan-Germanism," a comment that triggered a wave of protest in Bonn.[111]

The renewed nationalism in the CDU/CSU made it increasingly difficult for Chancellor Kohl to continue his policy of separating conservative ideology from pragmatic policies without compromising his credibility. The chancellor exacerbated this dilemma by accepting an invitation to speak at the annual convention of expellees from Silesia, which was scheduled for April 1985. Not only did Kohl set a symbolic act that was bound to irritate the East European states, but he made himself hostage of the extremists within the Silesian movement. For a theme of the convention, the Silesians had first chosen the provocative slogan, "Silesia remains ours." Although Kohl insisted, after fervent protests both in West Germany and abroad, on a different motto with a less blatant revisionist message, the incident still raised doubts over the government's commitment to the fundamentals of *Ostpolitik*. Equally strong was Kohl's embarrassment when a young writer contributed to the official newspaper of the Silesian movement a fictional essay about German troops "liberating" the eastern territories. Besides playing into the hands of the Soviet revanchism campaign, these events further damaged the already strained West German relations to Eastern Europe as a whole, and particularly to Poland. When Foreign Minister Genscher was forced to cancel a visit to Warsaw in December over several disputes concerning human rights and the participation of a conservative West

German journalist, West German-Polish relations had reached their lowest point since 1970.[112]

Despite these developments and the shock of Honecker's cancellation, inter-German relations remained surprisingly stable throughout the fall of 1984. Honecker made some concessions to the Soviets by joining their attacks against revanchist groups in the Federal Republic and by emphasizing socialist solidarity at the GDR's 35th anniversary celebrations in East Berlin on October 7. A joint communiqué with Gromyko, who headed the Soviet delegation, called for more "effective" coordination of Soviet and East German foreign policies. On the practical level, German-German ties demonstrated significant continuity. Although negotiations on cultural exchange, environmental protection, and scientific exchange stagnated, all traffic and transit agreements continued to function, a new border checkpoint was opened and an agreement on potassium mining was signed in December. Apparently upon the request of the East German leadership, however, these events were rendered as inconspicuous as possible.[113]

A chance for a new opening between Bonn and East Berlin came with the decrease in tensions between the two superpowers after Reagan's reelection in November 1984. The resumption of U.S.-Soviet arms control talks in Geneva in the spring of 1985 was greeted with relief by both German governments. The East German leadership took immediate advantage of the improvement in the international climate by resuming a more assertive policy toward the West. But apparently concerned about the rise of right-wing rhetoric in the CDU/CSU and the continuous anti-Bonn propaganda coming from Moscow, Honecker at first almost completely bypassed the FRG in favor of contacts to other West European states. In December Austrian Chancellor Fred Sinowatz visited the GDR. British Foreign Minister Sir Geoffrey Howe was Honecker's guest in March. In April Honecker met with Italian Premier Craxi in Rome. It was his first official visit ever to a NATO country, and he was even received by Pope John Paul II. In June French Prime Minister Laurent Fabius became the first head of government of one of the three Western allied powers to make an official visit to the GDR.[114]

When the GDR decided to reach out to the Federal Republic again, it chose as its partner not the government in Bonn, but members of the SPD. Whether Honecker had become genuinely disillusioned with the policies of the Kohl government or whether this approach was another way of appeasing Soviet suspicions is not clear. Some observers even speculated that after the demise of the peace movement, the Soviet Union had adopted a version of the Popular Front strategy by seeking a coalition between communist and socialist parties in order to alienate Western Europe from its U.S. allies.[115] Whatever the cause, SPD members were the main beneficiaries of the renewed East-West thaw. In January the social democratic prime minister of North Rhine-Westfalia, Johannes Rau, was the first high-level West German official to visit the GDR since Honecker's cancellation.

In early spring representatives of the SPD and the SED opened official discussions over an agreement to ban chemical weapons from Central Europe. While the sheer existence of such talks was not extraordinary, the circumstances were. Since the mid-1970s, East and West German officials had periodically discussed disarmament issues with each other, a practice that was even continued by the CDU/CSU. Most observers saw these talks as devices to improve the political atmosphere rather than as elements of a genuine arms control process. With the negotiations on chemical weapons, however, high-level political representatives from both countries worked for the first time toward a concrete agreement that would impose specific requirements on the two German states. The agreement challenged the policies of the two military blocs, both of which had plans for the stationing and use of chemical weapons in a crisis. Another unprecedented element was the East German concession to allow on-site inspections on its own territory. Although the Kohl government sharply criticized the SPD for usurping the role of the government in the course of the negotiations and thus undermining official West German policy, it never assailed the agreement as such.[116]

Just as some SPD officials had hoped, the talks on chemical weapons served as a catalyst for inter-governmental relations between the two states. When Hermann Axen, the foreign policy expert in the SED Politbureau, arrived in Bonn in the beginning of March for the purpose of talks with the SPD, he used this opportunity also to meet with Genscher and the under-secretary for inter-German affairs in the chancellor's office, Wolfgang Schäuble. This occasion was not only the first high-level meeting between the FRG and GDR since Honecker's cancellation, but the first time that a West German foreign minister had received a leading member of the Politbureau in Bonn.[117]

Kohl's state of the nation address on February 27, in which he confirmed his government's recognition of the post-war borders and even used the term "Poland's western border" for the Oder-Neiße line, contributed to the end of the "quarantine" that the Soviets had imposed on Eastern Europe's relations with the FRG. East Berlin responded positively to the speech, which had been Kohl's strongest endorsement of the Eastern Treaties since the beginning of his tenure, although it was harshly criticized by TASS. In early March Genscher visited Poland and Bulgaria after meeting with Gromyko in Moscow. At the spring fair in Leipzig, which proved again to be an accurate gauge for inter-German ties, Honecker visited the booth of a West German company where he commended Kohl for his speech and expressed optimism about inter-German relations. Two days later the West German minister of trade and newly elected chairman of the FDP, Martin Bangemann, travelled to Leipzig to become the first government official to meet with Honecker in more than a year.[118]

Bangemann's talks on trade and humanitarian issues were interrupted by the news of Chernenko's death and his immediate succession by Mikhail Gorbachev. This announcement was received with relief all over Eastern Europe. Although few people dared to predict what course the new general secretary would pursue toward the West, most East European leaders expected that a reinvigorated leadership in the Kremlin would facilitate the development of East–West detente. These hopes were enhanced by the relaxed atmosphere at Chernenko's funeral in Moscow and the prospect of a U.S.-Soviet summit meeting. As with their encounter at Andropov's funeral a year earlier, Kohl and Honecker conducted a noticeably friendly conversation and released a communiqué that was both commendatory of the past and optimistic about the future of inter-German relations. The two leaders stressed the inviolability of the European borders and their desire to work toward peace. Although a future visit by Honecker to the FRG was not officially discussed, commentators immediately began speculating over the prospects for such a trip.[119]

Kohl's meeting with Gorbachev, however, was overshadowed by a new issue that particularly preoccupied the Soviets: the U.S. Strategic Defense Initiative (SDI). Two years after Reagan had first suggested the construction of a defensive shield against a nuclear attack, the West European states came under increasing pressure to take a position on the plan. The SDI (popularly dubbed "Star Wars") was one of the main issues at the Geneva arms control negotiations, and the U.S. government had begun to actively solicit support and cooperation from its allies. While both political elites and public opinion in most West European countries had at first been strongly opposed to the Star Wars concept, years of anemic economic growth and an increasing lag behind the United States and Japan in high technology had introduced a new factor into the debate. An increasing number of people in business and politics argued that participation in SDI research was Europe's only chance to return to the frontiers of technological research and to remain economically competitive.

While France under President François Mitterand declared early its firm opposition to the SDI scheme, the Kohl government was still undecided at the time of Chernenko's funeral. But what was for the West German government a disturbing and often perplexing issue was perceived by the Soviet leadership as a question of life and death. The fear that the expenses of an unrestrained arms race in space would cripple the Soviet economy and forestall the necessary economic recovery had already induced the Soviets to return to the nuclear bargaining table in Geneva. Thus undercutting West European support for the SDI became one of Gorbachev's highest priorities in his foreign policy, just as the Kremlin had supplemented the INF negotiations in 1982 and 1983 with a propaganda campaign aimed at West European public opinion. Although Gorbachev was aware that the NATO allies did not play the same crucial role in SDI as they did in the deployment of the Pershing and cruise missiles, the question of their participation was a central concern for both Washington and Moscow. Fortunately for the Soviets, the space weapon's system promised to have a similar emotional appeal to the peace-inclined West European population in Western Europe as the INF did. And just as in the case of the Pershing II and cruise missiles, the superpowers were most interested in the decisions taken by the Federal Republic, which was also the country most vulnerable to popular pressure at home.

It was therefore not surprising that Kohl found himself caught in a crossfire between East and West. At Kohl's meeting with Gorbachev at Chernenko's funeral, the Soviet leader made progress in both West German-Soviet and inter-German relations dependent on West German abstention from SDI. An editorial in *Pravda* restated this point a few days later: "Of decisive importance will be what policy the Federal Republic will conduct in respect to the security interests of the USSR and of its allies." The icy atmosphere during Kohl's meeting with Gorbachev was also interpreted as warnings from Moscow against U.S.-West German cooperation in SDI. In June Honecker confirmed this message in a letter to Kohl, in which he noted that West German participation in Star Wars would inevitably have a negative effect on inter-German relations.[120]

Kohl's vacillating attitude in the following months only increased his vulnerability to pressures from all sides. President Reagan, upon Kohl's request, did not cancel his controversial visit to the military cemetery in Bitburg during his trip to Europe commemorating the 40th anniversary of the defeat of Nazi Germany. The chancellor tried to show his gratitude by supporting Reagan's space weapons plans. In a speech in the German *Bundestag* on April 18, Kohl announced his government's cooperation with the United States in the SDI. Moscow immediately denounced the German move; Gromyko told Genscher at a meeting in Vienna that the Germans "had to bear the full responsibility for the consequences" of participation in the SDI. But Kohl's decision was also controversial within the FRG. Not only did the SPD maintain its total rejection of Star Wars, but even Genscher opposed West German participation out of concern for West German relations with the Eastern bloc and with France. In May, Kohl partly reversed his position when he stated at a NATO meeting in Stuttgart that the SDI was "both a chance and a risk for the alliance."[121] As the prospect of large research grants to German corporations and access for German scientists to information on U.S. advances in space technology became more tempting in the course of the summer, the West German government again moved closer to the U.S. position. In October, the FRG and Britain sent missions simultaneously to Washington in order to discuss their countries' involvement in the space weapons project. By the end of 1985, the Federal Republic had already committed itself to some form of participation in SDI.[122]

Whether to punish Kohl's SDI decision or just to continue its ongoing revanchism campaign, the Soviet leadership consciously excluded the West German government from its accommodating moves toward Western Europe. At Chernenko's funeral, Kohl was the last of the major Western statesmen to meet Gorbachev. While the Soviet leader accepted Mitterand's invitation to Paris, he made no indication of planning a visit to Bonn, although such a move would have strongly enhanced the prospects of inter-German relations. Like the East Germans, the Soviets passed over the Kohl government in favor of the Social Democratic opposition. Gorbachev received SPD leader Willy Brandt with the highest honors during his trip to Moscow in May, and responded with a personal letter to Brandt's message commemorating the tenth anniversary of the Moscow Treaty in August. In stark contrast, he practically ignored similar notes from Kohl and Genscher. Brandt received a similar reception from Honecker when he visited East Berlin in September.[123]

Whether the arrival of a new Soviet leadership actually gave the East Germans more room for maneuver in their relations with the West was difficult to establish at first. A meeting between East German Foreign Minister Fischer and his Soviet colleague Gromyko shortly after Gorbachev's ascent did not suggest an imminent improvement in inter-German relations. The two politicians cited the continuing INF deployment in the FRG as well as West German participation in the SDI as major obstacles to detente in Europe. East German maneuverability was also limited by Gorbachev's attempts to strengthen his control over Eastern Europe, following years of rather loose rein. After months of behind-the-scenes negotiations, the Warsaw Pact was renewed for another 20 years on April 26. Despite pressure from some East European states, particularly Romania, the terms of the pact were neither changed, nor were the small states given more input into military decisions. At several meetings of the CMEA, the Soviet Union demanded stepped-up deliveries on high-quality goods from Eastern Europe, a measure that makes export to the West more difficult, and stressed the need for more internal economic integration as compared to extensions of trade relations with the West. Although some commentators speculated that Gromyko's move in June from the post of foreign minister to the primarily representative position of state president would result in a liberalization of Soviet policies, these expectations were soon disappointed. An article under the pseudonym of "O. Vladimirov" in *Pravda* on June 21 sharply attacked national economic experiments and the detente policies of unnamed East European states. Calling for increased bloc solidarity, the article constituted the strongest affirmation of Soviet dominance in Eastern Europe since the attacks against the GDR in the summer of 1984.[124]

Still, other events indicated different trends in East–West relations. When in May Honecker welcomed the Romanian state and party leader Ceaucescu in East Berlin, the two leaders expressed their complete agreement on foreign policy issues. While the joint communiqué, which supported most Soviet positions on arms control, indicated Romania's interest to come closer to the foreign policy mainstream of the Eastern bloc, it was simultaneously a demonstration of Honecker's continuing quest for independence. The meeting showed that the axis East Berlin-Bucharest, which had developed during the Soviet revanchism campaign in the summer of 1984, had become a permanent feature of East European politics and had the potential to strengthen the GDR's position *vis-à-vis* the Soviet Union.[125]

Also, Gorbachev's emphasis on improved economic performance and particularly his efforts to overcome Eastern Europe's lag in high technology created new opportunities for the GDR's Western policy. Since inter-German trade constitutes one of the main windows for Western technology and is a major factor for the GDR's economic stability, it was difficult for the Kremlin to call for advances in technology while at the same time discouraging inter-German ties. Thus in the months after Gorbachev's ascent, the GDR softened its rhetoric toward Bonn and actually achieved significant progress in a number of issues with the FRG. In contrast to the Soviets and other East European governments, the GDR refrained from the usual attacks against West German revanchism in their celebrations for the end of World War II, although the occasion lent itself well for this purpose. Officials from the FRG and GDR agreed on resuming the youth exchange program between the two states, which had been interrupted in the year before. In exchange for less than DM 50 million in annual payments, the GDR consented to the construction of a glass fiber cable and a radio relay system between the FRG and West Berlin. Visits of East Germans to the FRG for urgent family matters increased by almost 20 percent in the first half of 1985, while the number of West Germans who traveled to the GDR increased by 10 percent. Inter-German trade in the first half of 1985 amounted to DM 8 billion, 7 percent more than in the previous year.[126]

In April Günter Mittag, the economics expert in the SED, came to Bonn to discuss an extension of the swing agreement that was due to expire in late 1985. Without a renewal, the swing would have automatically fallen from the current DM 600 million to a base level of DM 200 million. Negotiations continued until July, when the FRG and the GDR agreed to increase the interest-free loan from DM 600 million to DM 800 million annually. In return, East German officials promised to restrict the influx of Asian refugees, in particular of Tamils from Sri Lanka, who had flown into the East Berlin airport of Schönefeld and crossed the zonal border to the West with the tacit approval of East German authorities. Since Western customs officials do not check passports of people entering West Berlin, there was no way to curb this influx from the western side. Although this agreement promised to alleviate a serious problem for West Berlin, the concession of the GDR was still relatively small and reflected its strong bargaining position. In the previous two years, the GDR had never used more than a third of the swing credit line. It had also demonstrated its independence from West German funds by borrowing $1 billion in new loans on the international capital markets in the first half of 1985. Most of this money was immediately deposited in East German bank accounts in West

European banks, a measure that was supposed to strengthen the GDR's credit rating.[127]

The most significant breakthrough came in the field of cultural relations. Throughout the year, a number of inter-German cultural events had fueled new hopes for the conclusion of a cultural exchange agreement. In the course of the fall, East and West German negotiators finally broke the deadlock that had thwarted an agreement for 14 years. In December 1985, a few weeks after the United States and the Soviet Union reopened bilateral cultural relations at the Geneva summit, the FRG and the GDR presented the framework for an accord to intensify cultural relations between the two German states.

While cooperation on economic issues continued to function swiftly, the fundamental ideological aspects of the inter-German relationship again proved their ability to disrupt practical agreements. In mid-June Kohl finally gave his address at the congress of the Silesian expellees in Hannover. His speech emphasized the West German recognition of the post-war borders but also mentioned the CDU/CSU's proviso concerning a unified Germany. Although West German officials later insisted that Kohl had only repeated earlier statements, the East German press responded with heavy criticism and accused Bonn of disregarding East German sovereignty. In the same month, the GDR launched another propaganda offensive against the West German interpretation of the Elbe border. The GDR was able to cite a recently released SPD report which supported the East German position that the inter-German border was situated in the middle of the river. Although the two sides were still far away from an agreement, the pressure on Bonn to compromise on the Elbe border was constantly growing. It was widely believed that a concession on this issue would be one way of inducing Honecker to reschedule his visit to the Federal Republic.[128]

A test of a different kind for the German-German relationship came with the uncovering of a major spy scandal in the FRG in August after the chief of West German counterintelligence service, Hans Joachim Tiedge, defected to the GDR. Despite the explosive consequences of the scandal for Western security, officials in East and West Germany managed to isolate their bilateral relations from the events. At the height of the debate over the affair, Franz Josef Strauß travelled to Leipzig to confer with Honecker at the annual fall fair.

The meeting between these two unlikely partners symbolized best the direction that inter-German relations had moved in the 1980s. For it is the domestic consensus in West Germany on better ties with the GDR, the unswerving interest of the SED leadership in this relationship for purposes of economic benefits and legitimacy, and the growing ability of both German states to isolate their relations from the constraints created by their memberships in hostile military alliances which holds the promise that the inter-German rapprochement will continue despite sizable domestic and international obstacles. This process was facilitated by the normalization of U.S.-Soviet relations since Gorbachev's ascent. With the summit meeting between Reagan and Gorbachev in Geneva on November 19 and 20, 1985, East-West relations seemed to have come full circle since 1979. The United States and the Soviet Union had returned to a state of affairs similar to the one before Afghanistan and Poland. Each was again in basic agreement with its allies over the correct policy toward the other bloc. At least for the moment, the gap between Europe and the superpowers seemed to have narrowed. Under these conditions, the road for Honecker's visit to the Federal Republic was finally paved.

Yet the FRG and the GDR have come a long way since the end of the "era of consensus" in 1979. Although inter-German relations are still sensitive to fluctuations in U.S. and Soviet policies, they have developed a life of their own that transcends the uncertainties of superpower relations.

NOTES

1.   See A. James McAdams, "Surviving the Missiles: the GDR and the Future of Inter-German Relations," *Orbis* 27 (Summer 1983): 351; and Angela Stent, "Soviet Policy toward the German Democratic Republic," in Sarah M. Terry, ed., *Soviet Policy in Eastern Europe* (New Haven: Yale University Press, 1984), p. 56.

2.   See *Der Spiegel,* April 7, 1980.

3.   Klaus Bölling, *Die fernen Nachbarn: Erfahrungen in der DDR* (Hamburg: Gruner & Jahr, 1983), pp. 78–82, 179. Schmidt said after the meeting: "I was moved to hear from Honecker and [Polish party leader] Gierek the same things that I told them: that we shouldn't let ourselves be pulled in if we can avoid it somehow." Similarly, Honecker emphasized "the responsibility of both German states for preserving peace" after the meeting. See *Neues Deutschland,* May 22, 1980.

4.   Pierre Lellouche, "Europe and her Defense," *Foreign Affairs* 59 (Spring 1981): 823.

5.   See Wolfgang Seiffert, "Polen bedroht das Machtmonopol der SED," *Der Spiegel* 43 (October 20, 1980); and Peter Jochen Winters, "Kurswechsel Ost-Berlins gegenüber Bonn," *Europa-Archiv* 1 (1981): 31-4.

6.   *Literaturnaya Gazeta,* July 23, 1980. Quoted in *Der Spiegel,* October 20, 1980.

7.   Bölling, *Die fernen Nachbarn,* pp. 124-5.

8. For example, Günter Gaus, *Wo Deutschland liegt: Eine Ortbestimmung* (Hamburg: Hoffmann und Campe, 1983), pp. 264-7.

9. Erich Fastenrath, "Erhöhung des Zwangsumtausches und vertragliche Bindungen," *Deutschland Archiv* 14 (January 1981): 44-9.

10. The GDR still denies every connection between this measure and the crisis in Poland. See, for instance, Honecker's interview in *Neues Deutschland,* February 13, 1981.

11. *Neues Deutschland,* October 14, 1980.

12. *Der Spiegel,* October 20, 1980.

13. See Seiffert, "Polen bedroht das Machtmonopol der SED," and McAdams, "Surviving the Missiles," pp. 355-8.

14. Bölling, *Die fernen Nachbarn,* pp. 83-4, 120-1.

15. In his remarks, the SED leader indicated his approval the FRG's loyalty to the West, but singled out the INF decision for criticism: "We have never considered to loosen the relations of the Federal Republic to its allies, especially to the United States. We also do not dream of the possibility to maintain good relations to the Federal Republic of Germany, one of the strongest states in NATO, when the relations between the USA and the USSR are aggravated by an unpredictable, confrontational policy of the United States." See *Neues Deutschland,* April 12, 1981.

16. *Neues Deutschland,* August 4, 1981. See also McAdams, "Surviving the Missiles," p. 362; and *Der Spiegel,* August 10, 1981.

17. McAdams, "Surviving the Missiles," pp. 361-2.

18. Bölling, *Die fernen Nachbarn,* pp. 118-9.

19. Wilhelm Bruns has published a whole range of articles on German-German relations and disarmament. For the facts cited, see Wilhelm Bruns, "NATO-Doppelbeschluß und Deutsch-deutsche Beziehungen," *Die Neue Gesellschaft* 28 (September 1981): 839-40; and Wilhelm Bruns, "Die beiden deutschen Staaten und die Abrüstung," *Die Neue Gesellschaft* 29 (April 1982): 365-6.

20. Peter Jochen Winters, "Das deutsch-deutsche Verhältmis 1981," *Deutschland Archiv* 14 (December 1981): 1234.

21. Joseph Joffe, "All Quiet on the Eastern Front," *Foreign Policy* 37 (Winter 1979-80): 172.

22. Strobe Talbott, *Deadly Gambits* (New York: Knopf, 1984), p. 47, 79-81.

23. Ibid., pp. 90-1.

24. Bölling, *Die fernen Nachbarn,* p. 134; and Bruns, *Deutsch-deutsche Beziehungen: Prämissen — Probleme — Perspektiven* (Opladen: Leske & Budrich, 1982), p. 122, 127.

25. *Neues Deutschland,* December 14, 1981. See also Bruns, *Deutsch-deutsche Beziehungen,* pp. 124-5.

26. McAdams, "Surviving the Missiles," p. 365.

27. Bölling, *Die fernen Nachbarn,* pp. 120-5.

28. Andrzej Korbonski, "Soviet Policy toward Poland," in Terry, ed., *Soviet Policy in Eastern Europe,* p. 82.

29. Ibid., pp. 80-1.

30. Ibid., pp. 88-9.

31. Sarah M. Terry, "Theories of Socialist Development in Soviet-East European Relations," in Terry, *Soviet Policy in Eastern Europe,* p. 251.

32. Interview with Hans-Peter Schwarze, West Berlin, July 18, 1984.

33. Ronald Asmus, "The Dialectics of Detente and Discord: The Moscow-East Berlin-Bonn Triangle," *Orbis* 28 (Winter 1985): 768.

34. Bölling, *Die fernen Nachbarn*, pp. 261-2.

35. Bruns, *Deutsch-deutsche Beziehungen*, pp. 90-1.

36. Bölling, *Die fernen Nachbarn*, p. 210.

37. See Gerhard Wettig, *Entspannungskonzepte in Ost und West* (Köln: Berichte des Bundesinstitutes für internationale und ostwissenschaftliche Studien, 1979), pp. 26-7. Brzezinski still holds this view. See Zbigniew Brzezinski, "The Future of Yalta," *Foreign Affairs* 63 (Winter 1984-85): 295-300.

38. Raymond Garthoff, "Eastern Europe in the Context of U.S.-Soviet Relations," in Terry, *Soviet Policy in Eastern Europe*, pp. 338-9.

39. Interview with Hanns Jacobsen, Washington D.C., October 30, 1984. See also op-ed article by Jacobsen and Angela Stent in the New York *Times,* June 7, 1984.

40. Joseph Joffe, "Europe and America: The Politics of Resentment," *Foreign Affairs* 61 (Winter 1982): 581.

41. Gerhard Wettig, *Die Friedensbewegung der beginnenden Achtziger Jahre* (Köln: Berichte des Bundesinstitutes für internationale und ostwissenschaftliche Studien, 1982), p. 15.

42. Jonathan Dean, "How to Lose Germany?" *Foreign Policy* 55 (Summer 1984): 55.

43. *Neues Deutschland*, December 31, 1982.

44. Pierre Hassner, "Zwei deutsche Staaten in Europa: Gibt es gemeinsame Interessen in der internationalen Politik?" in Werner Weidenfeld, ed., *Die Identität der Deutschen,* (Bonn: Schriftenreihe der Bundeszentrale für politische Bildung, 1983), pp. 313-15.

45. See Michael Sodaro, *In the Shadow of the Missiles: East German and Soviet Perceptions of West German Foreign Policy,* (unpublished manuscript); and Bruns, "Der Grundlagenvertrag ist 10 Jahre in Kraft," *Die Neue Gesellschaft* 30 (January, 1983): 68-9.

46. For a good discussion of the East German peace movement see Ronald Asmus, "Is There a Peace Movement in the GDR?" *Orbis* 27 (Summer 1983): 301-41.

47. Robert English, "Eastern Europe's Doves," *Foreign Policy* 56 (Fall 1984): 49.

48. Interview with Dirk Schneider, Bonn, July 11, 1984.

49. Winters, "Die DDR in Moskaus Doppelstrategie," *Deutschland Archiv* 16 (February 1983): 113-5.

50. Bölling, *Die fernen Nachbarn*, p. 195.

51. Dettmar Cramer, "Ein deutsches Signal?" *Deutschland Archiv* 14 (May 1981): 561-3.

52. *Zur Lage der Nation im geteilten Deutschland.* Speech by Helmut Kohl, June 23, 1983 (Bonn: Presse-und Informationsamt der Bundesregierung), p. 26.

53. See Jonathan Dean, "How to Lose Germany?" *Foreign Policy* 55 (Summer 1984): 54-6, 58-9.

54. Maria Haendcke-Hoppe, "DDR-Außenhandel im Zeichen schrumpfender Westimporte," *Deutschland Archiv* 16 (October 1983).

55.   See Franz Loeser, "Der Rat der sozialistischen Götter." Excerpts published in *Der Spiegel,* August 6-27, 1984.

56.   Wolfgang Seiffert, "DDR: Wandel durch Abgrenzung," *Der Spiegel,* June 28, 1982.

57.   See McAdams, "Surviving the Missiles," p. 368, and Peter Jochen Winters, "Aufgeshoben, nicht aufgehoben," *Deutschland Archiv* 16 (June 1983): 561-6.

58.   Interview with Anne-marie Schlemper-Kubista, Bonn, July 11, 1984. Libor (London interbank offered rate) is the interest rate with which debtors with the highest credit rating are charged.

59.   For a description of intragovernmental fights around the loan, see *Der Spiegel,* July 7, 1983. For analysis of the impact of the loan on the GDR, see Ilse Spittmann, "Der Milliardenkredit," *Deutschland Archiv* 16 (August 1984): 785–8.

60.   The science and technology negotiations offer one of the rare examples where U.S. policy directly interfered with inter-German relations. The FRG had failed to reach an accord with both the GDR and the Soviet Union because of the dispute over the inclusion of West Berlin. In late 1982, Moscow indicated its approval for an arrangement for Berlin that was acceptable to Bonn. A West German-Soviet agreement would have induced the GDR to accept the same arrangements. However, Foreign Minister Genscher decided against concluding an agreement with the Soviets while the Reagan administration was pursuing a policy of confrontation. The science and technology agreement with the GDR has still not been signed. See Wilhelm Bruns, "Der Grundlagenvertrag ist 10 Jahre in Kraft," *Die Neue Gesellschaft* 30 (January 1983): 69.

61.   See Dean, "How to Lose Germany?" pp. 63-4, and Peter Jochen Winters, "Ungewisser Herbst," *Deutschland Archiv* 16 (November 1983): 121-3.

62.   Wolfgang Seiffert, "Die DDR kämpft um ihre Existenz," *Der Spiegel,* October 10, 1983.

63.   *Neues Deutschland,* November 26-27, 1983. See also Honecker's new year's address in which he repeated these themes, *Neues Deutschland,* December 31, 1983.

64.   In 1982, Hungary became the second East European country, after Romania, to join the International Monetary Fund. Poland's application is still pending.

65.   Letters to the editor in communist newspapers always enjoy official approval and are sometimes written by the editorial staff. See *Der Spiegel,* August 13, 1984.

66.   Robert English, "Eastern Europe's Doves," *Foreign Policy* 56 (Fall 1984): 51-3.

67.   The occasion was an article by the two Soviet defense experts Portugalov and Berymesky entitled, "Should We Put Our Foot Down?" See Oldenburg, "Moskaus Schatten werden länger," *Deutschland Archiv* 17 (August 1984): 835-8.

68.   English, "Eastern Europe's Doves," pp. 56-7.

69.   This last quote, in the original German, "Wir möchten dieses Teufelszeug hier nicht haben," has never been definitely confirmed. See *Der Spiegel,* August 13, 1984. For other East German reactions to the Soviet missile deployment see Ronald Asmus, "The Dialectics of Detente and Discord: the Moscow-East Berlin-Bonn Triangle," *Orbis* 28 (Winter 1985): 747-8; and *Neues Deutschland,* November 26-27, 1983.

70.   See Matyas Szüros, "The Reciprocal Effect of National and International Interests in the Development of Socialism in Hungary," published in *Taesadalmi*

Szemle (January 1984): 13-21. Quoted in Ronald Asmus, *East Berlin and Moscow: the Documentation of a Dispute* (Munich: Radio Free Europe, 1985), pp. 21-4.

71. Carl-Christian Kaiser, "Kontinuität mit Hindernissen," *Die ZEIT* 1 (January 4, 1985). For a discussion of the emigrants' motives and social background, see Anne Köhler und Volker Ronge, "Einmal BRD — Einfach: Die DDR-Ausreisewelle im Frühjahr 1984," *Deutschland Archiv* 17 (December 1984).

72. The scenario was suggested by Manfred Ackermann of the West German permanent mission in the GDR in an interview on July 17, 1984 in East Berlin. Although it is based on speculation, like all explanations of East German policy-making, it seems to be one of the most plausible interpretations of the sudden emigration wave.

73. Being eligible, of course, does not mean that one can leave immediately. This process can take many months or even years.

74. Walter Leisler Kiep, "The New Deutschlandpolitik," *Foreign Affairs* 63 (Winter 1984-85): 317-18, and Ilse Spittmann, "Die deutsche Option," *Deutschland Archiv* 17 (May 1984): 449.

75. See Maria Haendcke-Hoppe, "Konsolidierung der DDR-Außenhandelswirtschaft," *Deutschland Archiv* 17 (October 1984): 1060; and interview with Anne-Marie Schlemper-Kubista, July 11, 1984.

76. A more unorthodox explanation is that the loan of 1983, in which the FRG had received no direct concessions in exchange, had aroused Soviet suspicions over West German designs. In light of Kohl's reunification rhetoric, the Soviets had reason to believe that the loan was not a generous present, but was intended as an inducement for the East Germans to seek reunification. Thus the obvious trade between concessions in their travel policies and the loan could have served to reassure the Soviets that the inter-German relationship had not fundamentally changed.

77. The interview was reprinted in full length in *Neues Deutschland*, July 9, 1984.

78. Although some old (i.e. pre-1969) maps are likely to be still in use in some West German schools, this does not express a general policy, nor does it apply to any newly-produced maps.

79. *Pravda* actually modified the articles slightly. The world "particularism" was replaced by "pragmatism," a slightly more moderate term that is normally used in the context of the Hungarian reform. See Fred Oldenburg, "Moskaus Schatten werden länger," *Deutschland Archiv* 17 (August 1984): 840.

80. See Ronald Asmus, *East Berlin and Moscow*, pp. 25-30.

81. Oldenburg, "Moskaus Schatten werden länger," p. 838.

82. Interview with Dieter Dettke, Bonn, July 12, 1984. See also an article by Juri Kornilow in TASS, reprinted by *Neues Deutschland*, May 16, 1984.

83. See *Neues Deutschland*, May 24-25, 1984; and Herbert Neubert, "The Actual Task of Communists," *Horizon* (1984) quoted in Asmus, *East Berlin and Moscow*, p. 52.

84. Oldenburg, "Moskaus Schatten werden länger," p. 338.

85. Asmus, *East Berlin and Moscow*, pp. 46-9.

86. *Neues Deutschland*, August 1, 1984.

87.   See Asmus, *East Berlin and Moscow*, pp. 53-4; and *Süddeutsche Zeitung*, August 3, 1984.

88.   *Frankfurter Allgemeine Zeitung*, August 6, 1984. For quotation of Tulkonov's article, see Asmus, *East Berlin and Moscow*, p. 55.

89.   *Süddeutsche Zeitung*, August 11/12, 1984.

90.   *Neues Deutschland*, August 19, 1984.

91.   *Frankfurter Allgemeine*, August 21, 1984; and Asmus, "The Dialectics of Detente and Discord," pp. 762-3.

92.   *Die Welt*, August 24, 1984.

93.   *Die Welt*, August 23, 1984; and *Süddeutsche Zeitung*, August 25/26, 1984.

94.   *Frankfurter Allgemeine*, August 29, 1985.

95.   *Die Welt*, September 3, 1984; and *Frankfurter Allgemeine*, September 4, 1984.

96.   *Neues Deutschland*, September 5, 1984. For more background see Wolfgang Seiffert, "Die Natur des Konflikts zwischen der SED-Führung und Moskau," *Deutschland Archiv* 17 (October 1984): 1043.

97.   For a discussion of this academic and political debate, see Michael Sodaro, *In the Shadow of the Missiles,* (unpublished manuscript).

98.   See, for instance, Honecker's speech in Gera, *Neues Deutschland,* October 14, 1980.

99.   For a general description of the SED leadership, see Bölling, *Die fernen Nachbarn,* pp. 202-20. For an analysis of the balance of power in the Politbureau in 1984, see Peter Jochen Winters, "Honeckers Kalkulation," *Frankfurter Allgemeine,* July 7, 1984.

100.   In general, there seemed to exist a split between party and government that became apparent through the divergent reporting of the party organ *Pravda* and the government daily *Istwestija.* See Seiffert, "Die Natur des Konfliktes zwischen der SED-Führung und Moskau," *Deutschland Archiv* 17 (October 1984): 1043-59.

101.   See Asmus, "The Dialectics of Detente and Discord," p. 769.

102.   Ibid., pp. 766-7; and *Der Spiegel*, September 10, 1984.

103.   Seiffert, "Die Moskauer 'Revanchismus'-Vorwürfe und die Gültigkeitsklauseln des Warschauer Paktes," *Deutschland Archiv* 17 (September 1984): 900-3.

104.   For a discussion of the motives for the Soviet revanchism campaign, see Seiffert, "Jetzt is Honecker gefordert," *Der Spiegel,* August 8, 1984; Seiffert, "Die Natur des Konflikts zwischen der SED-Führung und Moskau," *Deutschland Archiv* 17 (October 1984); and *Der Spiegel,* August 13, 1984.

105.   Interview with Hugo Portisch, Vienna, August 21, 1984.

106.   *Frankfurter Allgemeine*, August 9, 1984.

107.   Transcript of interview with Helmut Kohl on the Austrian television network ORF, August 14, 1984.

108.   *Der Spiegel*, September 10, 1984.

109.   *Neues Deutschland*, September 7, 1984.

110.   *Süddeutsche Zeitung*, August 31, 1985.

111.   Theo Sommer, "Lieber zweimal Deutschland als einmal?" *Die ZEIT,* 39 (September 28, 1984).

112. Mari Gräfin Dönhoff, "Wie Vertrauen verspielt wird," *Die ZEIT* 38 (September 21, 1984); and Peter Bender, "Deutsche und polnische Hupkas," *Die ZEIT* 5 (December 14, 1984).

113. See Asmus, "The Dialectics of Detente and Discord," p. 765; Joachim Nawrocki, "Rückschläge, aber kein Kurswechsel;" and Carl-Christian Kaiser, "Kontinuität mit Hindernissen," *Die ZEIT* 1 (January 4, 1985).

114. Harald Kleinschmid, "DDR in Westen aktiv," *Deutschland Archiv* 17 (December 1984): 1233-5; Peter Probst, "Werben um NATO-Staaten geht weiter," *Deutschland Archiv* 18 (May 1985): 454-60; and *Frankfurter Allgemeine,* June 12, 1985.

115. Peter Jochen Winters, "Am strafferen Zügel: Zur 10. Tagung des SED-Zentralkommitees," *Deutschland Archiv* 18 (July 1985): 676.

116. *Frankfurter Allgemeine,* June 20, 1985. For an analysis and two opposing views on the SPD-SED agreement, see also *Deutschland Archiv* 18 (September 1985).

117. For negotiations on a chemical weapons ban, see *Frankfurter Allgemeine,* March 2 and June 20, 1985.

118. For Kohl's address on the "State of the Nation in Divided Germany," see *Deutschland Archiv* 18 (April 1985): 437-45. For Genscher's trip, see *Süddeutsche Zeitung,* March 4, 5, 8, 9-10, 1985. For Honecker's comments at the Leipzig fair, see *Süddeutsche Zeitung,* March 11, 1985; and *Frankfurter Allgemeine,* March 13, 1985.

119. *Süddeutsche Zeitung,* March 13, 1985.

120. See *Der Spiegel,* March 18 and September 23, 1985.

121. Ibid., May 6 and May 27, 1985.

122. *Frankfurter Allgemeine,* October 19 and November 15, 1985.

123. *Frankfurter Allgemeine,* May 29 and August 13, 1985; Interview with Willy Brandt, *Der Spiegel,* June 3, 1985; and *Frankfurter Allgemeine,* September 19, 1985.

124. See Peter Probst, "Der Warschauer Pakt wird verlängert," *Deutschland Archiv* 18 (June 1985): 568-70; and *Frankfurter Allgemeine,* July 1 and 4, 1985.

125. See *Frankfurter Allgemeine,* June 1, 1985; and Peter Probst, "Rumänischer Staatsbesuch in der DDR," *Deutschland Archiv* 18 (July 1985): 686-8.

126. See Peter Jochen Winters, "Nicht Eiszeit, aber Pause," *Deutschland Archiv* 18 (March 1985): 227-8; *Süddeutsche Zeitung,* March 16, March 22, April 12, April 23, 1985; *Frankfurter Allgemeine,* June 22, August 22, 1985; and *Der Spiegel,* April 8, 1985. For the summer of 1986, the GDR is planning a major exhibition of Baroque art in Dresden. See Michael Stürmer, "Wem wird die deutsche Geschichte gehören?" *Frankfurter Allgemeine,* August 3, 1985.

127. In mid-1985, the GDR had outstanding foreign debts of $8.36 billion, compared to a $4.49 billion balance in foreign bank accounts. See *Frankfurter Allgemeine,* August 22, 1985. For information on the swing negotiations, see Probst, "Werben um NATO-Staaten geht weiter," pp. 457-8, and *Frankfurter Allgemeine,* March 20, July 6, July 10, 1985.

128. For East German reactions to Kohl's speech at the Silesian Congress, see *Frankfurter Allgemeine,* June 18, June 22, 1985. For the debate on the Elbe border see Ibid., March 26 and June 14, 1985.

7 CONCLUSION: TWO GERMANIES IN A CHANGING WORLD

Thirty-five years after the final division of Germany and 15 years after the beginning of the new *Ostpolitik,* inter-German relations still unleash fierce debates in the two German states and among their allies. Most recently, the inter-German thaw, the Soviet revanchism campaign in 1984, and the rise of a new leadership generation in the Soviet Union have drawn politicians, journalists, and social scientists from all different fields back to the old "German question." These events have raised some of the questions that were outlined in an earlier chapter: Is the Federal Republic still a reliable ally, or will it move toward neutralism and self-Finlandization? Is there room for more independence for the East European countries? Can the two German states go separate ways, and will they ever be reunited? Even observers with a less visionary bent are debating how far inter-German relations can move and if they will be able to prosper even during periods of U.S.-Soviet tensions.

The debate on these questions will probably never come to an end, for the answers are as relevant as they are unclear. Neither the consequences of the Polish crisis nor the East German-Soviet quarrel of 1984 and its aftermath have answered any of these questions. On the contrary, they have made the issues appear even more complex and obscure. All the events described in the last chapter can be used to support contradictory positions. Their interpretation depends more on the ideological bias of the debaters than on the facts themselves. Without claiming to avoid these pitfalls, this chapter will analyze the development of inter-German relations in the last six years and define their prospects by relating them to a larger development within and between the two alliances: the Europeanization of detente.

The most intriguing questions concerning the prospects for an autonomous European detente, which in turn constitutes the precondition for an autonomous inter-German detente, relate to the future of the Eastern bloc. One of the premises of a Europeanization of detente is that the Soviets are slowly loosening their iron grip over their European empire, and that the East European countries will be able to institute economic reforms and even permit the establishment of pluralistic political systems. Eastern Europe will then increasingly change its orientation from the Soviet Union to Western Europe, leading to an erosion of the division of the continent. This scenario of Eastern Europe's future is naively optimistic: real democracy will be elusive as long as the Soviets enjoy effective military control of the region. The events of 1956 in Hungary, 1968 in Czechoslovakia, and 1981 in Poland leave no room for doubt about that issue.

Still, developments in the last two decades have proven that East European countries are allowed to reform provided they stay within certain bounds. Changes in the East since the 1950s are remarkable. The argument does not hold that Eastern Europe can only reform after the Soviet Union has been fundamentally transformed. Already today, the life styles, atmospheres and standards of living in the Soviet Union and some East European countries belong to completely different realms. Hungary, in particular, shows the almost unlimited possibilities of economic reform. Tolerating political pluralism is more difficult, but the cases of Hungary and Poland, even after the period since the imposition of martial law, demonstrate that flourishing autonomous institutions like the Catholic church, a certain amount of free speech, and less repressive policies toward political opposition need not immediately evoke Soviet wrath.

The most prominent argument made about the prospects for reform relates to the economic needs of Eastern Europe. Gorbachev's stress on improving economic efficiency in the Eastern bloc, in particular, has aroused new hopes of liberalization and detente with the West. The experiences of the Soviet Union in the 1920s and Hungary since 1968 illustrate that genuine economic reform is almost always accompanied by the relaxation of political controls and the toleration of cultural pluralism. The two are closely intertwined. Economic reform can only succeed in an atmosphere of individual responsibility and thus requires increasing political freedoms and individual rights. And as the turmoil in Poland in the 1970s and 1980s has shown, political liberalization cannot be sustained in the presence of an inefficient economic system and the resulting economic difficulties.

Although some of Gorbachev's early statements have pointed in the direction of reform, such hopes could turn out to be immature. It is not yet clear that Gorbachev will give a green light to market-oriented economic reform measures similar to the Hungarian model. His actions have emphasized increasing efficiency and discipline within the central planning system as the key to more productivity rather than instituting free market mechanisms. The GDR, in particular, has been demonstrating for many years how relatively high-level economic productivity can be achieved with very little liberalization and reform.

Similarly, a more open foreign policy by itself need not result in internal economic and political reform. Brezhnev's detente policy in the 1970s was accompanied by an extremely conservative domestic course and economic stagnation. Today, Romania's maverick foreign policy and Stalinist political system demonstrate that a country can pursue detente without reform. Also, the GDR's relatively autonomous *Westpolitik* has not yet been followed by domestic liberalization.[1] In the reverse case, however, the link between external and internal relaxation is much stronger. For political and economic reform in an East European country will almost inevitably result in closer political, economic and cultural relations with Western Europe. Whenever an East European country embarks on a course of reform, it also increases its stake in detente.

The key to detente with Eastern Europe therefore lies in the success of economic reform. Only a profound change in the economy can change the political climate in these countries and allow a genuine opening to the West. For Western policymakers, this means that they should be more concerned with internal liberalization in Eastern Europe than with signs of independence in the foreign policy of these states. Western interests are hardly affected by the voting patterns of a WTO country in the United Nations. Where Western Europe's and the United States' interests, both economic and moral, come into play is in the transformation of the domestic climate in Eastern Europe. It makes sense for the West to expand trade relations and help Eastern Europe achieve a higher standard of living because the economic interests of the regime and population are the main determinants for this climate. Although economic benefits do not translate immediately into greater detente and better human rights policies, in the long run it is the only chance to move Eastern Europe toward reform. Even if some Communist party leaders would like to see Western trade and loans as a substitute for changes in the economic system, there is reason to believe that the former will ultimately stimulate the latter.

Nor is conflict between the Soviet Union and its Eastern European allies, such as the Soviet-East German dispute of 1984, always in the interest of the West. Just because a WTO country defies Moscow on some issues, it does not mean that it has embarked on the road toward liberalization. Ulbricht's last years in power were of a quest for independence, not in the name of detente, but of further demarcation. Although quarrels in the Eastern bloc might satisfy Western observers because they show that the Soviets also have trouble managing their alliance at times, they will not help the prospects of detente in the long run if they are not accompanied by more profound reforms within the countries themselves.

It is also questionable that a movement toward reform in Eastern Europe must automatically lead to conflict with the Soviets over detente with the West. As we have seen, the debate over detente is not simply between Moscow and its client states; it is also an ideological debate that cuts through practically every Communist party. It is not clear that the liberal factions in all East European countries will gain the upper hand. In the CSSR, for example, such a change seems rather unlikely; nor is the GDR a prime candidate for economic and political reform for reasons discussed earlier. Similarly, if Gorbachev actually adopts a policy of better relations with Western Europe in the coming years, it is possible that the disagreements over detente in the East will wither away.

Still, certain fundamental differences in interests and perspectives between the Soviets and East Europeans that go beyond ideological preferences of certain political leaders will persist even under a new Soviet strategy. East European states are by necessity more dependent on Western trade and more vulnerable to Western influences due to their more exposed positions. Given their political traditions, they are more open to political pluralism than are their Soviet counterparts, more likely to encounter resistance in the population, and thus more likely to show concern for reaching domestic consensus. This should not be interpreted as a sign of declining Soviet hegemony in Eastern Europe; rather, it should be seen as a fundamental transformation in the Soviet-East European relationship from dependence to interdependence, a reflection of the growing strength of the smaller states in their dealings with Moscow.[2] This need not, and should not, lead to open conflict over foreign policies, such as the events of summer 1984. Contrary to the common view among Western policymakers that friction in the Eastern bloc is of value in itself, a reform movement that is coordinated with Soviet policy has a much better chance of long-lasting success. Attempts by East European states to defy the Soviet Union too blatantly, even if done to defend detente, could actually hurt the cause of detente and should therefore not be encouraged by the West. What is needed are not vicious media campaigns between Moscow and East European capitals, but a differentiation of the countries' policies toward the West based on a pragmatic assessment of divergent interests.

In regard to such divergence in national policies of the Western alliance towards the East, the conflict of interest between United States and Western Europe seems today much less severe than it appeared between 1979 and 1982. This is primarily the consequence of changes in leadership in many NATO countries. In the FRG, Britain, Belgium, and the Netherlands, conservative governments received electoral mandates, the Socialist leaders of France and Italy have proven themselves to be the staunchest supporters of the Atlantic alliance in Europe, and the Reagan administration has moved toward a more conciliatory policy toward the Soviet Union. While there is still disagreement on specific issues, the fears within the alliance of a general drifting apart have faded.[3] This change in the overall climate in the alliance since the beginning of the INF deployment has taken the bitterness out of the trans-Atlantic quarrels over East-West relations, and has reduced the suspicion that inter-German relations aroused among the FRG's Western allies. Helmut Kohl enjoyed more leeway to advance inter-German relations than Helmut Schmidt ever did, mainly because he could not be accused of anti-Western sentiments.

The solution of the INF issue was a major reason for easing of political friction within the alliance. Given the absence of real military conflict in Europe, military hardware and doctrines have never caused conflicts by themselves. Few people in Europe care enough about detailed weapons technology and strategic doctrine to rally a mass movement in protest. The real problem is that Europe's defense ultimately depends on two political "gimmicks": the U.S. nuclear umbrella (the U.S. political commitment to defend Europe with its own strategic nuclear weapons), and the political unity of the Atlantic alliance. Both requirements are rather precarious and difficult to sustain in an intense political debate. Every time a new military issue is introduced, whether it is the multilateral force, the neutron bomb, or the INF, the old political dilemmas are brought back to the public eye: Will the U.S. really sacrifice New York for Hamburg? Will a nuclear war remain limited to Europe? Should Europe subordinate its own foreign policy to U.S. defense designs? Given the asymmetry of the alliance, no fully satisfying solution exists to this problem. The only way to prevent damage to the alliance is to keep military issues out of the political debate, thus offering no occasion to question NATO's viability. Had Schmidt followed this tenet in 1977, the whole INF controversy might have been avoided; and given the unclear military purpose of the INF, the political gain would not have been accompanied by any sacrifice in military security.

There is a good chance that history will repeat itself with the Strategic Defense Initiative (SDI). In contrast to the INF, the Star Wars project is not primarily concerned with European security; the Western European states play only a secondary role in the debate. Still, the controversy over SDI has already caused friction within the Western alliance, has sown suspicion between Europe and the United States, and has divided France and Italy from the Federal Republic and Great Britain. Most important, it has given the Soviet leadership another opportunity to undermine the unity of NATO by aiming its propaganda both at West European governments and West European populations. On several occasions, Gorbachev has tried to thwart the development of SDI by appealing to public opinion in Western Europe, most conspicuously before the U.S.-Soviet Geneva summit in November 1985. As always in such cases, the main prize in the U.S.-Soviet propaganda war has been the Federal Republic. In the course of 1985, when the government in Bonn tried to decide on its participation in the space weapons project, Soviet-West German relations were basically shaped by the Soviet preoccupation with SDI. Although the GDR, just like the other East European states, managed to insulate their policy toward Bonn from the Soviet campaign, it definitely slowed progress in inter-German relations.

If recent history can serve as a guide, Western Europe, and the Federal Republic in particular, should stay clear of the SDI debate. The effects of the project on West European security are complex and ambiguous. The argument that it would lead to a decoupling between Europe and the United States is simplistic and probably incorrect. A fully effective defense shield could strengthen extended deterrence by making the United States invulnerable to a Soviet retaliatory strike, while a partial effective shield would not have any stronger destabilizing effects on Europe than it would on the two superpowers. And since the concept of a tactical defense shield for European cities is even more far-fetched than the original Star Wars project, the question of European participation in research and development has little bearing on European vulnerability to a nuclear attack.

The economic and technological benefits of SDI for Europe are even more uncertain. A concerted plan to overcome the high-tech gap with the United States and Japan, like the French-initiated "Eureka" project, is likely to yield much higher payoffs. The costs that Western Europe would have to pay for direct participation are much more tangible: a temporary decline in detente in Europe, and, even more important, the reviving of the European peace movements and the devisive debates on armament policies, relations to the United States, and even the membership in the alliance. While the benefits of the SDI are years away, if ever to come, these developments will have an immediate and detrimental effect on the strength of the Western alliance, and particularly on the FRG. Neither is it advisable for Western European governments to be too outspoken in their opposition to the SDI. In contrast to the INF missiles, where Western Europe enjoyed a de facto veto power over the deployment, the future of SDI can only be decided in Washington. Strident criticism in West European capitals would only arouse U.S. mistrust of their allies, fuel isolationist tendencies, and prove ultimately futile in affecting the future of the space weapons program. Faced with this no-win situation, the best European leaders can do is adopt a neutral stand, or at least avoid any irreversible commitment.

One can apply a similar line of reasoning to designs of a "Europeanization of the European defense." It is an illusion to believe that a partial U.S. troop withdrawal linked to a stronger emphasis on European defense efforts will either improve Europe's defense posture or solve the political problems of the alliance. Not only do economic constraints in Europe make a large conventional buildup rather improbable, but tinkering with the structure of the alliance could cause another round of devisive defense debates in Western Europe and thus could alienate the allies from each other. Given the disunity within the European Community, a stronger European defense would neither provide Western Europe with more power in the international sphere, nor facilitate the pursuit of an independent policy toward the East. As long as Western Europe depends on the U.S. nuclear shield (and there exists no viable design yet that could replace this arrangement), the political dilemmas of the alliance will persist. Indeed, one can argue that these political problems are inherent in any alliance of this kind. And designs for the extension of the French and British nuclear shield to cover all Western Europe, particularly the Federal Republic, is likely to fail due to inter-European rivalries and the continuing German problem — the dilemma of finding an appropriate place on the continent for the state that is the strongest power but must always be kept in check by its neighbors.

While this analysis calls for better and less politicized alliance management with regard to policies toward the East, NATO's geographical conditions create certain divergent interests that cannot be overcome even by the most adroit political leaders. Western Europe and the United States espouse a different view of East-West trade. Western Europe, and particularly the FRG, regards the East as a natural market for its economic products, an interest that is not shared by the United States. Given their economic stakes, West European governments are unlikely to use trade as a political weapon, and thus will clash with the United States every time the latter tries to do so. This dispute becomes particularly sensitive in the area of technology transfer where it is intertwined with military concerns. Quarrels on these issues will be shaped by the policies and styles of various political leaders, but their periodic occurrence seems to be structurally determined.

This geographical proximity also influences West European political relations with the Soviet Union. The United States can afford to pursue a confrontational course with the Soviets, even over a sustained period. For Western Europe, and for the FRG in particular, such an approach has become extremely costly. There are too many economic, human, and psychological interests at stake to justify the abandonment of detente under current political conditions. To call this "self-Finlandization" is an insult to Western Europe's political, economic, and military power. Detente with the Soviet Union is not an irreversible surrender, but a policy geared to specific political and economic interests that are present at a given moment. European leaders only pursue a more conciliatory policy toward the Soviet Union because they believe that confrontational policies would not enhance their security and would damage other humanitarian and economic goals. But nothing would rally the West European countries around the United States and return them to a "policy of strength" toward Moscow faster than Soviet attempts to intimidate or threaten Western Europe. The only condition for this recourse is that NATO will not cease to exist. Thus Western Europe has to steer a fine line between pursuing its own detente with the East without jeopardizing the existence and viability of the alliance. This process is possible because Europe need not make radical choices, neither between loyalty to the alliance and neutralism nor between the United States and the Soviet Union. Not every West European opposition to a given U.S. policy foreshadows a drift toward neutralism, nor does every conflict with the

Soviet Union require a return to the Cold War. If the United States and Western Europe recognize that their interests diverge sometimes, just as West European and Soviet interests converge sometimes, then Europe will be able to pursue its own detente with the East without risking a breakdown of the Western alliance system.

This conclusion also holds for the Federal Republic. Despite innumberable warnings, this country is still not any closer to adopting a neutralist position than it ever was. Even the current SPD leadership, with its opposition to the INF deployment and its attempts to establish independent arms control links with the East, is strongly committed to the Atlantic alliance. Protests against the arms race and even the rampant anti-Americanism among parts of the West German population are primarily an expression of discontent with certain U.S. policies and attitudes and do not always imply the desire for neutralism. Again, polls showing a third of West Germans in favor of neutrality are more a result of these feelings of unease than of an interest in a fundamental reorientation of West German foreign policy. But attempts by their allies to deny West Germans the right to express these views only exacerbate the feeling of powerlessness that has pervaded the FRG in recent years and can thus foster resistance against the Western alliance itself. Thus the political emancipation of the Federal Republic and the West German population becomes a precondition for the future viability of NATO.

In the specific case of the FRG's relations with the GDR, the United States has rarely proven to be an obstacle to progress, even during periods of East-West tensions. Although U.S. officials sometimes fear that the FRG will make too many concessions to the Soviet Union in order to maintain inter-German relations, the relations themselves enjoy the support of all Western governments. Hence the main reason that inter-German relations are shaped by superpower relations is East Germany's foreign policy dependence on Soviet approval and leadership. As it has demonstrated many times, Moscow possesses de facto veto power over inter-German relations and does not hesitate to use it in the pursuit of its interests. This veto has been applied most frequently during periods of U.S.-Soviet conflict, when Moscow also sought a conflict with Western Europe. And due to the exposed position of both German states between the two blocs, they have never succeeded in insulating themselves from global tensions.

Despite this obvious link, it is too simplistic to say, as many analysts do, that inter-German relations can only prosper if the superpowers get along. The previous chapter demonstrated that inter-German relations are not always a reflection of superpower relations, but rather have a dynamic of their own. Twice in recent years, in 1980 and 1984, the FRG and the GDR managed to continue a thaw despite global tensions. The parallels between the two cases are surprisingly strong. Both times U.S.-Soviet relations deteriorated due to events in the late fall of the previous year — in 1979 because of the invasion of Afghanistan, and in 1983 because of the breakdown of the INF talks. Both times the inter-German thaw continued until early September, when it was terminated by Soviet pressure. Does this mean that Moscow allows its German ally eight months of freedom before it forces it to return to the fold of the alliance? Or does it take that long until Moscow's orders to break off relations reach East Berlin?

The answer is obviously more complex. Power in the Eastern bloc is not so centralized that each time the Soviets are in conflict with the West, all other member countries automatically follow suit. Instead, Moscow must first mobilize its allies so that they adopt a confrontational policy toward the West. But if such a policy is against the interests of the East European countries, then mobilization can become expensive. While GDR is highly dependent on the Soviet Union, this dependence is mutual. The USSR needs East Germany for its technology, economic strength, and strategic location. The Kremlin needs a stable regime in the GDR, as well as a population that is willing to cooperate with the government and work efficiently. If the Soviet Union regards it as necessary, it can force the GDR to do almost anything; the Soviet troops on East German territory are the ultimate lever. However, each time it uses this kind of force, the Soviet Union loses some of the consensus, some of the stability, and consequently some of the economic efficiency that it needs to manage its empire.

Whenever the Soviets wish to disrupt inter-German relations in order to mobilize the bloc against the Western alliance and punish the FRG for supporting certain U.S. policies, they must ask themselves whether the benefits are worth the costs. In 1984 they obviously decided that it was. In retrospect, their calculations may have been wrong, having been made by a weak regime without effective leadership or direction. For if the goal was to demonstrate to the West the unity of the Warsaw Pact, the attempt undoubtedly failed. Given this result, one must doubt whether Moscow will disrupt the harmony in the alliance every time that it wishes to cause a new Cold War. There are strong indications that the costs of mobilization have risen significantly and are likely to rise even further.

Thus to explain the downturn in inter-German relations in 1980 and 1984 by the Soviet desire to impose a uniform foreign policy on its bloc is generally unsatisfactory. A common front against the West cannot be reason enough for such heavy-handed intervention. Instead, it is much more plausible to explain the events of these two years by developments *within* the Eastern alliance. This is most evident in 1980. While the crisis between the superpowers had only limited effect on inter-German relations, the German-German thaw broke down in response to the Polish crisis. In Moscow's view, the Polish situation undoubtedly had important East-West aspects, since the strikes were partly blamed on Western influence. However, the real aim of the bloc-wide demarcation policy was not to demonstrate Soviet resolve to the West, but to protect the stability of the alliance. The crackdown on inter-German relations was a move against an internal, not an external, threat. And given that the East Germans shared the Soviet concerns over the Polish situation, mobilization was neither difficult nor expensive in this case.

In 1984, one is more tempted to argue that the campaign against inter-German relations was part of a strategy directed against the West. Undoubtedly, this was one of Moscow's rationales, but internal concerns again seem to have been more prominent. Due to its leadership crisis, the resistance of the East European countries to the deployment of Soviet missiles and the approaching expiration of the Warsaw Pact, the Soviets had reason to fear that they were losing control over their own alliance. The problem with Honecker's course was not that it helped the West Germans, but that it called into question the Soviet hold on the Eastern bloc. In order to reassert their power, the East Germans, the most recalcitrant of the allies, had to be disciplined. Inter-German relations became a victim, not of East-West tensions, but of the Soviet struggle for control over its own empire.

It is not clear whether the Soviets will intervene the same way in inter-German relations the next time that relations with the United States deteriorate. Given this analysis, one can imagine that they might very well arrive at a different conclusion. But even if the Kremlin demands bloc solidarity during every crisis, this need not affect inter-German relations as much as it appears on the surface. If we look beyond the two most dramatic moments in 1980 and 1984 and analyze the whole period since the breakdown of U.S.-Soviet detente, it becomes apparent that the two German states have cultivated much closer bilateral relations than the superpowers did. In the last 15 years, the FRG and GDR have developed an intricate web of mutual interdependence that promises more continuity in inter-German relations than global East-West relations will ever achieve.

It is the discontinuity in U.S-Soviet relations that hurts the two German states most. Every time the superpowers change their general policy toward each other, they need solidarity among their allies in order to lend credibility and momentum to this about-face. But once the change has taken place, alliance mobilization becomes less important and withers away. This dynamic allows the German states to continue their relations on a long-term basis regardless of superpower policies. And while the international situation can induce Honecker to cancel a visit, it does not fundamentally change the net of mutual interests between the two states. The fact that in areas such as cultural exchange inter-German relations still lag behind comparable relations between other East and West European countries is a function of their unique bilateral problems, not of the relations between the superpowers.

One should also be suspicious of sudden improvements in inter-German relations that seem to be part of a Soviet strategy to use them as a lever over West German policies. While the GDR adopted a more conciliatory position on some issues at the height of the Soviet INF campaign in 1982 and 1983, this rapprochement was conditioned on "correct" behavior by the government in Bonn — the carrot part of the Soviet double-track policy which was destined to be succeeded by the stick of an inter-German freeze if the West Germans deployed the Euromissiles. That this was the original plan became apparent in the Soviet reaction to inter-German relations after the INF deployment in December 1983. Only then, when East Berlin defied Moscow and continued the inter-German thaw, did the "false rapprochement" of the previous two years turn into a "genuine rapprochement," one that was based not on Soviet propaganda tactics but on the real interests of the two German states. Despite the short-term benefits a false rapprochement of that kind can bring to inter-German relations, it also introduces another element of volatility and discontinuity. Therefore it does more damage than good to the relationship between Bonn and East Berlin.

Among other developments most likely to interfere with inter-German relations is a continuing arms race in Europe, not because of the weapons buildup as such but because it inevitably exacerbates tensions and provides the superpowers with an incentive to interfere in their allies' foreign policies. The INF deployment has shown how difficult it is for both German states to carry on bilateral relations while their alliances deploy new weapons systems on their territories. The general question is whether the German states can improve their relations while the arms arsenals that are directed against each other are constantly increased. Hence, some experts have become interested in what inter-German relations can contribute to arms control in Europe. As we have seen in the case of INF negotiations, their role is very limited. The two German states have neither the forum, nor the authority and consensus necessary to conduct constructive bilateral consultations on arms control issues.

Even within their alliances, the two German states have little influence on the defense policies of the superpowers. The GDR's opposition to the new Soviet missiles probably went as far as it could go, and yet it had no significant effect on the outcome. Although the FRG was central in the original INF decision in 1979, it was essentially restricted to the role of an observer once the Geneva talks were under way. Decisions concerning the talks were made in the White House, the State Department and the Pentagon. Theoretically, the *Bundestag* could have voted against the deployment. But such a step would have provoked strong doubts over West Germany's reliability. It would have raised the specter of neutralism and would have fueled support for a U.S. troop withdrawal in the U.S. Congress. Then the survival of NATO would have been endangered, not due to shifts in the military situation, but only to a political crisis. Ultimately, the FRG may have been forced to sacrifice autonomy in its foreign policy in order to placate its allies and save the alliance. We do not know what would have happened if the SPD, which voted against the deployment, had been in power at that time. But one can imagine that if it had had to bear government responsibility, it could not have afforded this vote.

Similar restrictions on the FRG and the GDR exist in the MBFR talks and in negotiations on confidence-building measures. German-German influence is strongly limited by the multilateral nature of the talks, Bonn's hesitation to take any initiative that would emphasize Germany's unique position in Europe, and East Berlin's unwillingness to swerve from the Soviet course. There are also irreconcilable differences between the two German counterparts on the issues of force estimation, practical confidence-building measures, and the transparency of military moves. This example should also make West Germans wary of putting too much hope in recent negotiations between the SPD and the SED on arms control issues, such as a chemical weapons ban. While inter-German agreements of that kind might serve atmospheric purposes, their influence on progress in actual arms reduction is questionable. And given the negative response such unilateral German advances on sensitive issues can create abroad, the Social Democrats might do more harm than good to the cause of detente with these talks.[4]

Still, there are ways in which the two German states, and particularly the FRG, can exert some influence on progress in arms control negotiations between East and West. Just by asserting its opposition to U.S. defense policies and thus causing tensions within the alliances, the FRG can induce its ally to be forthcoming in the arms control process. Although such a strategy runs the risk of doing more damage to the unity of NATO than it can benefit the cause of disarmament, the prospect of intra-alliance disputes has had some effect on U.S. policy, particularly as it concerns European security. The shift of the Reagan administration from rejecting the whole arms control process to seeking agreements with the Soviets in Geneva was due not only to U.S. domestic pressures but also to the constant criticism from Western Europe. In other examples, the role of Western Europe, and the Federal Republic in particular, is even clearer. The MBFR talks have continued for many years despite their lack of success, mainly because the FRG wished to maintain this forum for East-West consultations. Without persistent lobbying by Foreign Minister Genscher of his U.S. allies, the CSCE conference in Madrid would probably not have produced a final document. Finally, Reagan's speech in Dublin in June 1984, in which he endorsed the idea of a resolution for the renunciation of force between NATO and the Warsaw Pact at the Stockholm Conference on Disarmament, was largely a result of pressure from his European allies.[5]

It is often argued that all these negotiations and resolutions are futile and contribute little to the reduction of arms and troops in Europe. Nevertheless, the value of these talks should not be underestimated. Consultations and dialogue on military matters might not result in any military reductions, but through their impact on the political atmosphere they can be essential for progress in political detente and thus do more for Europe's security than the most effective disarmament measures. Short of radical cutbacks in the number of troops and weapons in Europe — and given the existence of two hostile alliances, this is a utopian concept — marginal arms reductions can do little to prevent wars. Whether the European states, including the Soviet Union, feel secure and therefore *are* secure depends primarily on the political climate between the two blocs. Even the threat of potential first-strike weapons becomes critical only in times of political crisis. Although the number of troops and weapons in Europe is much larger today than it was in the 1950s, Europe was much more insecure during the Berlin crisis from 1958 to 1961 than in the 1970s and 1980s. The codification of the political and territorial status quo and the growing net of economic interests and political contacts between Eastern and Western Europe have made a conflict in Europe an extremely unlikely prospect. In this process of building interdependence and confidence, the two German states can play a central role. And as long as military questions, such as the INF deployment, do not become political controversies, the arms race between the United States and the Soviet Union need not interfere with inter-German relations even if it involves European alliance members.

Returning to the earlier question of a "Germanization of detente," one might ask what the chances are that the FRG and GDR will link their interests in uniquely German national issues with those in peace and disarmament. Could the two German states collude against the interests of their alliances? As discussed earlier, reunification as a practical political goal is not a relevant issue in the inter-German relationship, nor is it a widely shared aspiration of the public in either country. In the realm of national goals, we are thus left only with economic and humanitarian interests. The former are held primarily by the GDR, the latter only by the FRG. Not surprisingly, West German economic services in exchange for East German humanitarian concessions have been the basic pattern of inter-German relations over the past 15 years.

While this process could continue without ever threatening the European bloc system, there remains the question of German desires to step out of the alliance system. Insofar as neutralism and anti-Americanism actually constitute a serious political force in West Germany, and the verdict on this question is still out, these aspirations have little to do with German nationalism and even less with inter-German relations. Even if some thinkers of the National Left talk about solidarity of Germans in East and West against the blocs as the first step toward reunification, pan-German nationalism seems to be only a means to make neutralism more attractive. What these theorists care about is not an all-German national state, but the dissolution of both Eastern and Western blocs. The driving force behind West German neutralism is a dissatisfaction with U.S. defense and foreign policies, as well as with the whole concept of a system of dual hostile alliances. Other West Europeans and Americans who are concerned about Germany's reliability should deal with these attitudes instead of approaching an inter-German rapprochement with suspicion or engaging in arguments about the danger of German reunification. If West German society is able to reestablish a consensus on defense policies, then neutralist arguments will soon lose their appeal.

The phenomenon of an all-German peace movement has drawn attention to the concept that Germans in East and West might collaborate in their attempts to make their homeland more secure. Such a vision is highly unrealistic. First, as long as the Soviets are the dominating military power in Eastern Europe, the GDR will never be able to withdraw from the WTO, or even disassociate itself as Romania did. And it is even unclear whether East Germans would desire such a step. Given their economic difficulties and their restricted freedoms, the aspirations of the East German people seem to be more practical: a higher standard of living, freedom to travel, more political freedom, and more pluralism in arts, literature, and popular culture. The striving for peace becomes a central concern only in a country that enjoys all these previous benefits, like the Federal Republic. Even the East German peace movement seemed to have been driven more by the general desire for political and religious self-expression than by a specific pacifist program.

The key to the future of inter-German relations lies in the internal conditions of the FRG and the GDR. In the West, the question is one of ideology. The more the Federal Republic moves away from reunification rhetoric and the more it recognizes East German sovereignty, the further inter-German relations can progress. This question is particularly pertinent to conservative governments. In the last few years, careless remarks by West German politicians and their stubborn refusal to even address any of the status problems have done more damage to the relationship with the GDR than many of the Soviet interventions. They have neither enhanced West German interests nor brought Germans on both sides of the border closer together. Even Honecker's cancellation in 1984 was at least as much the product of problems in the inter-German relationship as of Soviet intervention. Suggestions about German claims to the Polish territories east of the Oder-Neiße line, as they have been frequently voiced by members of the CDU/CSU, are as unrealistic as they are damaging to the FRG's relations with the East.

The faults for these superfluous conflicts lie on both sides. The GDR must understand that the relationship between the two states can only be "special" and must ultimately resign itself to the West German refusal to establish normal diplomatic relations between the two sides. There is reason to hope that under the right political circumstances East Berlin will agree to some concessions, for in recent years Honecker has shown considerable flexibility on the issues of diplomatic recognition and citizenship whenever he wanted to advance inter-German rapprochement. Still, despite its claims to represent the forces of realism, the SED is still far away from a genuinely pragmatic policy toward Bonn. The points on which the FRG must yield are the problems of the Elbe border and the documentation center at Salzgitter. Bonn would not sacrifice any genuine interests by compromising on these questions and could gain considerable concessions from the East Germans in return. Both issues are much more important for East Berlin than for Bonn — the Elbe because of Soviet strategic interests, Salzgitter because of a basic need for self-respect. On the citizenship question, a compromise could be found if the Federal Republic would commit itself to fully respecting East German citizenship without depriving any East Germans of their "German citizenship." Although an official agreement that is fully consistent with both the West German and East German constitutions is probably unattainable, so many legal issues in inter-German relations have been fudged in the past that there is no purpose to obstruct these relations for the sake of constitutional purity.

The central East German problem concerning inter-German ties is still the GDR's "stability dilemma," the paradoxical situation that a rapprochement with the FRG is at the same time essential for and detrimental to the stability of the East German regime. Whether the GDR moves toward an opening to the West or toward further demarcation, this stability will be in jeopardy. Demarcation is the easier course, and popular dissatisfaction with it can easily be suppressed. Contrary to some expectations in the West, such a policy can be reconciled with the need for a better economic performance. For many years the GDR has demonstrated considerable success in achieving relative prosperity, and thus creating the main condition for political stability, without resorting to genuine economic reform measures. In contrast to the Hungarian model, recent East German economic innovations have been concerned with improving the central planning process and creating a more effective incentive system but have included neither real decentralization nor the institution of an adequate price system.[6]

But the success of the East German economy depends to a large degree on West German payments and inter-German trade. Generally, it is inconceivable that in today's and tomorrow's world the Eastern economies can function without Western trade and Western technology. Throughout its history, however, the GDR has shown the ability to separate trade from politics. Until 1972 it enjoyed the benefits of inter-German trade without any political relations with the FRG. In the 1970s, it combined growing economic relations with the West with a strict demarcation policy. Ironically, it was precisely the detente with the Federal Republic and other West European states which strengthened the East German regime sufficiently so that today it can resist most pressure to reform. When East German party leaders look at the results of liberal experiments in Poland, they are tempted to conclude that their domestic stability can best be guaranteed only by a continuation of a hard line.

Thus the SED is undoubtedly capable of continuing its demarcation policy, even in the face of economic constraints and popular discontent, and is unlikely to choose a different course in the near future. Despite some measure of relaxation, the GDR is still ruled by one of the most repressive dictatorships in Europe, a regime that grants no political freedoms to its citizens and constantly violates their basic human rights. For several reasons, the bleak prospect for liberalization also constitutes a major obstacle to an inter-German rapprochement. First, demarcation makes the regime more suspicious of Western influence; it is inevitable that the SED will periodically crack down on contacts with the FRG in order to secure domestic order. Second, West Germans will ultimately resist any stepping up of economic and political relations if they are not accompanied by significant humanitarian concessions, especially the freedom to travel and to emigrate but also political liberalization in the GDR. Finally, without an opening up of East German society, inter-German relations lack the substance that would make them valuable. Without some freedom of expression, a cultural agreement is an empty piece of paper; and without the freedom to travel, the meetings between high-level officials become increasingly worthless gestures.

Still, there is some hope that the SED leaders will one day realize that Western influences will not lead to popular unrest; that if people are allowed to travel, almost all will gladly return; that a less rigid censorship would actually improve the credibility of the East German press and thus would provide the party with more influence over the people; and that it is easier to reach economic targets through a decentralized economy than with a rigidly planned system. Much of it will depend on the self-assurance of the East German regime, and that has been steadily growing. It is up to the East German policymakers to choose between the Hungarian and the Czech way. The GDR is at the crossroads today and could turn in either direction. If they choose the road toward liberalization and succeed, then there is considerable hope for inter-German relations.

The field in which the interests of two German states most strongly converge is the reduction of political tensions in Europe. But as long as the two superpowers do not pursue an excessively aggressive policy on the continent, this desire should not conflict with the requirements of the alliances. The best way for both the United States and the Soviet Union to maintain the stability of their alliances and keep the genuine loyalty of their respective German allies is to refrain from such policies and respect their national interests, whether it is economic relations, human contacts, or the pursuit of political detente.

It is not necessary for the United States and the Soviet Union to overcome all their differences in order to allow inter-German relations to prosper. All that the two German states need are stable and pragmatic relations between the superpowers that are not affected by swings in ideology, public opinion, or a general outlook on foreign policy. Fortunately, there exist signs that such a state has been reached in the mid-1980s. U.S. attitudes in the 1970s were characterized by exaggerated hopes for detente and subsequent disillusionment, while the Soviets neglected their responsibilities to preserve stability in their urge to transform themselves into a world power. If the Reagan-Gorbachev summit in November 1985 was an indication that both sides have actually become more realistic about the chances and limits of their relationship, then the era of wild fluctuations in U.S.-Soviet relations could soon be over. This does not mean that no East-West crises will occur, but it suggests that such incidents will not cause a major about-face in either side's foreign policy and thus a large mobilization effort within the alliances.

What will undoubtedly change is the structure of the alliances. Whether NATO will move toward a more dual structure in which Europeans gain more input both in political and military matters is difficult to foresee. But even fundamental changes are unlikely to alter the common interests that hold NATO together. This prospect is reassuring, for the main threat to European security comes neither from Soviet expansionism nor from superpower confrontations, but from the prospect of a breakdown of the alliance system. Whether it was intended or not, the bipolar system has secured peace and stability on the continent since the end of World War II.[7] While a slow weakening of the political division is in the interest of most Europeans, any move that would threaten the alliance system in itself, whether decoupling in the West or revolt in the East, would create an unstable power vacuum that could incite military conflicts on the continent.

The situation is more disconcerting in the East. There, the crucial question is whether Eastern Europe will be able to reform without upsetting the security interests of the Soviet Union. If these states, and particularly the GDR, succeed, then inter-German relations can progress further until they have reached a state of genuine good-neighborly relations. But a failure of Eastern Europe to reform, or a reform that jeopardizes the fundamentals of Soviet power and Soviet security interests, represents perhaps the most severe threat to European security for the future. It could lead to instability and unrest that would not only disrupt inter-German relations but also endanger the European post-war political order which has preserved peace for 40 years.

NOTES

1. See Georg Schöpflin, "Die Reformfähigkeit von Sowjetsystemen: Ist Ungarn ein Modell?" *Europa-Archiv* 4 (1984): 111–8.

2. For an excellent discussion of these different interpretations of Soviet-East European relations, see James McAdams, *Conceptualizing Change in Soviet-East European Relations* (unpublished manuscript).

3. Hans-Peter Schwarz, "'Europäische Interessen' im Ost-West-Verhältnis: Ein Scheinproblem," *Beiträge zur Konfliktforschung* 1 (1982): 5–28.

4. See Reimund Seidelmann, "Möglichkeiten und Grenzen der MBFR-Politik der Bundesrepublik Deutschlands und der DDR," in Ilse Spittmann and Gisela Helwig, eds.*Die beiden deutschen Staaten im Ost-West-Verhältnis*, 15, Tagung zum Stand der DDR-Forschung in der Bundesrepublik Deutschland, 1-4, June 1982. (Köln: Edition Deutschland Archiv, 1982), pp. 124–47; Reimund Seidelmann, "Deutsch-deutsche Rüstungskontrollpolitik?" *Deutschland Archiv* 17 (May 1984): 480–7; Wilhelm Bruns, "Ohne Vertrauen keine Abrüstung: Zur Position der DDR gegenüber vertrauensbildenden Maßnahmen," *Deutschland Archiv* 15 (June 1982): 596–605.

5. Interview with John Kornblum, Vienna, October 30, 1984; and with Dieter Dettke, Bonn, July 12, 1984.

6. For the debate on East German economic reform measures in the 1980s, see Karl Thalheim, "Gegenwärtige Reformansätze im Wirtschaftssystem der DDR — Renaissance des 'Neuen Ökonomischen Systems'?" *Deutschland Archiv* 18 (February 1985): 151–8; and Doris Cornelsen, Manfred Melzer and Angela Scherzinger, "DDR-Wirtschaftssystem: Reform in Kleinen Schritten," *Deutschland Archiv* 18 (February 1985): 140–51. In the same issue, see also Hans-Dieter Schulz, "Auch Honecker sieht eine Wende," pp. 113–7.

7. For an extensive presentation of a similar argument, see Anton De Porte, *Europe between the Superpowers: The Enduring Balance* (New Haven: Yale University Press, 1979).

Bibliography

BOOKS AND ARTICLES

Asmus, Ronald. "Bonn und Washington aus Washingtoner Sicht." *Deutschland Archiv* 18 (March 1985): 257–63.

____. "Is There a Peace Movement in the GDR?" *Orbis* 27 (Summer 1983): 301–41.

____. "The Dialectics of Detente and Discord: the Moscow-East Berlin-Bonn Triangle." *Orbis* 28 (Winter 1985): 743–74.

____. *East Berlin and Moscow: the Documentation of a Dispute.* RFE Occasional Papers, Number One. Munich: Radio Free Europe, 1985.

Bahr, Egon. "Neuer Ansatz der gemeinsamen Sicherheit (Rede vom 23.5. 1982)." *Die Neue Gesellschaft* 29 (July 1982).

____. *Was wird aus den Deutschen? Fragen und Antworten.* Hamburg: Rowohlt, 1982.

Bender, Peter. *Das Ende des ideologischen Zeitalters: Die Europäisierung Europas.* Berlin: Severin und Siedler, 1981.

____. "Deutsche und polnische Hupkas." *Die ZEIT* 5 (December 14, 1984).

Bertram, Michael. "Eine Lehre für die Deutschen." *Die ZEIT* 37 (September 14, 1984).

Bethkenhagen, Jochen, und Horst Lambrecht. *Die Außenhandelsbeziehungen der DDR vor dem Hintergrund von Produktion und Verbrauch.* Köln: Berichte des Bundesinstitutes für internationale und ostwissenschaftliche Studien, 1982.

Bethkenhagen, Jochen, Siegfried Kupper, Horst Lambrecht. "Über den Zusammenhang von außenwirtschaftlichen Interessen der DDR und Entspannung." In *13. Tagung zum Stand der DDR-Forschung in der Bundesrepublik Deutschland*, May 27–30, 1980. Köln: Edition Deutschland Archiv, 1980.

Bibliographie zur Deutschlandpolitik 1975–1982. Dokumente zur Deutschlandpolitik. Bonn: Bundesministerium für innerdeutsche Beziehungen, 1983.

Bölling, Klaus. *Die fernen Nachbarn: Erfahrungen in der DDR.* Hamburg: Gruner & Jahr, 1983.

Brandt, Peter, und Peter Ammon (Hrsg.) *Die Linke und die nationale Frage: Dokumente zur deutschen Einheit seit 1945.* Hamburg: Rowohlt, 1981.

Bruns, Wilhelm. "Die beiden deutschen Staaten und die Abrüstung." *Die Neue Gesellschaft* 29 (April 1982).

_____. *Deutsch–deutsche Beziehungen: Prämissen — Probleme — Perspektiven.* Opladen: Leske & Budrich, 1982.

_____. "Der Grundlagenvertrag ist 10 Jahre in Kraft." *Die Neue Gesellschaft* 30 (January 1983): 66–70.

_____. "NATO-Doppelbeschluß und deutsch-deutsche Beziehungen." *Die Neue Gesellschaft* 28 (September 1981).

_____. "Ohne Vertrauen keine Abrüstung: Zur Position der DDR gegenüber vertrauensbildenden Maßnahmen." *Deutschland Archiv* 15 (June 1982): 596–605.

_____. "Die Position der DDR auf der Stockholmer KVAE." *Deutschland Archiv* 18 (February 1985): 169–77.

Brzezinski, Zbigniew. "The Future of Yalta." *Foreign Affairs* 63 (Winter 1984/85): 279–302.

Büchler, Hans. "Was nutzt der DDR der Grundlagenvertrag?" *Die Neue Gesellschaft* 28 (April 1981): 338–41.

Buchnan, David. *Western Security and Economic Strategy Toward the East.* Adelphi Paper No. 192. London: International Institute for Strategic Studies, 1984.

Cornelsen, Doris, Manfred Melzer, Angela Scherzinger. "DDR-Wirtschaftssystem: Reform in kleinen Schritten." *Deutschland Archiv* 18 (February 1985): 146–51.

Cramer, Dettmar. "Ein deutsches Signal?" *Deutschland Archiv* 14 (May 1981): 561–63.

_____. "Eine überflüssige Diskussion: Über den angeblichen Bonner Revisionismus." *Deutschland Archiv* 17 (December 1984): 1272–74.

_____. "Ostpolitik im Wartestand." *Deutschland Archiv* 14 (January 1981): 1–3.

De Porte, Anton. *Europe between the Superpowers: The Enduring Balance.* New Haven: Yale University Press, 1979.

Dean, Jonathan. "How to Lose Germany?" *Foreign Policy* 55 (Summer 1984): 54–72.

Dönhoff, Marie Gräfin. "Wie Vertrauen verspielt wird." *Die ZEIT* 38 (September 21, 1984).

Döschner, Jürgen. "Zehn Jahre bundesdeutsche Korrespondenten in der DDR." *Deutschland Archiv* 17 (August 1984): 859–69.

Ehmke, Horst. "Sozialdemokratische Außenpolitik." *Die Neue Gesellschaft* 29 (March 1982): 206–12.

_____. "Überlegungen zur Selbstbehauptung Europas: Ein Diskussionspapier." *Politik: Aktuelle Informationen der Sozialdemokratischen Partei Deutschlands* No. 1 (January 1984).

English, Robert. "Eastern Europe's Doves." *Foreign Policy* 56 (Fall 1984): 44–60.

Fastenrath, Erich. "Erhöhung des Zwangsumtausches und vertragliche Bindungen." *Deutschland Archiv* 14 (January 1981): 44–9.

Fedder, Edwin H. *Defense Politics of the Atlantic Alliance*. New York: Praeger, 1980.

Gaddis, John Lewis. *The United States and the Origins of the Cold War 1941-1947*. New York: Columbia University Press, 1972.

Gati, Charles. "Soviet Empire: Alive But Not Well." *Problems of Communism* 34 (March-April 1985): 73–86.

Gaus, Günter. "Der Mann, der nicht von drüben kam." *Die ZEIT* 38 (September 21, 1984).

_____. "Wir dürfen an den Einflußsphären in Europa nicht rühren: NG-Gespräch mit Günter Gaus." *Die Neue Gesellschaft* 29 (August 1982): 712–20.

_____. *Wo Deutschland liegt: Eine Ortbestimmung*. Hamburg: Hoffmann und Campe, 1983.

Hacke, Christian. "Soll und Haben des Grundlagenvertrages." *Deutschland Archiv* 15 (December 1982).

Haendcke-Hoppe, Maria. "DDR-Außenhandel im Zeichen schrumpfender Westimporte." *Deutschland Archiv* 16 (October 1983).

_____. "Konsolidierung der DDR-Außenhandelswirtschaft." *Deutschland Archiv* 17 (October 1984): 1060–69.

Hassner, Pierre. "Was geht in Deutschland vor?" *Europa-Archiv* 17 (1982): 517–26.

Hoesch, Jan. "Ein Erfolg im Schatten." *Deutschland Archiv* 15 (October 1982): 1917–19.

Jacobsen, Hans-Adolf, Gert Leptin, Ulbrich Scheuner, Eberhard Schulz, eds. *Drei Jahrzehnte Außenpolitik der DDR.* München: Oldenbourg, 1979.

Die Integration der beiden deutschen Staaten in die Paktsysteme. Bonn: Friedrich-Ebert-Stiftung, 1980.

Joffe, Joseph. "All Quiet on the Eastern Front." *Foreign Policy* 37 (Winter 1979-80): 161–75.

_____. "Europe and America: The Politics of Resentment (cont'd)." *Foreign Affairs* 61 (Winter 1982/83): 569–90.

_____. "European-American Relations: The Enduring Crisis." *Foreign Affairs* 59 (Spring 1981): 835–49.

Kaiser, Carl-Christian. "Kontinuität mit Hindernissen." *Die ZEIT* 1 (January 4, 1985).

Kiep, Walter Leisler. "The New Deutschlandpolitik." *Foreign Affairs* 63 (Winter 1984/85).

Kissinger, Henry. *White House Years.* Boston: Little, Brown, 1979.

Kistler, Helmut. *Die Ostpolitik der Bundesrepublik Deutschland 1966-1973.* Bonn: Bundeszentrale für politische Bildung, 1982.

Kleinschmid, Harald. "DDR im Westen aktiv." *Deutschland Archiv* 17 (December 1984): 1233–35.

Kohl, Helmut. "Bericht der Bundesregierung zur Lage der Nation im geteilten Deutschland." *Deutschland Archiv* 18 (April 1985): 437–45.

_____. *Zur Lage der Nation im geteilten Deutschland.* Bericht der Bundesregierung abgegeben von Bundeskanzler Dr. Helmut Kohl vor dem Deutschen Bundestag am 23 June 1983. Bonn: Presse-und Informationsamt der Bundesregierung. Reihe Berichte und Dokumentationen.

Köhler, Anne, und Volker Ronge. "Einmal BRD — Einfach: Die DDR-Ausreisewelle im Frühjahr 1984." *Deutschland Archiv* 17 (December 1984): 1280–6.

Krippendorf, Ekkehart, and Volker Rittberger, eds. *The Foreign Policy of West Germany: Formation and Contents.* London: SAGE Publications, 1980.

Lellouche, Pierre. "Europe and her Defense." *Foreign Affairs* 59 (Spring 1981): 813–33.

Livingston, Robert Gerald, ed. *The Federal Republic of Germany in the 1980s: Foreign Policies and Domestic Changes.* New York: German Information Center, 1983.

Löwenthal, Richard. "The German Question Transformed." *Foreign Affairs* 63 (Winter 1984/85): 279–302.

Mahnke, Hans Heinrich. "Die besonderen Beziehungen zwischen den beiden deutschen Staaten." *Recht in Ost und West* 23 (July 1979): 137–51.

Mallinckrodt, Anita. "Bonn und Ost-Berlin: Andere Sichten aus Washington." *Deutschland Archiv* 18 (May 1985): 385–9.

McAdams, A. James. "Surviving the Missiles: the GDR and the Future of Inter-German Relations." *Orbis* 27 (Summer 1983): 343–70.

McGraw Olive, Marsha, and Jeffrey D. Porro, eds. *Nuclear Weapons in Europe: Modernization and Limitation.* Lexington, Mass: Lexington Books, 1983.

Menudier, Henri. "Das Deutschlandproblem aus französischer Sicht." *Politik und Kultur* 6 (1983): 20–37.

Mleczkowski, Wolfgang. "Die Enwicklung der innerdeutschen Beziehungen aus DDR-Sicht." *Deutsche Studien* 18 (1980): 108–23.

Nawrocki, Joachim. "Rückschläge, aber kein Kurswechsel." *Die ZEIT* 1 (January 4, 1985).

Niclauß, Karlheinz. *Kontroverse Deutschlandpolitik: Die politische Außeinandersetzung in der Bundesrepublik Deutschland über den Grundlagenvertrag mit der DDR.* Frankfurt/Main: Alfred Metzner, 1977.

Oldenburg, Fred. "Moskaus Schatten werden länger." *Deutschland Archiv* 17 (August 1984): 834–43.

Probst, Peter. "Warschauer Pakt verlängert." *Deutschland Archiv* 18 (June 1985): 568–70.

_____. "Werben um NATO-Staaten geht weiter." *Deutschland Archiv* 18 (May 1985): 454–60.

Rösch, Franz and Fritz Homann. "Thirty Years of the Berlin Agreement — Thirty Years of Inner-German Trade: Economic and Political Dimensions." *Zeitschrift für die gesamte Staatswissenschaft* 137 (1981): 525–55.

Roth, Margit. *Zwei Staaten in Deutschland: Die sozialliberale Deutschlandpolitik und ihre Auswirkungen 1969-1978*. Studien zur Sozialwissenschaft. Opladen: Westdeutscher Verlag, 1981.

Royen, Christoph. "Die Aussichten für einen Systemwandel in Osteuropa." *Europa-Archiv* 2 (1985): 31–40.

Schmidt, Helmut. "A Policy of Reliable Partnership." *Foreign Affairs* 59 (Spring 1981): 743–55.

Schmitz, Michael. "Das Beste für den großen Bruder." *Die ZEIT* (January 25, 1985).

Schöpflin, Georg. "Die Reformfähigkeit von Sowjetsystemen: Ist Ungarn ein Modell?" *Europa-Archiv* 4 (1984): 111–18.

Schulz, Hans-Dieter. "Auch Honecker sieht eine Wende." *Deutschland Archiv* 18 (February 1985): 113–17.

_____. "Honeckers 'Firma' muß lavieren: Innerdeutsche Handel braucht neue Impulse." *Deutschland Archiv* 15 (October 1982).

Schwartz, David. *NATO's Nuclear Dilemmas*. Washington, D.C.: Brookings, 1984.

Schwarz, Hans-Peter. "Europäische Interessen im Ost-West-Verhältnis: Ein Scheinproblem." *Beiträge zur Konfliktforschung* 1 (1982): 5–28.

Schweigler, Gebhard. *West German Foreign Policy: The Domestic Setting*. The Washington Papers 106. New York: Praeger, 1984.

Seidelmann, Reimund. "Deutsch-deutsche Rüstungskontrollpolitik?" *Deutschland Archiv* 17 (May 1984): 480–7.

Seiffert, Wolfgang. "Die DDR kämpft um ihre Existenz." *Der Spiegel*, October 10, 1983.

_____. "Jetzt ist Honecker gefordert." *Der Spiegel*, August 8, 1984.

_____. "Die Moskauer 'Revanchismus'-Vorwürfe und die Gültigkeitsklauseln des Warschauer Paktes." *Deutschland Archiv* 17 (September 1984): 900–3.

_____. "Die Natur des Konflikt zwischen der SED-Führung und Moskau." *Deutschland Archiv* 17 (October 1984): 1043–59.

_____. "Polen bedroht das Machtmonopol der SED." *Der Spiegel* 43 (October 20, 1980): 35–9.

_____. "Was bedeutet die Respektierung der Staatsangehörigkeit?" *Deutschland Archiv* 17 (November 1984): 1121–5.

Sommer, Theo. "Alte Krämpfe." *Die ZEIT* 49 (December 7, 1984).

_____. "Wie offen ist die deutsche Frage?" *Die ZEIT* 33 (August 17, 1984).

Spittmann, Ilse. "Andere müssen bleiben." *Deutschland Archiv* 17 (August 1984): 785–6.

_____. "Die deutsche Option." *Deutschland Archiv* 17 (May 1984): 449–55.

_____. "Großdeutsche Sprüche." *Deutschland Archiv* 15 (Januar 1982): 225–7.

_____. "Der Milliardenkredit." *Deutschland Archiv* 16 (August 1983): 785–8.

_____. "Weichenstellung." *Deutschland Archiv* 18 (August 1985): 785–8.

Spittmann, Ilse, and Gisela Helwig, eds. *Die beiden deutschen Staaten im Ost-West-Verhältnis*. 15, Tagung zum Stand der DDR-Forschung in der Bundesrepublik Deutschland. 1-4, June 1982. Köln: Edition Deutschland Archiv, 1982.

Stent, Angela. *From Embargo to Ostpolitik: The Political Economy of West German-Soviet Relations 1955–1980*. Cambridge: Cambridge University Press, 1981.

Talbott, Strobe. *Deadly Gambits*. New York: Knopf, 1984.

Terry, Sarah M., ed. *Soviet Policy in Eastern Europe*. New Haven, Yale University Press, 1984.

Thalheim, Karl. "Gegenwärtige Reformansätze im Wirtschaftssystem der DDR — Renaissance des 'Neuen Ökonomischen Systems?'" *Deutschland Archiv* 18 (February 1985): 151-8.

Vernohr, Wolfgang, ed. *Die deutsche Einheit kommt bestimmt*. Bergisch-Gladbach: Gustav Lübbe, 1982.

_____. "Deutschlands Mittellage." *Deutschland Archiv* 17 (August 1984): 820–9.

_____. "35 Jahre DDR und die nationale Frage." *Deutschland Archiv* 17 (December 1984): 1263–71.

Weidenfeld, Werner, ed. *Die Identität der Deutschen*. Bonn: Schriftenreihe der Bundeszentrale für politische Bildung, 1983.

Wettig, Gerhard. *Ansätze zu einer Theorie der Entspannung.* Köln: Berichte des Bundesinstitutes für internationale und ostwissenschaftliche Studien 27, 1979.

_____. *Die Beziehungen der Sowjetunion zur Bundesrepublik Deutschland.* Köln: Berichte des Bundesinstitutes für internationale und ostwissenschaftliche Studien 10, 1982.

_____. *Entspannungsinteressen in Ost und West.* Köln: Berichte des Bundesinstitutes für internationale und ostwissenschaftliche Studien 16, 1981.

_____. *Entspannungskonzepte in Ost und West.* Köln: Berichte des Bundesinstitutes für internationale und ostwissenschaftliche Studien 32, 1979.

_____. *Die Friedensbewegung der beginnenden 80er Jahre.* Köln: Berichte des Bundesinstitutes für internationale und ostwissenschaftliche Studien 9, 1982.

_____. *Instrumentarien der Entspannungspolitik.* Köln: Berichte des Bundesinstitutes für internationale und ostwissenschaftliche Studien 17, 1981.

_____. "Das Problem der Bindungen West-Berlins bei der Anwendung des Viermächteabkommens." *Deutschland Archiv* 12 (September 1979): 920–37.

Wilke, Michael-Kay. *Bundesrepublik Deutschland und Deutsche Demokratische Republik: Grundlage und ausgewählte Probleme des Gegenseitigen Verhältnisses der beiden deutschen Staaten.* Berlin: Duncker & Humblot, 1976.

Windsor, Philip. *Germany and the Western Alliance: Lesson from the 1980 Crises.* Adelphi Paper No. 170. London: International Institute for Strategic Studies, 1981.

Winters, Peter Jochen. "Aufgeschoben, nicht aufgehoben." *Deutschland Archiv* 16 (June 1983): 561–6.

_____. "Die DDR in Moskaus Doppelstrategie." *Deutschland Archiv* 16 (February 1983): 113–5.

_____. "Das Deutsch-deutsche Verhältnis 1981." *Deutschland Archiv* 14 (December 1981): 1233–6.

_____. "Kurswechsel Ost-Berlins gegenüber Bonn." *Europa Archiv* 1 (1981): 31–4.

_____. "Nicht Eiszeit, aber Pause." *Deutschland Archiv* 18 (March 1985): 225–8.

_____. "Ungewisser Herbst." *Deutschland Archiv* 16 (November 1983): 121–3.

____. "Vereinbarungen und Verhandlungen mit der DDR im Gefolge des Grundlagenvertrages." *Deutschland Archiv* 15 (December 1982).

Zahlenspiegel: Bundesrepublik Deutschland//Deutsche Demokratische Republik — Ein Vergleich. Bonn: Bundesministerium für innerdeutsche Beziehungen, 1983.

NEWSPAPERS AND MAGAZINES

Frankfurter Allgemeine Zeitung, Frankfurt/Main, 1983–85.

Neues Deutschland, Berlin (Ost), 1980–84.

Der Spiegel, Hamburg, 1980–85.

Süddeutsche Zeitung, München, 1983–85.

Die Welt, Hamburg, 1984.

Die ZEIT, Hamburg, 1981–85.

UNPUBLISHED MATERIALS

Dean, Jonathan. *Inter-German Relations — Will They Change the Political Map of Europe?* October 4, 1985.

Kohl, Helmut. Interview with the Austrian television network ORF in St. Wolfgang, August 14, 1984.

McAdams, A. James. *Conceptualizing Change in Soviet-East European Relations.* Prepared for delivery at the 1985 Annual Meeting of the American Political Science Association, The New Orleans Hilton, August 29-September 1, 1985.

Royen, Christoph. *Change and Immobility in Poland, the CSSR and the GDR — Problems and Choices for Western Policy,* 1984.

Sodaro, Michael. *In the Shadow of the Missiles: East German and Soviet Perceptions of West German Foreign Policy,* 1984.

Schneider, Dirk. *Seid umschlungen, Millionen: Wie das Stichwort "Wiedervereinigung" Linke und Rechte zusammenführt.* July 3, 1984.

INTERVIEWS

Ackermann, Manfred. Specialist on GDR domestic policy at the West German permanent mission in the GDR. July 17, 1984 in East Berlin.

Dean, Jonathan. Former political counselor at the U.S. Embassy in the FRG. October 30, 1984 in Washington, D.C.

Dettke, Dieter. Foreign policy expert for the SPD parliamentary party. July 12, 1984 in Bonn.

Dolezal, Joseph. Federal Ministry for Inner-German Relations, Public Information Department. July 6, 1984 in Bonn.

Jacobsen, Dr. Hanns. Stiftung Wissenschaft und Politik, Ebenhausen. October 30, 1984 in Washington, D.C.

Kornblum, John. Director for Central European Affairs, U.S. Department of State. June 24, 1984 in Vienna; October 30, 1984 in Washington, D.C.

Kreisky, Bruno. Former Chancellor of Austria. August 29, 1984 in Mallorca, Spain (telephone conversation).

Okun, Herbert. Former U.S. Ambassador to the GDR. October 29, 1984 in Washington, D.C.

Portisch, Hugo. Journalist and author. August 21, 1984 in Vienna.

Schlemper-Kubista, Anne-Marie. Federal Ministry for Inner-German Relations, Economics Department. July 11, 1984 in Bonn.

Schneider, Dirk. Member of the *Bundestag,* specialist on inter-German relations of the parliamentary party of the Greens. July 11, 1984 in Bonn.

Schulze, Gerhard. Member of the *Bundestag* (CDU-West Berlin). July 16, 1984 in West Berlin.

Schwarze, Hans-Peter. Director of the ZDF studio, West Berlin, and president of the West German PEN-Club. July 18, 1984 in West Berlin.

Schweigler, Gebhard. Deutsche Gesellschaft für auswärtige Politik, Bonn. October 29, 1984 in Washington, D.C.

Schweiger, Gerwin. Institut für internationale Beziehungen. July 17, 1984 in East Berlin.

Sodaro, Michael. Associate professor of Politics and International Relations, George Washington University. October 29, 1984 in Washington, D.C.

Stent, Angela. Associate professor of Government, Georgetown University. October 31, 1984 in Washington, D.C.

Strasser, Helmuth. Austrian ambassador to the GDR. July 17, 1985 in East Berlin.

Ziegler, Uwe. Department for domestic policy in the GDR, Friedrich-Ebert-Stiftung (SPD). July 7, 1984 in Bonn.

Index

About the Author

Eric G. Frey, born in Vienna, Austria, received his B.A. in international affairs from Princeton University and his Master's in Public Affairs from the Woodrow Wilson School of Public and International Affairs at Princeton University. He is currently a reporter for AP-Dow Jones News Service in Frankfurt/Main, West Germany.